Servants of Christ and Stewards of the
Mysteries of God

Time Alone

A Daily Devotional

by

Gordon L. Densmore

TIME ALONE
Copyright © 2011—Gordon L. Densmore
ALL RIGHTS RESERVED

This book is protected under the copyright laws of the United States of America and may not be copied or reprinted for commercial gain or profit. The use of short quotations or occasional page copying for personal or group study is permitted and encouraged. Permission will be granted upon request. No part of this publication may be stored in a retrieval system, transmitted, or reproduced in any way, including but not limited to photocopy, photograph, magnetic or other record, without prior agreement and written permission from the author.

Unless otherwise noted, all scripture references are from the *New International Version of the Bible,* copyright © 1973, 1978, 1984 by International Bible Society, Colorado Springs, Colorado. Portions marked KJV are from the *King James Version* of the Bible.

Published by:

McDougal & Associates
18896 Greenwell Springs RD
Greenwell Springs, LA 70739
www.thepublishedword.com/bayou

McDougal & Associates is an organization dedicated to the spreading the Gospel of the Lord Jesus Christ to as many people as possible in the shortest time possible.

ISBN 978-1-934769-80-5

Printed on Demand in the US, the UK and Australia
For Worldwide Distribution

WELCOME TO TIME ALONE

Welcome to this devotional,
Of TIME ALONE with Him;
May it bring you joy every day,
And be a daily hymn.

As time is set to be alone,
With His great Majesty;
May you be blessed each coming day,
To live in victory.

There is a scripture to be read,
The Word of God to Know;
That we're to live by every day,
And in His Spirit grow.

There is a challenge to consider,
And give you food for thought;
To think about the life you live,
And what it is you've sought.

There is a rhyme for you to read,
And take it all to heart;
Let the rhyming words bless your soul,
To enjoy every part.

There is a prayer for you to pray,
In seeking out our LORD;
To give yourself to Him again,
Receive His love outpoured.

So put it all together now,
Enjoy it day by day;
My prayer for you that it would be,
A blessing every day.

Whether you read by day or date,
To keep in spiritual trim;
Welcome to this devotional,
Of TIME ALONE with Him.

Now Spend
TIME ALONE
With Him

A NOTE FROM THE AUTHOR

Dear one,

It has been my desire to bring you a very unique devotional.

I always encourage the reading of a daily devotional. In fact, I personally use two or three each morning as I first begin my time in devotion, Bible and prayer. I have often stated that it helps to get the "juices" flowing.

This devotional, *Time Alone,* is designed so that you can follow it by the date or go through it, starting at any time, and just follow by the week and day.

However you do it, I pray you will enjoy it and that it will help you along your spiritual journey each day. I always welcome your comments.

I hope you will first read the dedications, acknowledgments and meter explanation.

For those interested in music, the meter is listed after each rhyme, and there is also a meter index at the rear of the book.

The Lord has been in this from the beginning to the end. He inspired me to write it, gave me the strength in body and imparted the wisdom to put down the words. I give Him all the credit, for without Him, this book would not exist.

May the Lord bless you greatly in your faithfulness to Him.

Gordon L. Densmore

DEDICATION

I dedicate this book to my wife Vernice, who became a "writing widow" through the hours, days, weeks and months that were involved in composing it all. I do love her and appreciate her more than words can describe. At first she did the proofing of all the rhymes as they were created, then later proofed the daily devotions as they were created and put together. And she did the final proofing, finding all my punctuation and grammatical errors.

She has had good practice at this since, over fifty years ago, I home published a mimeographed news booklet called *Buckeye Beacon* for the square dancers in the northeastern Ohio area. So began her proofing of her husband's writings at that time.

I am so grateful for her "eagle eye" in spotting many little errors that I have not seen. As I write this, we have celebrated 63 years of marriage. She stuck with me all those years, and I'm also very grateful for that. Thank you, Vernice, my love.

I also dedicate this book to our daughter, Robyn Kaye Wall. She does excellent work at editorial critique. When I had a page returned with all of her notes, I couldn't deny that she was right 98% of the time. (Once in a while old Dad felt he was right and let something remain.) She spent untold hours over several months, as I wrote this book, critiquing each day's devotion, and I am eternally grateful to her for this being a better book than it otherwise would have been.

I'm a very fortunate man to have a daughter with this talent, and one who is willing to spend the necessary hours to do her critique, even though it caused me some re-writing and correcting. Thank you, Robyn.

I thank the Lord daily for these two most important women in my life. They have helped me to become what I am.

ACKNOWLEDGMENTS

Vernice Densmore, Burton, TX ~ Initial and final proofreader
Robyn Kaye Wall, Burton, TX ~ Editorial critique

A tremendous "thank you" goes to the testing team. They also helped to make this book what it is. Their input was so very valuable, informative and productive. What a privilege to have such a wonderful team to help formulate some ideas and thoughts, especially in the early stages of writing this devotional.

The Testing Team (in alphabetical order)

Vivian (Dwayne) Barber	Sulphur Springs, AR
Jim and Pat Causey	Liberty, MS
David (Tamara) Densmore	Wadsworth, OH
Don and Karen Densmore	Perry, OH
Richard Frey	Perry, OH
Glenda (Allen) Green	Farmdale, OH
Kelly (Marie) Irish	Painesville, OH
Myron and Sharon Ricketts	Clarksville, AR
George and Charlotte Sanford	Carrollton, OH
Jim and Jeanette Smith	Jerusalem, OH

METER

You will note that at the end of each rhyme, the meter is given. For example:

CM = 86.86
SM = 66.86
LM = 88.88

Or the rhyme could have a meter such as:
10 8.10 8 (just one example)

In case you are interested in looking up a particular meter, the meter index at the end of the book lists the meter for each rhyme. This is particularly useful to those interested in music and desiring to put these rhymes to musical tunes they have composed or are composing. In some cases one may have a musical tune without words, and if this is true, they can go to the Meter Index and pick out the rhymes of that meter.

One actual example is "Amazing Grace" which is CM (86.86). Most rhymes of Common Meter could be sung to that tune.

CONTENTS

Welcome to Time Alone... Page 5
A Note from the Author 6
Dedication 7
Acknowledgments and "Meter" Explanation 8
Rhyming from the LORD 11
Time Alone Prelude´... 12

THEMES BY DATE INDEX

WK	DATE	THEME	PAGE #
1	Jan 1 - Jan 7	Beginning a New Journey	13
2	Jan 8 - Jan 14	Walk with Him	21
3	Jan 15 - Jan 21	Be Still/Quietness	29
4	Jan 22 - Jan 28	His Voice	37
5	Jan 29 - Feb 4	Faith	45
6	Feb 5 - Feb 11	Hope	53
7	Feb 12 - Feb 18	Love	61
8	Feb 19 - Feb 25	Grace	69
9	Feb 26 - Mar 3	Follow Him	77
10	Mar 4 - Mar 10	His Peace	85
11	Mar 11 - Mar 17	His Plan	93
12	Mar 18 - Mar 24	Need	101
13	Mar 25 - Mar 31	Serve	109
14	Apr 1 - Apr 7	Gratitude for Resurrection	117
15	Apr 8 - Apr 14	Prayer	125
16	Apr 15 - Apr 21	His Presence	133
17	Apr 22 - Apr 28	Submission	141
18	Apr 29 - May 5	Righteousness	149
19	May 6 - May 12	Heaven Bound	157
20	May 13 - May 19	Fear Not	165
21	May 20 - May 26	Listen to His Voice	173
22	May 27 - Jun 2	Help from the LORD	181
23	Jun 3 - Jun 9	Healing/Miracles	189
24	Jun 10 - Jun 16	Giving	197

25	Jun 17 - Jun 23	He Is My Victory	205
26	Jun 24 - Jun 30	Forgive/Pardon	213
27	Jul 1 - Jul 7	His Clear Voice	221
28	Jul 8 - Jul 14	Our JESUS	229
29	Jul 15 - Jul 21	His Will	237
30	Jul 22 - Jul 28	Release	245
31	Jul 29 - Aug 4	Witness	253
32	Aug 5 - Aug 11	His Call	261
33	Aug 12 - Aug 18	Thanksgiving	269
34	Aug 19 - Aug 25	Gathering	277
35	Aug 26 - Sep 1	His Rest	285
36	Sep 2 - Sep 8	Comfort	293
37	Sep 9 - Sep 15	Friend	301
38	Sep 16 - Sep 22	In His Love	309
39	Sep 23 - Sep 29	Salvation	317
40	Sep 30 - Oct 6	Heaven Ahead	325
41	Oct 7 - Oct 13	Renewal	333
42	Oct 14 - Oct 20	His Word	341
43	Oct 21 - Oct 27	Contentment	349
44	Oct 28 - Nov 3	Praise	357
45	Nov 4 - Nov 10	Jesus	365
46	Nov 11 - Nov 17	Victory	373
47	Nov 18 - Nov 24	Trust	381
48	Nov 25 - Dec 1	Thanks	389
49	Dec 2 - Dec 8	His Light	397
50	Dec 9 - Dec 15	Joy	405
51	Dec 16 - Dec 22	His Final Return	413
52	Dec 23 - Dec 29	His Presence and Peace	421
	Dec 30 - Dec 31	Eternity	429

Time Alone Postlude	431
Themes, Alpha Index	432
Titles, Alpha Index	433
Scripture Index, Old Testament	437
Scripture Index, New Testament	438-439
Metrical Index	440
1 Thessalonians 5:23-24	441

RHYMING FROM THE LORD

People have asked me over time,
About my writing rhyme;
How could I write so many lines,
And all those words combine?

Therefore I put it down in rhyme,
To make it very clear;
That how I get these words to say,
Explanation follows here.

Before I ever write a rhyme,
I go to Him in prayer;
To seek His counsel and His gifts,
To make it His affair.

I know that I have not the art,
To put words into rhyme;
That's why I need to go to Him,
And seek Him all the time.

As I surrender all to Him,
And seek His words to write;
I sense His voice speaking to me,
To shed on me His Light.

Then comes a mighty flow of words,
He lays them on my heart;
I record them as they come to me,
That I may do my part.

Therefore I give Him all the praise,
In all the words I write;
I know it's not by my own power,
It's only by His Might.

Thank You, Lord, for giving to me,
Your words to put in rhyme;
I give You all the glory due,
And praise You all the time.

TIME ALONE
Prelude

How is it with your worship time,
In privacy of your home;
When you can sing praises to Him,
In time with Him alone?

Worldly things have been put aside,
Nothing to interfere;
To praise Him with your words and song,
Just you and Him to hear.

It could be a closet of prayer,
Or corner of a room;
Where you and He can meet alone,
Relationship to bloom.

The secret is in privacy,
To talk just you and He;
Developing a fellowship,
A close cam'raderie.

This is a mark of maturity,
In journey of your faith;
As you spend time in secrecy,
With Him as face to Face.

There is no more important task,
To give time of your own;
With Him to grow and love Him so,
In spending Time Alone.

❖

And now, in these daily devotions that follow,
I pray you will experience
A closer walk with the LORD,
A greater sensitivity to His Spirit, and
A deeper appreciation of that which He has wrought for you.

BEGINNING A NEW JOURNEY

This is a new beginning,

A journey new to blaze;

As down this road you travel,

To Him be all your praise!

A DAILY JOURNEY WITH YOU

HIS WORD: "Then he said to them all:
'If anyone would come after me, he must deny himself and
take up his cross daily and follow me.'"
Luke 9:23

MY CHALLENGE: *To take up my cross and follow Him daily!
These words, uttered by Jesus, challenge me to do just what He asks.*

To My Beloved Lord:

A daily journey with You, Lord,
That is what life's about;
Walk in the light of Your Presence,
To trust You without doubt.

I'll not focus on worldly ways,
With its selfish desire;
But rather give it all to You,
Let You set me afire.

For I am determined to walk,
The path You've carved for me;
With You by my side guiding me,
It is a daily journey.

I know You will take care of me,
No matter what I face;
It matters not the circumstance,
You lead me by Your Grace.

I take my walk with You today,
With You, my walk is grand;
To follow as You lead me on,
I'll hold on to Your hand.

I'll never fear to call Your Name,
Whatever comes my way;
For You're my One and only One,
My Journey's with You today.

Your Loving Child

CM

PRAYER AND PRAISE: *"Lord Jesus, it is my will to do what You say and
to follow after You on a daily basis. Energize me with Your
Holy Spirit, to empower me to do just what You ask.
It is my desire to follow You today and forevermore."*

Week 1 ✦ Day 1   Theme: Beginning a New Journey   Jan 1

A NEW BEGINNING

HIS WORD: "I write to you, dear children,
because your sins have been forgiven on account of his name.
I write to you, fathers, because you have known him
who is from the beginning.
I write to you, young men, because you have overcome the evil one.
I write to you, dear children, because you have known the Father.
I write to you, fathers, because you have known him
who is from the beginning.
I write to you, young men, because you are strong, and the word of God
lives in you, and you have overcome the evil one."
2 John 1:12-14

MY CHALLENGE: To surrender my life to Him today and receive His new beginning. There is only one true new beginning, and that is the new life that I gain when I give my life to Christ. Jesus, Who is from the beginning, is the only one Who can truly give me this opportunity. He is my Savior. He is my LORD.

If you want a new beginning,
To start your life anew;
The only place to seek it, child,
Is Jesus to renew.

In times you feel exhaustion come,
There's no place else to go;
It's true in times of weaknesses,
God's Word can truly flow.

For then to Him you give your all,
To cast all else aside;
To hear His voice speak out His love,
And let Him be your Guide.

So look to Him and Him alone,
In life for everything;
For He's the One Who gives to you,
A new life beginning.

CM

PRAYER AND PRAISE: LORD Jesus, I give my life to You today.
I believe You are the Savior of the world,
and I receive You as LORD of my life.
I thank You for giving me a new beginning today, as I follow Your way,
live in Your will, and worship at Your feet. Thank You, Jesus!

Week 1 ❖ Day 2   Theme: Beginning a New Journey   Jan 2

AWAITING THAT DAY

HIS WORD: "But our citizenship is in heaven.
And we eagerly await a Savior from there,
the Lord Jesus Christ, who, by the power that enables him
to bring everything under his control,
will transform our lowly bodies so that
they will be like his glorious body."
Philippians 3:20-21

MY CHALLENGE: *To eagerly await my Savior's return.
I must ask myself: Am I truly eagerly awaiting?
Am I anticipating with joy that coming great and wonderful day?*

I've longed for His appearing,
And I've fought the good fight;
My life is nearly over,
The end is now in sight.

I've kept the faith through this life,
His Name I have professed;
He gives to me His blessings,
The Crown of Righteousness.

That Day is fast approaching,
When I shall hear His call;
I'll leave this world behind me,
Be face to face enthralled.

As that time comes closer still,
Waiting to hear His voice;
I'll be singing His praises,
My soul will shout "Rejoice!"

His beauty I'll behold there,
And we'll walk side by side;
In His majesty and glory,
I'll eternally abide.

Singing Glory Hallelujah!
He's won the victory;
Praises to His Holy Name,
Through all eternity.

76.76

PRAYER AND PRAISE: *My coming Lord Jesus, how I long to see You and that Great Day coming soon. So many times the cares of this world interfere with my focusing on You. Help me now to eagerly await Your coming again as I focus daily on You. Just to think that I will be transformed with a glorious new body that will be for eternity, gives me cause to rejoice. To rejoice and eagerly await. Thank You, my Lord!*

Week 1 ❖ Day 3   Theme: Beginning a New Journey   Jan 3

A TRAINING GROUND

HIS WORD: "Do you not know that in a race all the runners run, but only one gets the prize? Run in such a way as to get the prize. Everyone who competes in the games goes into strict training. They do it to get a crown that will not last; but we do it to get a crown that will last forever."
1 Corinthians 9:24-25

MY CHALLENGE: *To run the race of life in such a way as to get the prize; and that prize is eternal life with Him. As Christians, we are already guaranteed eternal life with Him. Can I run my race of life in such a way that will bring Him glory? For I'll receive the crown of everlasting life, and how glorious that will be!*

Our earthly life a training ground,
For that which is to come;
We look to that Day of the LORD,
And hear the words "well done."

We're to grow and mature in Him,
Without going astray;
Following the path laid out for us,
Learning to walk His Way.

The LORD empowers us to serve Him,
As we remain steadfast;
And keep our faith with others too,
Until we're Home at last.

To prepare us for life with Him,
A coming time profound;
We accept struggles here on earth,
As being a training ground.

CM

PRAYER AND PRAISE: *LORD Jesus, I confess that I do not always "run the race" as though to win; but succumb to the way of the world. It is my desire to run the race of my life to bring glory to You, my LORD Jesus, as I look forward to eternal life with You. You have given me the race to run and entrusted it to my care. May I follow You in such a way that my race of life will glorify You!*

Week 1 ❖ Day 4   Theme: Beginning a New Journey   Jan 4

MY WEAKNESSES, I REJOICE

HIS WORD: "But he said to me, 'My grace is sufficient for you, for My power is made perfect in weakness.' Therefore I will boast all the more gladly about my weaknesses, so that Christ's power may rest on me. That is why, for Christ's sake, I delight in weaknesses, in insults, in hardships, in persecutions, in difficulties. For when I am weak, then I am strong."
2 Corinthians 12:9-10

MY CHALLENGE: *To receive His gift of grace with joy. I need to worry less about my weaknesses and be more concerned with God's power within me to carry me through. His grace is more than sufficient. His power is made perfect in my weakness.*

I do not have the physical strength, As others to whom I compare; I do not have the "fix-it" gifts, Nor have a mechanical flare.	He'll use the shortcomings that I fret, To bring about His will for me; And use the lacking found therein, That I will gain the victory.
But I rejoice in knowing the fact, That God will use my weaknesses; To bring about His Life through me, In being one of His witnesses.	I bow my knees to You, Divine, And listen for Your gentle voice; My life I lay before You, Lord, In my weaknesses I rejoice.

LM

PRAYER AND PRAISE: Lord, I confess, that in this flesh it is difficult for me to grasp this biblical concept, since my mind has been saturated with the worldly notion that I must be strong on my own; that I must develop a strength that can overcome according to the world's way of thinking. I thank You for giving me new understanding to accept Your Word that it is to YOUR strength I must look to and accept.

Week 1 ❖ Day 5   Theme: Beginning a New Journey

SEEDS FROM SOLOMON

HIS WORD: "To the man who pleases him, God gives wisdom, knowledge and happiness, but to the sinner he gives the task of gathering and storing up wealth to hand it over to the one who pleases God."
Ecclesiastes 2:26

"He has made everything beautiful in its time.
He has also set eternity in the hearts of men; yet they cannot fathom what God has done from beginning to end."
Ecclesiastes 3:11

MY CHALLENGE: *To grasp all that God has done for His children. I am to know that He desires to give the very best to me.*

Proclaim His Presence to a waiting world,
Waiting for answers to life;
Look to our Savior, the Light of all men,
Took upon himself our strife.

God gives wisdom, knowledge and happiness,
To the man who pleases Him;
Man stores up treasures in His loving heart,
Living life in God's rhythm.

He made all things beautiful in its time,
Therefore stand in awe of God;
Know that He will meet every need you have,
As the path of life you trod.

His eternal life is the gift of God,
Is set in the hearts of men;
Do not delay in fulfilling your vows,
Looking to the Great Amen!

10 7.10 7

PRAYER AND PRAISE: *My LORD God, I am Yours and You are mine. Help me to grasp Your awesomeness, that I could begin to comprehend Your Great Love for me and Your desire that I live close to You.*

Week 1 ❖ Day 6   Theme: Beginning a New Journey   Jan 6

LIVE IN SIMPLICITY

HIS WORD: "Make it your ambition to lead a quiet life, to mind your own business and to work with your hands, just as we told you, so that your daily life may win the respect of outsiders and so that you will not be dependent on anybody."
1 Thessalonians 4:11-12

MY CHALLENGE: To conduct my life in such a way that "things" will not control me. But I am to live a quiet, simplistic life, free from unwarranted demands.

To My Beloved Child:

> You're to live in simplicity,
> That's what I ask of you;
> To walk in trust and confidence,
> And be contented too.
>
> The simplicity of living,
> Your life under My care;
> Will bring you many great rewards,
> With which I have to share.
>
> For I desire not your rushing,
> From one thing to the next;
> Until you're haggard and worn out,
> You feel you've been compressed.
>
> Now let's slow down the pace a bit,
> And put your eyes on Me;
> For I will guide you gently on,
> To show simplicity.
>
> Now can there be a better life,
> Than that which I direct?
> Follow the way that I will lead,
> It simply is correct.
>
> For that is a secret to life,
> To live abundantly;
> With joy and peace and love in full,
> In My simplicity.

Your Loving Dad
CM

PRAYER AND PRAISE: *My Lord and my God, how I need You! I confess that too often it seems that things are controlling me. Maybe it's because I have too many things. But whatever the case, my Lord, I ask You to help show me the way to a more simplistic life.*
A life that will be completely dependent upon You.
Thank You, my Lord!

Week 1 ❖ Day 7   Theme: Beginning a New Journey   Jan 7

WALK WITH HIM

We walk with Him on our life's road;

He is our Guiding Light.

If we'll but trust Him all the way,

All things will be all right.

WALK WITH HIM

HIS WORD: "Blessed are those who have learned to acclaim you, who walk in the light of your presence, O Lord."
Psalm 89:15

MY CHALLENGE: To walk with Him hand in hand. That is to have such a personal relationship with Him, that I sense His Presence in my daily life, and give Him the praise! Then I am challenged to praise Him all the more so that I can be blessed all the more! I will try that as I continue to walk His path, hand in hand, in His presence, giving Him praise!

To My Beloved Lord:

To walk Your way not wavering,
To left nor to the right;
But keeping on the narrow path,
To follow in Your Light.

Wide is the gate and broad the road,
Leads many to destruct;
The world has led them far astray,
Has given wrong instruct.

For narrow is the road we walk,
The gate is small we see;
But as we follow in Your steps,
You grant us victory.

Now fill us with Your Spirit, Lord,
Fill us to overflow;
To trod that narrow path with You,
To walk Your way aglow.

Your Loving Child
CM

PRAYER AND PRAISE: Lord, as I walk with You hand in hand, in Your Presence on a daily basis, I pray for Your guidance to stay Your path. The temptations of the world are great and its voices loud in my ears. I know the only answer is to stay close to You, to heed Your words and to walk hand in hand. Thank You, Lord!

Week 2 ❖ Day 1   Theme: Walk With Him   **Jan 8**

OUR FIRST RESORT

HIS WORD: "But I have had God's help to this very day, and so I stand here and testify to small and great alike. I am saying nothing beyond what the prophets and Moses said would happen—that the Christ would suffer and, as the first to rise from the dead, would proclaim light to his own people and to the Gentiles."
Acts 26:22-23

MY CHALLENGE: To put Christ first in my life. I know that Christ was the first to rise from the dead, and I am to put Him first in my life. That's the challenge I have—simply to put Him first—absolutely first—before all.

Do we seek Him only in times of need,
As we turn to Him only to concede;
We're at the end of our rope,
We've tried all, but there's no hope?
We cry to Him, our last resort indeed.

We discover we've been on the wrong track,
Going to Him only when there is lack;
Pleading with our heart and soul,
To answer and bring control.
We have exhausted all means is a fact.

Now we have learned our lesson from the past,
When we tried to break that ceiling of brass;
As friend to friend in this land,
Walk together hand in hand,
As we make Him our first resort at last.
10 10 7 7 10

PRAYER AND PRAISE: As we come to you, Lord, it is our prayer to put You first at all times in every aspect of our lives. We ask that You help us to do just that. When we stray left or right, please correct our course, because we desire to serve You, to be the most effective servants possible.

WALK IN HIS LIGHT

HIS WORD: "Come, O house of Jacob, let us walk
in the light of the Lord."
Isaiah 2:5

"But if we walk in the light, as he is in the light, we have fellowship with one another, and the blood of Jesus, His Son, purifies us from all sin."
1 John 1:7

MY CHALLENGE: To walk in His Light!
Both the Old and New Testaments speak of walking in the light of the Lord.
When I go it my own way, I am walking in the dark.
But when I follow His Way, I am walking in His Light.
Why is it, so often, I choose to travel my path of life without His light?
That's my challenge. I will do it!

The Lord is my Light to guide me,
Along His glorious way;
To keep me from a wayward path,
And from a needless stray.

If we will walk in holy light,
As He is in the Light;
We fellowship with each other,
And follow what is right.

"I AM Light of the world" said He,
"Come follow after Me;
You'll never walk in darkness then,
So keep your eye on Me."

For we all have the Light of life.
As children that's our right;
Our walk is on His promises,
As we walk in His light.

CM

PRAYER AND PRAISE: I thank You for Your promise of never walking in the dark, because You are my guiding Light, the Light of the world. Therefore I do not fear to follow You wherever you'd have me go. I pray for a willing heart to follow Your light on my path, wherever it may lead. Thank You, Lord.

Week 2 ❖ Day 3   Theme: Walk With Him   Jan 10

WALK YOUR WAY

HIS WORD: (Words of Jesus) "Enter through the narrow gate. For wide is the gate and broad is the road that leads to destruction, and many enter through it. But small is the gate and narrow the road that leads to life, and only a few find it."
Matthew 7:13-14

MY CHALLENGE: *To walk the way of the Lord!*
There's no gray area in these words spoken by Jesus!
I'm either walking His narrow road to life and entering His small gate,
or I'm on the broad road with the wide gate that leads to destruction.
Quite obviously, my challenge is to live my life in such a way
that my walk keeps on the narrow road and
leads me through His small gate.

Now walk with Jesus hand in hand,
Make this your daily task;
To hang on to His every word,
Hold firmly to His grasp.

It matters not the world gives you,
Its glitter and its glee;
That turns your head aside to look,
At things from which to flee

You know the world calls out to you.
Daily you hear it's sound;
We close our eyes and turn our head,
To heed His words profound.

It's only by His loving grace
That we can take our stand
And overcome all worldly thoughts,
Go with Him hand in hand.

CM

PRAYER AND PRAISE: *Lord Jesus, I praise You for Your saving Grace, as I know I am walking Your narrow road of faith. I know that this flesh of mine wants to waver, to go left or right. But I stand on Your Word, stick to Your Way and hold unwaveringly to Your Will.*

Week 2 ❖ Day 4   Theme: Walk With Him   **Jan 11**

WITH HIM AS ONE

HIS WORD: (Words of Jesus) "My prayer is not for them alone. I pray also for those who will believe in me through their message, that all of them may be one, Father, just as you are in me and I am in you. May they also be in us so that the world may believe that you have sent me. I have given them the glory that you gave me, that they may be one as we are one: I in them and you in me. May they be brought to complete unity to let the world know that you sent me and have loved them even as you have loved me."
John 17:20-23

MY CHALLENGE: *To have a personal dialogue with Him. If I claim to have a personal relationship with Jesus, I then should be experiencing a personal dialogue with Him, especially in my devotional time. Although the fact remains that I can converse at any time, all the time, whatever the time. Am I? Will I?*

Relationship is what He wants,
To be with Him as one;
To share one's thoughts throughout the day,
As Father with His son.

A dialogue He so desires,
As Friend with friend to talk;
To share one's heart of warmth and love,
While on our daily walk.

His love is more than we can know.
How can we understand
He loved so deep He gave His life?
He made the cross His stand.

When walking hand in hand with Him,
Until the crown we've won,
We'll find this earthly walk each day
Will be with Him as one.

CM

PRAYER AND PRAISE: *Dear Lord, as I look around the world at other religions, I find there is none like You! You alone became one of us, gave Your life for us, and now live and communicate with us daily. What a privilege! What an honor! What a Comforter! What a mighty God we have. Thank You, Lord!*

Week 2 ❖ Day 5   Theme: Walk With Him   **Jan 12**

WALKING THE ROAD OF LIFE

HIS WORD: "As they were walking along the road, a man said to him, 'I will follow you wherever you go.'"
Luke 9:57

MY CHALLENGE: *To follow Jesus wherever He goes. The man who spoke those words quoted in the verse above had good intentions. I know not whether he followed through on his word. However, I should say the same thing as he said, and then do it! Doing it is my challenge each day.*

In walking down the road of life,
Observing all I can,
I see a lot of people have
Forsaken God's own plan.

His plan to save the world from sin
Meant leaving golden throne
To live amongst the people here,
To be their very own.

His love was measured not in coin,
Nor any earthly way;
That love so great gave everything,
His life the price to pay.

Remember all He did for you
To take away your strife;
Now give your all to Him this day,
To walk the road of life.

CM

PRAYER AND PRAISE: *Lord, why is it so easy to say and so difficult to do. I also have good intentions. But I confess that my "good intentions" have often been placed in the back seat, while "self indulgence" is in the driver's seat. I pray for the strength and wisdom to convert these good intentions to good works for You. As I continue to walk this road of life, may it be by Your direction, with Divine power, as I give my all to You now. Thank You, Jesus!*

Week 2 ❖ Day 6   Theme: Walk With Him   Jan 13

CONSTANT COMPANION

HIS WORD: "What agreement is there between the temple of God and idols? For we are the temple of the living God. As God has said: 'I will live with them and walk among them, and I will be their God, and they will be my people.'"
2 Corinthians 6:16

MY CHALLENGE: To look at the first sentence of the scripture and know beyond a shadow of a doubt that there is no agreement between the temple of God (myself) and idols of any kind. Is there anything I put ahead of my living God? Do I have idols in my life that keep me from being a constant companion of Christ? I often focus on the second portion of this verse and the fact that God lives and walks among us and is my God.

To My Beloved Child:

I AM Your Constant Companion.
In your heart I abide;
And I also walk beside you,
Never to leave your side.

Therefore keep your focus on Me.
My child, please comprehend
That as we walk this road of life,
I'M more than just a friend.

Walk the path I have made for you
Through all the curves and bends,
Up all the hills and down the slopes.
I'm with you to the end.

Relax in My Presence, My child.
Give Me your attention,
For as we walk this path, I AM
Your Constant Companion.

Your loving Dad

CM

PRAYER AND PRAISE: I thank You, Jesus, that I know You personally and that You are my Constant Companion. As we walk this road of life together, I ask You to convict me of any idols I allow to come between me and You. I repent of them. I turn to You. My heart's desire is to follow You alone. Thank You, Jesus!

Week 2 ❖ Day 7   Theme: Walk With Him   Jan 14

3

BE STILL/QUIETNESS

There is a stillness in His Love,

With no one can compare.

In quietness He gives to us

His love for us to share.

BE STILL

HIS WORD: "Be still and know that I am God;
I will be exalted among the nations,
I will be exalted in the earth."
Psalm 46:10

MY CHALLENGE: *Can I be still, truly still, and know that He is God? In my prayer time, can I still my mind enough to hear His voice? This is always my challenge.*

To My Beloved LORD:

"Be still and know that I AM God"
Are words You did express,
As printed in the Word of God,
To believe and confess.

Take my thoughts into Your control,
That I'll not ramble on,
With thinking so small and useless
That leaves me quite undone.

Lord, I ask that Your Holy Light
Fill up this heart of mine,
Then penetrate this busy mind,
To make me wholly Thine.

May Your light in my very being
Bring peace internally,
To calm my fears and anxious thoughts,
Be set aglow for Thee.

I confess my need for You always,
God's sacrificial Lamb.
I'll follow Words of Life You've said,
"Be still and know I AM!"

Your Loving Child

CM

PRAYER AND PRAISE: LORD, I confess that many times my mind races around while I am trying to pray, so that I do not stop to listen. Help me now, LORD, to still this mind and heart, that I would hear Your still small voice. Thank You, Jesus!

I OFFER MY DEVOTION

HIS WORD: And you, my son Solomon, acknowledge the God of your
father, and serve him with wholehearted devotion and
with a willing mind, for the LORD searches every heart and
understands every motive behind the thoughts.
If you seek him, he will be found by you;
but if you forsake him, he will reject you forever.
1 Chronicles 28:9

MY CHALLENGE: *To offer my devotion to God.*
This was a challenge to Solomon directly from God through his father David.
Each one of us has the same challenge. Each one of us has the decision to make.
Will I follow the One True God, or will I go my own way as Solomon did?

I offer You my devotion,
To draw closer to You;
To know Your Holy will for me,
And give You what is due.

I offer You my thanksgiving,
The sacrifice of praise;
Lips that confess Your Holy Name,
Your banner high we raise.

I offer You my temple LORD,
To give You for Your will;
Take me and use me as You would,
Your glory to fulfill.

I offer You my Holy praise,
in all situations;
You are LORD of lords over all,
I offer my devotion.

CM

PRAYER AND PRAISE: LORD, the answer seems so simple. The choice is very
clear. We are to follow Your way, or follow the way of the world's enticements.
From the world's perspective the choice is difficult to make, and yet when
we are committed to You, the decision is an easy one. And that is to give our
devotion to You and to You alone. You are worthy of our praise.
Help me now to always make the decision to be devoted to You in all I do.

Week 3 ❖ Day 2   Theme: Be Still/Quietness   **Jan 16**

IN HUMBLE SERVICE

HIS WORD: "Do nothing out of selfish ambition or vain conceit,
but in humility consider others better than yourselves.
Each of you should look not only to your own interest,
but also to the interests of others.
Your attitude should be the same as that of Christ Jesus."
Philippians 2:3-5 (-8)

MY CHALLENGE: *To take the humble attitude of Jesus Christ.
One of my greatest roadblocks of service to God is my pride.
It is a challenge for me each day to walk in humility, submitted to the Lord.
I must set aside my prideful, selfish ways and put Him first in my life,
knowing that He will supply all my needs and will take care of me.*

Be not selfish nor conceited,
But humble in all ways,
That you may lead a life of love
In service every day.

Your attitude should be the same
As that of Jesus Christ,
Who gave His life for all of us,
Considered not the price.

He took the nature of a slave,
To serve His God, and then,
Obedient to the point of death,
Until the Great Amen!

That death He took upon Himself,
When nailed upon the cross.
He gave His life for you and me,
That we not suffer loss.

That we would gain eternal life,
To serve and to adore;
In freedom from the bonds of sin
And live forevermore.

When we consider all of this,
Should it not break us still,
That we would come in humbleness,
And serve Him here until?

CM

PRAYER AND PRAISE: *Lord, I confess I have, in selfish pride, put myself
ahead of everything else—especially You.
I pray for Your strength and guidance,
to serve You as an humble servant, putting aside all selfishness,
and allow You to lead and guide.
I am Yours and You are mine. I thank You, Lord, all the time.*

Week 3 ❖ Day 3   Theme: Be Still/Quietness   Jan 17

GIVE YOU HONOR DUE

HIS WORD: "In the sight of God, who gives life to everything, and of Christ Jesus, who while testifying before Pontius Pilate made the good confession, I charge you to keep this command without spot or blame until the appearing of our LORD Jesus Christ, which God will bring about in his own time—God, the blessed and only Ruler, the King of kings and LORD of lords , who alone is immortal and who lives in unapproachable light, whom no one has seen or can see. To him be honor and might forever. Amen."
1 Timothy 6:13-16

MY CHALLENGE: To acknowledge Him as King of Kings and LORD of lords, giving Him the honor due, at all times and in all circumstances! As the scripture says, "He alone is immortal and lives in unapproachable light." My challenge is to celebrate His Majesty continually, giving Him glory for all things and in all circumstances.

Hail, Your Majesty, LORD Jesus,
Our everlasting King!
Your glory reigns far above all
And over everything.

There is none other can compare
To Your glory supreme,
And to Your Glory here on earth.
You set the Holy theme.

Then, as we take our every breath,
To set our hearts aflame,
May it bring You glory on earth,
And praise Your Holy Name!

There is no greater happiness,
But to glory in You.
We praise You for all things in life,
And give You honor due.

CM

PRAYER AND PRAISE: *LORD, I give You the glory, the praise and the honor, for You are due it all, at all times and for all things. May Your Name be praised throughout the world, and may it bring salvation to thousands of people who are looking for answers in their lives. Yes, LORD, all honor is due Your Name!*

Week 3 ❖ Day 4   Theme: Be Still/Quietness   Jan 18

HIS MIGHTY MERCY

HIS WORD: "When the kindness and love of God our Savior appeared, he saved us, not because of righteous things we had done, but because of his mercy. He saved us through the washing of rebirth and renewal by the Holy Spirit."
Titus 3:4-5

MY CHALLENGE: *To recognize the mercy of our God, and all that means to me in my Christian walk. His mercy—unmerited love—is far greater than I can imagine. My challenge is to reach out and receive it and give Him all the glory for it.*

A mighty mercy of our God
Is to redeem the time you've lost
And bring a fresh beginning now,
Just like the time at Pentecost.

The LORD brought down those flames of fire.
All there were made anew to serve.
It changed their lives to such extent
Their praising God was done with verve.

God took the weak and made them strong.
He changed their lives forevermore.
The past was gone, the new had come.
They gave their lives as ne'er before.

It matters not the time you've lost.
Our LORD redeems and makes anew.
Give all to Him and open up.
Receive His might mercy too!

LM

PRAYER AND PRAISE: *Oh mighty mercy of You, our God. It's because of Your mercy, Your unlimited and unwarranted love, that we stand before You in freedom of the spirit today. There has been no other who can remove our sins and set us free! We give You thanks for Your great mercy!*

Week 3 ❖ Day 5   Theme: Be Still / Quietness   Jan 19

HIS PERFECT WAY

HIS WORD: "As for God, his way is perfect;
the word of the Lord is flawless.
He is a shield for all who take refuge in him.
For who is God besides the Lord?
And who is the Rock except our God?
It is God who arms me with strength and makes my way perfect."
Psalm 18:30-32

MY CHALLENGE: *To receive that perfection He wrought for me and to live it everyday. In my Christian walk, I am in the process of being made perfect, in line with the perfection Christ wrought for me on the Cross. Jesus said, "Be perfect therefore, as your heavenly Father is perfect." He would not have said this if it were not possible. I am made perfect in Christ. I shall act like it!*

His way is perfect,
Though I not understand
Fully His way in my life.
Listening to His voice,
I take Him at His word,
Overcoming all my strife.

I oft fall so short
Of His Word, I know well,
Though I know He is the key.
That I'd comprehend
The greatness of His love,
in fully dealing with me.

To fathom His love,
Like a bottomless well,
Takes a lifetime to reflect.
Though the case may be,
We can't fully fathom,
His way is always perfect.

11 7.11 7

PRAYER AND PRAISE: *Lord, I come to You now and humbly bow before You admitting that I don't feel perfect, even though I know that is the position You have placed all of Your followers. I praise Your Name and thank You for Your sacrifice and Your power to create perfection in me. Amen!*

Week 3 ❖ Day 6   Theme: Be Still/Quietness   Jan 20

LISTEN FOR DISCERNMENT

HIS WORD: "And now this is my prayer: that your love may abound more and more in knowledge and depth of insight, so that you may be able to discern what is best and may be pure and blameless until the day of Christ, filled with the fruit of righteousness that comes through Jesus Christ—to the glory and praise of God."

Philippians 1:9-11

MY CHALLENGE: To start listening more intently and trust the Holy Spirit to guide me. Discernment can always be a challenge as I attempt to hear what the LORD is saying to me. As with so many other things in my life, it gets better with practice—plenty of practice. It's a gift I am to develop to be of greater service to Him.

To my beloved child:

When you're in a conversation,
Learn one thing you can do:
Listen closely to My prompting,
And hear My words come through.

Open up those ears to hear Me.
Learn what I have to say.
I will speak to you about them
To help them on their way.

For they hide from you their feelings
And their own tendencies,
To embellish actual truth then
And hide reality.

For when I speak My words to you,
Revealing what is true,
Then you'll know what words to utter.
I'll flow them on through you.

So now listen to My clear voice,
To learn the actual facts.
I'll reveal the words to give them,
That they'll know how to act.

Keep your ears wide open, hear Me,
That you will know and learn.
I will give you all you need then.
Now listen to discern.

Your loving Dad

CM

PRAYER AND PRAISE: My Father God, I am so blessed! You pour out unconditional love and You fill me with Your power to hear Your word to me. I pray that I would continually discern Your word to an ever-increasing degree. Thank You, LORD.

Week 3 ❖ Day 7   Theme: Be Still/Quietness   Jan 21

4

HIS VOICE

His voice is heard throughout the earth,

His message to impart.

As we quiet ourselves to listen,

The Lord will share His heart.

HEAR HIS VOICE

HIS WORD: "Now choose life, so that you and your children may live and that you may love the LORD your God, listen to his voice, and hold fast to him."
Deuteronomy 30:19b-20a

MY CHALLENGE: *To tune out the noises of the world,*
and listen for that loving, gentle voice.
I pray. I praise. I plead. But do I take time to listen?
The key is in taking time, plenty of time, to be still and listen.

To My Guiding LORD,

I know the world is calling me
To walk its road of life.
All I have found, along the way,
Is naught but pain and strife.

Therefore I leave that downward road,
To change my direction.
Then let You guide me on Your path,
And give me correction.

I walk in the Light of Your Presence.
I sense Your loving heart,
To live my life as You see fit,
To walk as one apart.

It matters not what others do,
As I have made my choice
To follow only after You,
That loving, gentle voice.

Your Listening Child

CM

PRAYER AND PRAISE: LORD, I bow to You, my Savior, and quiet the world around me to hear Your loving, gentle voice. What a joy! What a fellowship! What a privilege to hear from You, my LORD.
Amen!

Week 4 ❖ Day 1   Theme: His Voice   Jan 22

HEAR HIS GENTLE VOICE

HIS WORD: "The man who enters by the gate
is shepherd of his sheep.
The watchman opens the gate for him, and the sheep listen to his voice.
He calls his own sheep by name and leads them out."
John 10:2-3

MY CHALLENGE: *To hear His gentle voice!
I know that Jesus is my Savior and* LORD.
*I know that I have a personal relationship with Him
because I am a born-again Christian.
Yet a personal relationship requires dialogue. That is my challenge.*

Be still and know that He is God.
Be still and hear His voice.
Spend time before His throne of Grace.
Spend time with Him. Rejoice!

Live one day at a time with Him.
Is there a better choice?
Then hear Him speak into your heart,
To bring His love. Rejoice!

There is no other Name on earth
By which we can rejoice.
Let's spend some time with Him alone
And hear His gentle voice.

- - -

S-h-h-h-h! Hear His gentle voice!

CM

PRAYER AND PRAISE: *Thank You,* LORD, *as I quiet down, look to You,
pray to You and listen for Your voice. I thank You for speaking
loud and clear, thus piercing the noise of the world.
It's my desire to hear and follow You, as You direct me by Your Word,
Your teaching and Your gentle voice.*

Week 4 ❖ Day 2   Theme: His Voice   Jan 23

YOU ARE UNIQUE

HIS WORD: "Sixty queens there my be, and eighty concubines,
and virgins beyond number; but my dove, my perfect one, is unique,
the only daughter of her mother, the favorite of the one who bore her.
The maidens saw her and called her blessed;
the queens and concubines praised her."
Song of Songs 6:8-9

MY CHALLENGE: *To <u>know</u> I am special and unique in God's sight.
The lover in Song of Songs claimed his dove to be unique,
a one of a kind, a very special one. She was blessed,
and so am I. For I am unique in God's creation, as He has created
each one of us to be one of a kind, a very special one in His eyes.
My challenge is to know this, accept it and live it as such.*

*Know you are a person unique,
Created in God's image.
He gives you everything you need.
It's up to you to manage.*

*He'll guide you in the steps to take,
If you'll trust in Him always.
He speaks to you in gentle voice,
As He leads along His way.*

*Just step out in a walk of faith,
And listen for His guidance.
Hear His voice coming through the din.
He helps you in abundance.*

*As you train your ear to hear Him
And listen for His critique,
Know that He desires the best for you.
Your are a person unique.*

87.87

PRAYER AND PRAISE: *Thank You, LORD, for making me unique. I am
special in Your eyes. I am beautiful and one of a kind. How blessed I am! LORD,
help me to live out my life with this image. For You are my All in All.
You are my Lover, and I am unique.
Thank You, LORD!*

Week 4 ❖ Day 3   Theme: His Voice   **Jan 24**

HIS VOICE COMES BREAKING THROUGH

HIS WORD: "I am the good shepherd; I know my sheep and my sheep
know me—just as the Father knows me and I know the Father—and I
lay down my life for the sheep.
I have other sheep that are not of this sheep pen.
I must bring them also. They too will listen to my voice,
and there shall be one flock and one shepherd."
John 10:14-16

MY CHALLENGE: *To do everything possible that will allow His voice
to come breaking through.
There are so many sounds of the world in my mind
that it is difficult to quiet my soul enough to hear His voice.*

The difficulty in listening
Is sitting quietly,
To still the mind of its spinning
On things only earthly.

For just as soon as you're quiet,
A thought comes loud and clear.
But it's not the voice of the Lord;
It brings you doubt and fear.

You must take control of your mind,
Take a very firm stance,
To cast aside all wrongful thoughts,
To give His voice a chance.

That first quiet whisper you hear
Your heart is gently soothed.
You know you've heard Him once again.
His voice comes breaking through.

CM

PRAYER AND PRAISE: *My Lord Jesus, You are my Shepherd, and I'm one
of Your flock. You speak to us loud and clear, but I ask You to help me hear with
a waiting, listening ear. I sense You have much more to share with me,
if I will but quiet myself, wait and listen. I quiet myself now.
I'll wait until I hear Your voice come breaking through.
Then I'll listen with an open heart and mind.
Thank You, Jesus!*

Week 4 ❖ Day 4   Theme: His Voice   Jan 25

HEAR HIS LOVING VOICE

HIS WORD: "Come, let us bow down in worship,
let us kneel before the LORD our Maker;
for he is our God and we are the people of his pasture,
the flock under his care.
Today, if you hear his voice, do not harden your hearts
as you did at Meribah."
Psalm 95:6-8a

MY CHALLENGE: *To keep my heart soft, pliable and open to Him.
That's the key. That's the challenge. Not to harden my heart,
as I bow down in worship to hear His voice.
I will keep it open and pliable to
receive whatever He wants to share with me.*

To hear His voice speaking to you
Requires practice on your part.
The world has noise to overcome.
Then you can open your heart.

The secret is in casting out
Every sound you hear until
His peace has invaded your soul,
And you're absolutely still.

To focus on Him face to face,
Imagine Him if you will.
He holds you in His Holy arms,
As you accept His council.

His voice is so still and gentle.
To hear His words is your choice.
He will give you comfort untold,
As you hear His loving voice.

87.87

PRAYER AND PRAISE: *LORD, I thank You now for helping me keep a soft,
pliable heart, as I listen for Your voice.
I promise now to listen more closely,
to listen with greater intent,
and to listen with great expectation, LORD.*

Week 4 ❖ Day 5 Theme: His Voice **Jan 26**

THAT LOVING, GENTLE VOICE

HIS WORD: "Take my yoke upon you and learn from me, for I am gentle and humble in heart, and you will find rest for your souls." *Matthew 11:29*

"When he has brought out all his own, he goes on ahead of them, and his sheep follow him because they know his voice." *John 10:4*

MY CHALLENGE: *To respond to Jesus calling me to come to Him. The* LORD *is calling me to come to Him and rest. That is my continual challenge. Will I come? Will I listen to His voice?*

Hear His voice, calling to you
From all eternity,
Speaking to your heart today,
"My dear child, Come to Me."

"Take My yoke upon you, friend,
And learn from Me, my saint.
Follow Me implicitly.
Cast aside all restraint."

Jesus has said, "Come to Me,
If burdened and weary.
From Me, receive My promise
To live eternally."

For all that hear this message,
You can now make the choice
To turn your back on His offer
Or hear and heed His voice.

That decision is yours to make,
Going to Him in prayer,
Confessing Him as your Savior.
Will it you now declare?

I repent of all my sins,
From them I turn away.
Lord Jesus, You're my Savior
Forever and a day.

So, Lord Jesus, I thank You,
For having saved my soul,
As my name is written down
On the heavenly scroll.

Never will I walk alone.
Forever I'll rejoice.
I've given my all to Jesus.
Today I've heard His voice.

76.76

PRAYER AND PRAISE: *My* LORD, *I would dare pray You to take my life and do whatever is necessary to come to You, take Your yoke upon me, and to hear Your voice loud and clear. I want to learn from You, for You are gentle and humble in heart. I open up the ears of my heart and listen for Your voice now.*

Week 4 ❖ Day 6   Theme: His Voice   **Jan 27**

HEAR MY VOICE

HIS WORD: "And I heard a loud voice from the throne saying, 'Now the dwelling of God is with men, and he will live with them. They will be his people, and God himself will be with them and be their God.
He will wipe every tear from their eyes.
There will be no more death or mourning or crying or pain,
for the old order of things has passed away.'" *Revelation 21:3,4*

MY CHALLENGE: *To simply quiet myself enough to listen, hear and receive. When the scripture above actually takes place, it will be at the end of the 1000-year reign of Christ on earth, and the final victory is won. The Holy City, the New Jerusalem has descended, and the new heaven and earth are in place. I'll have no problem in hearing His voice at that time.*

To My Beloved Child:

There's no mystery about My voice;
I speak so it is clear.
It's just that the noise of the world
Is so loud you cannot hear.

There are those who teach the wrong thing,
That I don't speak today.
The written Word is all they need,
To walk the Christian way.

My written Word is true enough,
You base your faith on it.
Just follow what it says, my child.
To Me, you must submit.

We have a close relationship
That's personal as can be.
For when you gave your life to Me,
You're in My family.

Therefore I want to talk with you,
And talk as Friend with friend.
It means that we will dialogue,
All earthly blocks transcend.

Let me assure that You will hear
My voice speaking succinct,
As you set aside other sounds
And hear my voice distinct.

Your Loving Dad.

CM

PRAYER AND PRAISE: *L*ORD*, I thank You for the assurance that You speak to me today, and expect to be in dialogue. I confess that too often I go to pray but don't stop to hear what You may be speaking to me. I repent of that. Help me now to do everything necessary to hear You loud and clear. Thank You, L*ORD*.

Week 4 ❖ Day 7   Theme: His Voice   **Jan 28**

5

FAITH

By faith you are a child of God;

By faith you persevere;

By faith you give your all to Him;

To faith you must adhere.

TOUGH FAITH

HIS WORD: "For in the gospel a righteousness from God is revealed, a righteousness that is by faith from first to last, just as it is written: 'The righteous will live by faith.'"
Romans 1:17

"In addition to all of this, take up the shield of faith, with which you can extinguish all the flaming arrows of the evil one."
Ephesians 6:16

MY CHALLENGE: To develop the kind of faith to grow to maturity in Him. Most all believers, myself included, desire a strong, tough faith, one that will trust in the LORD for all things, all the time.

To My Beloved LORD:

O LORD, our God, we want a faith
That's tough enough to stand
Against all evil of this world
And all that it demands.

All things are working for our good,
No matter what befall.
We trust our faith be tough enough
To overcome it all.

A realistic faith is ours
And rooted in the fact
That You are in control of all.
You have the final act.

We thank You for Your wisdom now,
To fully comprehend
That we are filled with Your tough faith,
Resilient to the end.

Your Loving Child

CM

PRAYER AND PRAISE: Jesus, I pray that my faith would become "tough"— that it would be strong to withstand all the arrows coming my way. I pray this, even though I know that I've grown the most during times of adversity. But I dare to pray to bring anything across my path that will help to build in me a faith that is strong, tough and durable. Thank You, LORD.

Week 5 ❖ Day 1   Theme: Faith   Jan 29

SOME THINGS

HIS WORD: "Therefore, since we are surrounded by such a great cloud of witnesses, let us throw off everything that hinders and the sin that so easily entangles, and let us run with perseverance the race marked out for us. Let us fix our eyes on Jesus, the author and perfecter of our faith, who for the joy set before him endured the cross, scorning its shame, and sat down at the right hand of the throne of God. Consider him who endured such opposition from sinful men, so that you will not grow weary and lose heart."
Hebrews 12:1-3

MY CHALLENGE: *To keep my eyes focused on Jesus.*
It's so very important to keep my eyes focused on Jesus, central to my faith, that as I trod the path of faith, I'll promise to take a stand for Him, and, at the same time, I'll take a stand on His promises.

Some things come through our faith in Him,
And some things are of flesh,
While some things bring us joy untold,
And some things bring distress.

We wonder on the things to come:
Will we arise or fall?
Some things are understandable,
While some things not at all.

Be not worried or despairing,
With feelings of dismay.
It is only through our Jesus
We live above the fray.

Some things are based on worldly gain,
And some things from above,
While earthly things will fade away,
Revealing heaven's love.

There is no such thing as "Some Things"
In the Heav'nly domain,
For "Some things" become "All things"
In God's eternal reign.

So keep your eyes on Jesus, friend,
His promises endure.
He has changed our life of "Some Things,"
To all things good and pure.

CM

PRAYER AND PRAISE: *Lord Jesus, help me focus on You. I confess too often I focus on my own desires and cares of the flesh. Often, those things are neither good nor pure. I know it is You and You alone Who can show me right direction and guide me along the narrow path of life.*
Take my hand, as I take my stand, to walk closer to You this day.

Week 5 ❖ Day 2   Theme: Faith   **Jan 30**

BE WHAT GOD CALLED YOU TO BE

HIS WORD: "Be completely humble and gentle; be patient, bearing with one another in love. Make every effort to keep the unity of the Spirit through the bond of peace. There is one body and one Spirit—just as you were called to one hope when you were called."
Ephesians 4:2-4

MY CHALLENGE: *To make His will my will and to know that will. In my life, I most often live to be what I want to be, giving no thought to what the LORD desires. Daily I am faced with the challenge of seeking and following that which God wants for me.*

To complain and compare
Is to live in despair,
Draining you of life giving power.
As you carry this strife,
It damages your life
And wilts you, like a dying flower.

He brings to us new strength,
To go to any length,
To follow His will for our lives.
That victory we'll win,
In our life over sin,
And in His Kingdom we will thrive.

Only Him you should seek,
He made you quite unique,
Part of His loving family.
Answer His call to you,
Do what He'd have you do,
To be what God called you to be.

668.668

PRAYER AND PRAISE: LORD, I must confess that often I'm not exactly certain what You called me to be. But as I grow in my faith I also realize that as long as I follow Your Word, seek Your Will and do the work You've called me to do, I will most certainly be ALL You have called me to be.
Thank You, LORD!

Week 5 ❖ Day 3   Theme: Faith   **Jan 31**

SHIELD OF FAITH

HIS WORD: "In addition to all of this, take up the shield of faith, with which you can extinguish all the flaming arrows of the evil one."
Ephesians 6:16

MY CHALLENGE: *To use my shield of faith. Far too often we Christians allow Satan to hit us with his flaming arrows, causing a myriad of problems in our lives. This need not be, as we have the authority in the Name of Jesus to come against him. As the scripture says, I can extinguish all his flaming arrows with my shield of faith.*

Has fear and doubt come creeping in
And left you feeling odd?
Take up your shield of faith, my friend,
Then put your trust in God.

The arrows of the evil one,
Pursuing to impart
Fears and doubts and anxieties,
Their aim to pierce your heart.

His flaming arrows are meant to burn,
To kill and to destroy.
But God has other plans for you,
His Word for you employ.

Put out those flaming arrows now,
Hold on to your faith's shield;
Know that you have the power of heaven.
The enemy has to yield.

Confess your fears and doubts to Him,
Releasing to be free,
That He may lead you by the hand,
And bring you victory.

The adage to "fight fire with fire"
Continues to be true.
Although we're filled with fire of God,
Let Satan get his due.

Know that you have the victory,
The battle God has won.
The shield of faith has guarded you.
Proclaimed He, "It is done!"

Stand firm now on the Word of God
And all that He saith.
We look to Him, our precious Lord,
And hold that shield of faith.

CM

PRAYER AND PRAISE: *Satan, I come against you and all you try to do against me and my family. I bind you, in the name of Jesus, and order you out! You have no right to fling your flaming arrows at me. Jesus is my Savior, LORD and Deliverer. Thank You, Jesus, for the victory we have in You!*

Week 5 ❖ Day 4 Theme: Faith **Feb 1**

SALVATION

HIS WORD: "That if you confess with your mouth, 'Jesus is Lord,' and believe in your heart that God raised him from the dead, you will be saved. For it is with your heart that you believe and are justified, and it is with your mouth that you confess and are saved."
Romans 10:9-10

MY CHALLENGE: *To a) confess with my mouth that Jesus is LORD <u>and</u> b) believe in my heart that God raised Him from the dead. Many people confess with their mouths but don't believe down in their hearts. And that doesn't do it! So, I come to Him for His eternal life by confessing and believing. That's my challenge.*

Lord, I pray the following aloud:

My Lord God, I come to You now.
I'm sorry for my sins.
I turn from them and turn to You.
Forgive me once again.

Lord Jesus, come into my heart.
I give my life to You,
To be the one You'd have me be,
And live my life anew.

I thank You for Your forgiveness
And granting me new life,
That I may walk a brand new path,
Above all worldly strife.

Empower me, Holy Spirit,
To live my life Your way.
It's my desire to be faithful,
To follow every day.

Lord, thank You for saving my soul.
My Savior You've become.
Now know You as my Lord and God,
My new life has begun.

Thank You for living in my heart,
A gift eternally;
That I've been brought out of the depths
To live in victory.

In Jesus' Name, Amen!

CM

PRAYER AND PRAISE: *Praise to You, my Lord, for saving my soul and making me whole for eternity. What a joy to be a part of Your family! I give You all the praise and thanksgiving, now and for evermore!*

Week 5 ❖ Day 5   Theme: Faith   **Feb 2**

ON STEPPING STONES OF FAITH

HIS WORD: "But you, dear friends, build yourselves up in your most holy faith and pray in the Holy Spirit. Keep yourselves in God's love as you wait for the mercy of our LORD Jesus Christ to bring you to eternal life."
Jude 1:20-21

MY CHALLENGE: To build my faith.
Am I doing what the Word says, building up myself in my faith by praying in the Holy Spirit? If I lack faith and am not following in His steps, then my challenge is to do just that: pray in the Holy Spirit!

Our faith, a walk of stepping stones,
From first unto the end.
We go from one on to the next.
Our faith is not to bend.

We're to take one step at a time,
Not stumble in between,
But make our steps deliberate,
And follow Him unseen.

Even though we fall and stumble,
He helps us to regain,
To rise and step out once again,
And walk to His refrain.

He asks no more of us than this:
To keep our steps in line,
As then He'll guide and lead us through,
Each step in our own time.

He teaches us along the way,
Each stone a lesson learned.
This is the way we mature in faith,
These steps of faith in turn.

This path may wind its way uphill
And slow us in our pace,
But God will lead us through to end,
On stepping stones of faith.

CM

PRAYER AND PRAISE: LORD, it seems I've been on this path of faith a long time. It has been long, winding and upward.
But I thank You, for I know I haven't yet reached the top,
but also that I'm a long way from where I came.
I pray for the strength to keep on climbing;
for the wisdom to follow You correctly
and Your joy to permeate me continually.
Thank You, Jesus, as I follow in Your steps on the stepping stones of my faith.

Week 5 ❖ Day 6   Theme: Faith   **Feb 3**

HOLDING HIS HAND

HIS WORD: "If I go up to the heavens, you are there;
if I make my bed in the depths, you are there.
If I rise on the wings of the dawn, if I settle on the far side of the sea,
even there your hand will guide me, your right hand will hold me fast."
Psalm 139:8-10

MY CHALLENGE: To hold on to His hand!
What a comforting thought! His right hand is holding me fast.
He will guide me by His hand, as I take my steps of faith each day.
My challenge is to continually affirm this, in taking my daily steps of faith.

To My Beloved Child:

My Hand is holding you, My child,
To guide you on your way.
See the direction we are going.
I'll ne'er lead you astray.

I'll keep you on this path of Mine,
That I've laid out for you.
It is the very best, be sure,
My Way is always true.

This is a path of stepping stones,
For you to go My way.
Just take them step by step, My child,
And you'll not go astray.

Hold tight to the grasp of My Hand,
To follow as I lead.
I have so much ahead for you.
Now, come, let us proceed.

We will walk this path together,
As we wander the land,
To fill the call I have for you.
Now, hold on to My hand.

Go slowly now, as we proceed.
I am Your Cornerstone.
To help you follow Me each day,
I give you stepping stones.

Your Loving Dad

CM

PRAYER AND PRAISE: LORD, in humbleness I come to You and give You
thanks for being my Cornerstone, leading me each day on the
stepping stones You have laid out for me.
Yes, I'll go carefully one step at a time, as I grow in You.
I'll hold tight to the grasp of Your Hand. Thank You, Jesus!

Week 5 ❖ Day 7   Theme: Faith   Feb 4

6

HOPE

Our faith and our hope are in God.

We hold to the hope we profess.

This hope and anchor for the soul,

Jesus is the hope we confess.

MY HOPE IS IN YOU

HIS WORD: "No one whose hope is in you will ever be put to shame, but they will be put to shame who are treacherous without excuse. Show me your ways, O Lord, teach me your paths; guide me in your truth and teach me, for you are God my Savior, and my hope is in you all day long. May integrity and uprightness protect me, because my hope is in you."
Psalm 25:3-5,21

MY CHALLENGE: *To live in His positive hope each day. I am challenged to walk in the way of the Lord, i.e. to be guided and taught by Him and to trust Him completely, while maintaining my integrity in my Christian life. That is my challenge each day.*

To My Lord:

Lord, help me in my problems here,
As in this life I cope.
There is one thing I need from You:
Teach me Your paths of hope.

Through all of this, I came to learn,
More sin I can't afford.
That's why it is so urgent now.
Show me Your way, O Lord.

You are my God and my Savior,
I confess this very day.
My hope I put in You alone,
And let You have Your way.

Guide me in Your truth and teach me
My hope gives full release.
It springs eternal in my soul,
And brings a quiet peace.

From Your Child

CM

PRAYER AND PRAISE: *Lord, it is my desire and prayer to be guided by Your Truth, follow Your ways and to place my eternal hope completely in You. I pray to do with me whatever is necessary to see that this takes place in my life. Show me Your ways, O Lord!*

HOPE THAT IS OVERFLOWING

HIS WORD: "May the God of hope fill you with all joy and peace
as you trust in him, so that you may overflow with hope
by the power of the Holy Spirit."
Romans 15:13

MY CHALLENGE: *To overflow with God-given hope.
I must allow God, my God of hope, to fill me full of Him,
so that I will overflow with hope. My challenge is also to so trust
in His Holy Spirit to fill me that I will overflow with His hope.
When I overflow, it will flow to others.
That is what God wants: that I would be so full of His hope that it would
touch others, that they, too, would be filled to overflowing.*

The memories of past long gone
Bring hope for us today,
For they are the foundation stones
To fill our jars of clay.

Your Spirit fills us with Your Love,
And with Your guidance too,
That we would walk Your path of hope,
Each day to walk anew.

It's You alone Who fills us so,
With pow'r that we might cope.
We know that You are urging on,
To forward look with hope.

On this, our path of life, we trod,
To walk it merrily,
As You remind us of Your Love,
And hope from memories.

CM

PRAYER AND PRAISE: *Thank You, LORD, for so filling me with Your hope
that it would affect others and cause them to do the same.
That is a wonderful thought:
that my hope could be so plentiful as to touch others, that they would also
overflow, and this would be passed on to others.
LORD, I pray to be a part of what You're doing here, right now.
Fill me now. Thank You, LORD!*

Week 6 ❖ Day 2   Theme: Hope   **Feb 6**

HOPE IN HIS UNFAILING LOVE

HIS WORD: "But the eyes of the LORD are on those who fear him, on those whose hope is in his unfailing love, to deliver them from death and keep them alive in famine. We wait in hope for the LORD;
he is our help and our shield.
In him our hearts rejoice, for we trust in his holy name.
May your unfailing love rest upon us, O LORD.
Even as we put our hope in you."
Psalm 33:18-22

MY CHALLENGE: *To put my hope in His unfailing love.
The world has a lot to offer—seemingly. But the LORD has so much more to offer! His promises are far and above anything the world has to offer—such as His love, His provision, His joy—you name it. Therefore I am challenged to simply accept and put my hope in Him and His offering!*

Our hope in Your unfailing love
Has been our help and shield.
We wait in hope for You, our LORD,
And to Your Spirit yield.

Oh LORD, Your eyes are upon us.
We have a holy fear,
As we live and follow in Your Way,
And know You're always near.

That gives us hope beyond our dreams,
Installs that peace within.
It's then our hearts rejoice in You,
For we're Your holy kin.

Thereby we trust Your Holy Name,
Our Hope in You above.
You give to us eternal life
By Your unfailing love.

CM

PRAYER AND PRAISE: *LORD, I come to You now in humble adoration and with special request that You and You alone give me the impetus to know and accept everything You have to offer.
This is a positive hope. It is my hope in You.
Thank You, LORD!*

Week 6 ❖ Day 3　　　　Theme: Hope　　　　**Feb 7**

WE WAIT IN HOPE

HIS WORD: "… we ourselves, who have the firstfruits of the Spirit, groan inwardly as we wait eagerly for our adoption as sons, the redemption of our bodies. For in this hope we were saved. But hope that is seen is no hope at all. Who hopes for what he already has? But if we hope for what we do not yet have, we wait for it patiently."
Romans 8:23-25

MY CHALLENGE: To patiently wait in hope. That's the key! "Wait for it patiently!" We're always challenged to worship and follow a God we cannot see, but we do see what His Hand has done and is doing and know by His Word what it will do. What a great hope we have! I am to know that hope and apply it, even as I'm waiting patiently.

Know that waiting requires that we
Have patience on our part,
To be at peace in His domain
Until the time to part.

For in this hope, then, we were saved,
This hope that can't be seen.
For it is hidden from our view,
Yet on Him we will lean.

We hope for what we do not have,
And patiently we wait;
For it is trust in Him we must
Until we graduate.

We look forward to His glory
That waits beyond our scope;
For a new life is promised us,
But now we wait in hope.

CM

PRAYER AND PRAISE: I confess I need Your strength and guidance in every aspect of my life. May You grant me all I need to faithfully follow You as I look forward to my new life. I now wait in hope. Thank You, my LORD.

Week 6 ❖ Day 4   Theme: Hope   Feb 8

HOPE IS AN ANCHOR

HIS WORD: God did this so that, by two unchangeable things in which it is impossible for God to lie, we who have fled to take hold of the hope offered to us may be greatly encouraged. We have this hope as an anchor for the soul, firm and secure.
It enters the inner sanctuary behind the curtain, where Jesus, who went before us, has entered on our behalf.
Hebrews 6:18-20a

MY CHALLENGE: *To anchor my hope in Christ.
As a boat anchor is dropped overboard to hold it securely in place, even during storms, so my soul is anchored in the hope of the* LORD *Jesus Christ. I cling to Him and maintain a secure life, even in the midst of storms that may buffet me.*

When sailing on the seas of life,
With storms buffeting you,
Your boat being battered by the winds,
Survival to pursue.

Fear not that storms may break your ship,
And sink into the deep;
For Jesus is our blessed hope,
We know our soul He'll keep.

His anchor is secure and firm,
As we hold on to it;
It calms the raging waters down,
To Jesus we commit.

He lifts us far above the storms,
Brings all into control;
He calms the seas for us to sail,
An anchor for our soul.

CM

PRAYER AND PRAISE: LORD, *I confess that so many times the storms in my life have knocked me off course, and have threatened to sink me. I acknowledge that every time I looked to You and Your provision, You calmed the storm. Thank You* LORD *that I have this hope as an anchor for my soul, firm and secure.
Thank You again, my Jesus.*

Week 6 ❖ Day 5   Theme: Hope   **Feb 9**

PURIFYING HOPE

HIS WORD: "Dear friends, now we are children of God,
and what we will be has not yet been made known.
But we know that when he appears,
we shall be like him, for we shall see him as he is.
Everyone who has this hope in him purifies himself, just as he is pure."
1 John 3: 2-3

MY CHALLENGE: *To know the hope of the future promised to me.
I am a child of the Most High God!
My challenge is to think and act like it!
My challenge is to live like it, now!*

A glorious promise He gives us,
At time of His return,
That we shall see Him as He is,
Our King, for whom we've yearned.

What we will be we know yet not,
But with our faith in Him,
We'll sing with the angels above,
While earth behind grows dim.

We know we'll see Him dressed in white,
In leading heaven's band,
His army of the heavn'ly host,
On earth to take His stand.

When, as we see Him as He is,
We know we'll be like Him.
That promise He has given us
And all His gathered kin.

His words are true we can depend,
As on this hope we stand:
He purifies us like Himself.
It's all by His command.

Now, dear friends, as children of God,
We have His word on this.
When He appears and makes us pure,
We're Home in wedded bliss.

CM

PRAYER AND PRAISE: *I confess, my Lord, that I often look forward to that time I will see You face to face in Your heavenly Glory! What a day that will be! But, in the meantime, I thank You for Your hope instilled in me, as I walk the path given me in this life on earth. Thank You, my Lord.*

Week 6 ❖ Day 6   Theme: Hope   Feb 10

PUT YOUR HOPE IN ME

HIS WORD: "But those who hope in the Lord
will renew their strength. They will soar on wings like eagles;
they will run and not grow weary,
they will walk and not be faint."
Isaiah 40:31

MY CHALLENGE: *To put my hope in the Lord.
So often the word "hope" is used in a negative vein.
However, biblically, it is very positive, as in the verse above.
This verse gives me great promise, that if I will simply put my hope,
my trust, my confidence and all reliance on Him,
my strength will be renewed, and I will soar in my faith!*

To My Beloved Child:

Those who put their hope in the Lord,
Who put their trust in God;
Will once again renew their strength,
While on this earth they trod.

They will soar on wings like eagles,
Far above earthly fray;
And will run and not grow weary,
As they live out each day.

They'll walk with Me and not be faint,
Trusting My Holy Name;
Those who put their trust in the Lord,
Will always be the same.

Fear not for I AM with you now,
It will always be so;
Be not dismayed, I am your God,
Until it's time to go.

I will strengthen you and help you,
To do the best you can;
To walk the path I've planned for you,
Before the world began.

I'll uphold you with My right hand.
For all the world to see;
That I AM the loving true God,
So put your hope in Me.

Your Loving Dad

CM

PRAYER AND PRAISE: Lord, I confess, my hope in You isn't always what it ought to be. I pray to keep me filled with Your Holy Spirit, that my hope in You would be unconditional, unquestioning and always resting on You. Thank You, Jesus!

Week 6 ❖ Day 7   Theme: Hope   Feb 11

7

LOVE

Love the LORD God with all your heart,

With all your mind and soul.

Know that you are a child He loves,

So give Him full control.

WALK IN YOUR LOVE

HIS WORD: "Jesus replied: 'Love the LORD your God with all your heart and with all your soul and with all your mind.' This is the first and greatest commandment. And the second is like it:
'Love your neighbor as yourself.'"
Matthew 22:37-39

MY CHALLENGE: *To follow these two commandments that Jesus beautifully molded into one. That's how He loved; that's how I am to love. I am to do as He commanded.*

To My Beloved LORD:

Grace, mercy and peace from You,
And from Christ Jesus, Your Son.
Your truth lives in us forever,
Till last setting of the sun.

For me, Your child, You beckon,
To come and sit by Your side,
Placing Your truth in my life,
Until I am satisfied.

"Walk in love," You are calling,
"Do as I have done for thee,
Loving others as examples,
For my disciples follow Me."

You gave us a new command.
We're to love one another.
You said, "As I have loved you,
So you must love each other."

You said, "By this all men will know,
As disciples, you are Mine,
If you do what I have said,
Loving others all the time."

I thank You, my Lord Jesus,
For giving to me Your Name.
I'll follow You faithfully.
With You, my heart is aflame.

I thank You for forgiving,
Restoring me to Your grace.
For I will live eternally,
Your precious love to embrace.

Your love surpasses all things,
To highest heights far above,
Yet lowly living in me.
I'll ever walk in Your love.

Your Loving Child
77.77

PRAYER AND PRAISE: *My prayer, dear LORD, is simply to give me everything I need to love as You have loved, with all my heart and being. Thus I am obeying Your command. Thank You, LORD.*

Week 7 ❖ Day 1   Theme: Love   Feb 12

HIS PERFECT LOVE

HIS WORD: "God is love. Whoever lives in love lives in God, and God in him. In this way, love is made complete among us so that we will have confidence on the day of judgment, because in this world we are like him. There is no fear in love. But perfect love drives out fear."
1 John 4:16b-18a

MY CHALLENGE: *To love as Jesus loved.*
Jesus exemplified perfect love.
WOW! Now that's a challenge!

The destiny of perfect love
Fulfilled the highest call,
As Christ the LORD went to the cross
And gave His life for all.

He came into a fallen world,
With sin and all it's strife.
He paid the price as He forgave.
He paid it with His life!

He suffered unexplainably
The blows and agony.
His flesh was torn, His side was pierced.
He bore for you and me.

He paid the ransom with His life,
A debt He did not owe;
For He alone made sacrifice,
His perfect love to show.

CM

PRAYER AND PRAISE: *Dear God, I confess, this is more than I can comprehend at times. I am to love as Jesus loved. He laid down His life because He loved us so much. Holy Spirit, help me to comprehend. Help me to understand. Help me to be more like Jesus every day. Praise His Holy Name!*

Week 7 ❖ Day 2　　　Theme: Love　　　Feb 13

COMMANDED TO LOVE

HIS WORD: "If you obey my commands, you will remain in my love, just as I have obeyed my Father's commands and remain in his love. I have told you this so that my joy may be in you and that your joy may be complete. My command is this: Love each other as I have loved you."
John 15:10-12

MY CHALLENGE: To love others as He loved me.
That's my challenge, and what a challenge it is!
After all, Jesus loved me so much He gave His life for me.
Now He tells me to love others as He has loved me.
The closer I get to that goal, the closer I get to Him.

Your love is more than anything
We dream or comprehend.
It far surpasses human thought,
But has its dividend.

You fill us with such gratitude,
To love and to forgive
All those we meet along the path,
Of life You give to live.

There is no room for hate and strife,
No room to bring distress;
For You have filled our hearts with love,
And brought us Your caress.

Therefore we open up our lives,
Reach out with loving hand,
To bring to others Your pure love
And follow Your command.

CM

PRAYER AND PRAISE: Lord Jesus, I know of no greater goal than to love as You have loved. My prayer is that You melt me, mold me and enable me to love as You have loved.
I give myself to You now to do just that. Thank You, Jesus.

Week 7 ❖ Day 3   Theme: Love   Feb 14

I SING YOUR SONG

HIS WORD: "Sing joyfully to the Lord, you righteous;
it is fitting for the upright to praise him. Praise the Lord with the harp;
make music to him on the ten-stringed lyre.
Sing to him a new song; play skillfully, and shout for joy."
Psalm 33:1-3

MY CHALLENGE: *To sing and shout for joy in my personal devotional
time. Have you ever thought of singing joyfully? Of playing skillfully?
Even shouting for joy? Well—that's my challenge!*

Put your thoughts into my mind.
Put Your song into my heart;
So that praise will be my gift,
To the day I will depart.

There is nothing in this world
That will build my faith so great,
But to hear Your words of love,
Then Your love to demonstrate.

It's Your song I sing today,
In my joy, You bring to pass.
For Your Word is food for me,
To rejoice in Your repast.

As I make Your love be known,
You're the One to whom belong;
For Your grace has saved my soul,
As my heart sings out Your song.

77.77

PRAYER AND PRAISE: *I sing praises to You, my God, I sing praises;
I sing praises to You, my King, I sing praises.
I sing to You a psalm of praise for great are You, my Lord,
and most worthy of praise!*

Week 7 ❖ Day 4   Theme: Love   Feb 15

HIS NATIVE TONGUE IS LOVE

HIS WORD: "Whoever is wise, let him heed these things and consider the great love of the Lord."
Psalm 107:43

MY CHALLENGE: To know that Jesus is love.
Just think: JESUS is love. Jesus IS love. Jesus is LOVE!
May my native tongue be one of love.
To accept this and live it is my challenge.

Jesus was born in Israel,
Came from heaven above;
It is a land of many tongues;
His native tongue is love.

It matters not what tongue we speak,
Nor what our dialect;
For we're all born into this world
To bring Him great respect.

We're to look to Him as Master,
Creator of our souls,
That we'd praise Him eternally
And let Him have control.

E'en though we speak in several tongues
Or just our own unique,
What matters most in life we live:
What does our life bespeak?

Therefore no matter what the tongue
You use to speak today,
Choose to utter just words of love,
To be above the fray.

Follow Jesus and what He did,
The standard of our King,
To bring His Light to a dark world,
The Good News we're to bring.

Remember, as we follow Him
And do as He has done.
The tongue we speak is one of love,
Until the closing sun.

To sum it up in words of old,
Love each other alway.
Make your native tongue be of love;
Follow His way today.

CM

PRAYER AND PRAISE: My Lord, how great You are! I pray that my native tongue will be of love, in order that I may love as Jesus loved. I confess I don't always feel like loving. But then again You don't tell us to go on feelings, but rather go in accordance with Your Word. So help me, Lord, to follow You, showing Your love to all I meet. Thank You, Jesus.

Week 7 ❖ Day 5   Theme: Love   Feb 16

THE ROAD OF HIS LOVE

HIS WORD: "But if anyone obeys his word,
God's love is truly made complete in him.
This is how we know we are in him:
Whoever claims to live in him must walk as Jesus did."
1 John 2:5-6

MY CHALLENGE: *To walk as Jesus did!
WOW! Now that's a challenge!
"Whoever claims to live in him must walk as Jesus did!"
Could there be a greater challenge than this?*

*The road of His love is a road giving life
In service to others for Him.
Just as our Lord Jesus gave all at the cross,
We offer our lives as a hymn.*

*We sing with our lives as we walk in His way,
To follow His loving commands.
Our love is complete as His Word we obey
And walk in His way in this land.*

*What matters it, friend, if we fear what's ahead,
Or ponder the future to be?
We trust in the LORD as we walk side by side,
With Him in complete harmony.*

*Therefore it behooves us to walk by His guide,
And wait for His voice from above.
He'll give us our need, as He shows us the way,
In walking the road of His love.*

11 8.11 8

PRAYER AND PRAISE: LORD, I dare to pray for You to do whatever is necessary in me to live my life in such a way that it would reflect the life of Jesus. I want to do as Jesus did, but I can't do it alone. I need Your help. Thank You, LORD, for Your prompting in me, filling me with Your power and teaching me with Your patience.
I give myself to You now.
In Jesus' Name!

Week 7 ✦ Day 6   Theme: Love   Feb 17

GOD'S LOVE

HIS WORD: "For God so loved the world that he gave his one and only Son, that whoever believes in him shall not perish but have eternal life. For God did not send his Son into the world to condemn the world, but to save the world through him."
John 3:16-17

MY CHALLENGE: To receive His love and salvation. This most beloved verse gives me the challenge to believe in the Son for eternal life and thereby not perish. I am saved through Him. I accept this challenge! Right?

My beloved Child:

You know not why I love you so,
You cannot comprehend.
My ways are far above your ways.
Please hold on to My hand.

It matters not you cannot fathom
The greatness of My Love.
That's why I give to you My Spirit,
To guide you from above.

I fill you with My Loving heart,
To teach you everything,
And give to you MY Love and Grace.
Sing glory to your King!

Now put your trust in Me, my child.
Your needs are my concern.
It's all because I love you so.
For you I will return.

Your Loving Dad
CM

PRAYER AND PRAISE: Thank You, LORD, that I have received Jesus as my Savior and recognized Him as King of kings and LORD of lords. I pray for my lost loved ones who so desperately need Your saving grace. I lift them to You and dare to pray that You do whatever is necessary to bring them into Your family. Thank You, LORD!

8

GRACE

Grace and truth come through Jesus Christ.

His grace is sufficient for you.

It is by His grace we are saved.

The grace of our LORD be with you.

TRUE GRACE OF GOD

HIS WORD: "And the God of all grace, who called you to his eternal glory in Christ, after you have suffered a little while, will himself restore you and make you strong, firm and steadfast. To him be the power for ever and ever. Amen
With the help of Silas, whom I regard as a faithful brother,
I have written to you briefly, encouraging you and testifying that
this is the true grace of God. Stand fast in it."
1 Peter 5:10-12

MY CHALLENGE: To recognize and appropriate the true grace of God. Oh, if I could but begin to fathom His wonderful grace and the depths of it, then I could not help but shout to the world of what a great God He is!

To My Beloved LORD:

My God of grace, You've called me Your own,
To share in Your attributes,
That I would bring Your message of love,
Your promises to impute.

Your grace has carried me through thus far.
Then, throughout eternity,
This one thing we can ever be sure:
Your grace will always be free.

For Jesus paid the ultimate price.
For this He answered the call.
You paid the price You needn't have paid,
Because of Your love for all.

I sometimes wonder why You did it.
No greater love, there's no doubt.
Your love's beyond my comprehension.
That's what grace is all about.

My hope is set on wonderful grace,
And Your sacrifice sublime.
I humble myself under Your great hand.
You'll lift me up in due time.

There is no other on earth in which
I can trust and give my nod.
You gave Your all that I'd be set free.
That is the true grace of God.

Your Loving Child

97.97

PRAYER AND PRAISE: I praise You LORD for being the awesome God you are! I ask Your help in this challenge to always come to You with confidence and great expectations.
I confess, I'm not always confident. But I thank You for your mercy and Your grace poured into my life. Amen

Week 8 ❖ Day 1   Theme: Grace   **Feb 19**

IN FOOTSTEPS OF HIS GRACE

HIS WORD: "Or do you think Scripture says without reason that the spirit he caused to live in us envies intensely? But he gives us more grace. That is why Scripture says:
'God opposes the proud but gives grace to the humble.'"
James 4:5-6

MY CHALLENGE: To be humble and know that His grace is mine.
I have been saved by that grace.
I am sustained by that grace.
I walk in the footsteps of that grace.
I look forward to that great act of God's grace,
i.e. His coming again in all His glory.

The old has gone, the new has come,
We now live by His Grace;
For as we're led by Spirit power,
We bask in His embrace.

No longer we follow old law,
For Christ has had His say.
The Holy Spirit is our guide,
To lead us day by day.

Before the sacrifice of Christ,
The law was put in place.
Then Christ redeemed us from the curse.
He saved us by His Grace.

We need not sweat the rules of law.
In life, the steps we face
We follow as the Spirit leads,
In footsteps of His Grace.

CM

PRAYER AND PRAISE: Lord Jesus, as I follow in Your footsteps, I thank You for Your wonderful grace and all it means to me,
all it has done for me, and all it will ever do.
Thanks be to You for that beautiful gift that has changed my life.
In Jesus' Name.

Week 8 ❖ Day 2   Theme: Grace   Feb 20

HIS UNMERITED GRACE

HIS WORD: "Do not be anxious about anything, but in everything, by prayer and petition, with thanksgiving, present your requests to God. And the peace of God, which transcends all understanding, will guard your hearts and your minds in Christ Jesus." *Philippians 4:6-7*

"For the grace of God that brings salvation has appeared to all men. It teaches us to say 'No' to ungodliness and worldly passions, and to live self-controlled, upright and godly lives in this present age, while we wait for the blessed hope—the glorious appearing of our great God and Savior, Jesus Christ." *Titus 2:11-13*

MY CHALLENGE: *To know that His grace as well as His peace transcends all understanding, and also to know that they will guard my heart and mind while I wait for His glorious coming.*

Calamities cause change to the heart;
They will do one of two things:
They harden the hearts of many souls,
While others God's praises sing.

Those singing the praises of our God,
Seeking out His perfect will,
Find their hearts are softened and ready,
To go far with Him until.

Know His grace is more than sufficient,
Whatever may come their way;
Their power made perfect in weakness,
To carry them throughout each day.

They delight in daily weaknesses,
In hardship and life that's tough;
For when they're weak, then they are strong.
His grace is more than enough.

His Grace is beyond understanding,
His grace companion for all;
His grace is made perfect in weakness,
His grace like a waterfall.

His grace is unmerited favor;
His grace we could not afford;
His grace and the peace of our Savior,
The grace of Jesus, our LORD!

97.97

PRAYER AND PRAISE: *Thank You, Jesus, for all that You are, all You have done, and all You will do in Your Great Appearance. How blessed we are to experience Your grace and peace.*
Help me, LORD, to remain faithful to You until that Day. In Your Name, I pray.

Week 8 ❖ Day 3   Theme: Grace   Feb 21

THE GIFT OF LIFE

HIS WORD: "Because of the service by which you have proved yourselves, men will praise God for the obedience that accompanies your confession of the gospel of Christ, and for your generosity in sharing with them and with everyone else. And in their prayers for you their hearts will go out to you, because of the surpassing grace God has given you. Thanks be to God for his indescribably gift!"
2 Corinthians 9:13-15

MY CHALLENGE: To remember that His grace is a gift! I cannot earn it. I cannot buy it. I cannot finagle for it. I cannot work for it. No, it is by His grace and His grace alone.

We cannot earn the Kingdom of God,
Therefore gain by deserving.
It's not by our works we obtain it,
Nor by our persevering.

There's not enough money in the world
To purchase a membership.
You can't connive and seek other ways
To gain His companionship.

He loved us so much He gave His life,
Having paid redemption's price,
That we could live free eternally,
With Him in His Paradise.

We come into the Kingdom of God
By His grace and His grace alone,
As we believe in His sacrifice
And for our sins He atoned.

Therefore we open our hearts to Him,
And ask Him to enter in,
To take His place on our throne of life,
And make us one of His kin.

We come to Him in faith assurance.
We're His because we believed.
We praise Him and joy in His presence.
His gift we've gladly received.

97.97

PRAYER AND PRAISE: LORD, it's no wonder Your grace is called amazing! From the human standpoint, we can barely begin to understand what a great and gracious gift it is. But with warm love, open hearts and bended knees, we bring our thanks and praise to You now. So be it, forever!

Week 8 ❖ Day 4   Theme: Grace   Feb 22

HIS AWESOME GRACE

HIS WORD: "Let us approach the throne of grace with confidence, so that we may receive mercy and find grace to help us in our time of need."
Hebrews 4:16

MY CHALLENGE: *To approach His throne of grace with confidence, not with groveling and fear, but with certainty and assuredness.*

Can you see what's ahead of you,
When you're looking behind?
When you're focused on past events,
Are you not flying blind?

Maybe there are some things ahead
That you need to avoid.
They are obstacles in your path
That need to be destroyed.

So the secret, in all of this,
To forget what's behind.
Keep your eyes on the LORD, your God.
He's our great Master Mind.

You will trust in His guiding role.
You will keep eyes on Him.
That you'll follow His every step,
For He's your Elohim.

You need not look behind you, child,
Nor to fret what to face.
You must keep your eyes trained on Him
And on His awesome grace.

CM

PRAYER AND PRAISE: *LORD, that's what I need: more confidence. My prayer is that I take my eyes off present circumstances and focus them on You, Your grace and Your leading.
Your grace is truly awesome as I lean on You,
trust in You and follow after You.
Amen!*

Week 8 ❖ Day 5   Theme: Grace   **Feb 23**

HIS GLORIOUS GRACE

HIS WORD: "Grace and peace to you from God our Father and
the Lord Jesus Christ.
And you also were included in Christ when you heard the word of truth,
the gospel of your salvation. Having believed, you were marked in him with
a seal, the promised Holy Spirit, who is a deposit guaranteeing
our inheritance until the redemption of those who
are God's possession—to the praise of his glory."
Ephesians 1:2, 13-14

MY CHALLENGE: *To remember to praise Him continually for His salvation by grace. That also includes singing of His grace with my heart full of His love.*

Grace and peace to you from God, our Father
And from Jesus Christ, our Lord.
He has given to us His salvation,
Wrought by His double-edged sword.

It's by the grace of our Lord Jesus Christ
We're saved for eternity.
That grace reaches down from heaven above,
Gives favor to you and me.

We ask the Lord, as we await His time,
"Hold us in loving embrace."
We promise Him this one thing we will do:
Sing praise to His glorious grace.

10 7.10 7

PRAYER AND PRAISE: *Lord, I need Your loving embrace today.
And, as with every day, I need Your grace as I walk Your path.
I appreciate Your peace, I thank You for Your favor,
and most of all, I praise You for grace. Your wonderful grace.*

Week 8 ❖ Day 6   Theme: Grace   Feb 24

BY MY GRACE

HIS WORD: For it is by grace you have been saved, through faith—and this not from yourselves, it is the gift of God—not by works, so that no one can boast.
Ephesians 2:8-9

MY CHALLENGE: To acknowledge, receive and share His grace given me. It is by grace and His grace alone, that one day I'll be able to stand before my Father in heaven, and praise Him for His Grace!

To My Beloved Child:

By My grace you are saved,
By My grace you've been taught;
You have My provision for life,
By My grace you've been bought.

You'll always be My child,
You'll always be My own;
As I build My Spiritual house,
You'll always be a stone.

You are a living stone,
You are a praying soul;
By grace you're saved for eternity,
By love you've been made whole.

I AM your loving God,
I AM your living bread;
I gave to you My greatest gift,
My Life for yours instead.

Your Loving Dad

SM

PRAYER AND PRAISE: Father, I know it's almost impossible this side of heaven, to fully understand the depths of Your Grace.
But as I try to fathom Your Greatness, may I catch a glimpse of Your glory and receive a touch of Your Grace. Thank You, LORD!

Week 8 ❖ Day 7   Theme: Grace   Feb 25

9
FOLLOW HIM

"Take up your cross and follow Me,"

Our LORD Jesus has said.

We follow the way of His love,

And by His Spirit be led.

FOLLOW YOU IMPLICITLY

HIS WORD: "Slaves, submit yourselves to your masters with all respect, not only to those who are good and considerate, but also to those who are harsh. For it is commendable if a man bears up under the pain of unjust suffering because he is conscious of God. But how is it to your credit if you receive a beating for doing wrong and endure it? But if you suffer for doing good, and you endure it, this is commendable before God. To this you were called, because Christ suffered for you, leaving you an example, that you should follow in his steps." *1 Peter 2:18-21*

MY CHALLENGE: *To simply follow Jesus, to follow His way, to follow His Word.*

To My Beloved LORD:

Though I know not where You take me,
I will follow all the way;
For I know my selfish roadway
Leads to nothing but dismay.

It takes some effort on my part,
Determined to follow You,
And keep my faith firmly intact,
With no other to pursue.

With Your guidance my faith has grown,
With focus more on Your care,
Knowing that You will always supply,
My needs to use and to share.

It matters not in the present
That I cannot see ahead.
If I could see, I would not trust
In You to act in my stead.

Therefore I learn to follow blind,
Against teaching of the earth.
I see only my hand in Yours,
As each day we walk afresh.

My human instincts interfere
In trusting You completely.
I toss the world's caution aside,
To follow You implicitly.

Your Loving Child

87.87

PRAYER AND PRAISE: LORD, You know that it is my desire to follow You and You alone. Yet I confess there are times it doesn't look that way or sound that way. But that is my desire and goal—to follow You wherever You lead and whatever You'd have me to do.
I give myself to You now, step out in faith and follow You the best I can.
Thank You, my LORD.

FOLLOW HIS LEAD

HIS WORD: "Teach me, O LORD, to follow your decrees;
then I will keep them to the end.
Give me understanding, and I will keep your law
and obey it with all my heart.
Direct me in the path of your commands, for there I find delight.
Turn my heart toward your statutes and not toward selfish gain."
Psalm 119:33-36

MY CHALLENGE: *To follow Him daily!*
Not to get ahead of Him and in His way,
but simply to get behind Him and follow as He leads.

When you put anything ahead of God,
You've got trailer before the car.
You can try to push with all of your might,
But your travel will not be far.

Put things in order as God would have be,
Let Him be the car in the lead.
As you follow behind His sure guide,
The travel will be smooth indeed.

It's up to you how you journey this life,
Be it His Way or be it yours.
To go your own way is to go alone.
It will be the wrong way for sure.

Keep the car of God out in front of you,
To see and follow day by day.
We trailer behind on the road for us.
We follow His lead all the way.

10 8.10 8

PRAYER AND PRAISE: *Thank You, LORD, for helping to keep me on track.*
Thank You for helping me get behind and follow You and
not try to lead the way.
Submitting sounds so simple, but sometimes it's so difficult.
I thank You, LORD, for Your leading and teaching me.

Week 9 ❖ Day 2   Theme: Follow Him   **Feb 27**

I AM READY

HIS WORD: "Be dressed ready for service and keep your lamps burning, like men waiting for their master to return from a wedding banquet, so that when he comes and knocks they can immediately open the door for him. It will be good for those servants whose master finds them watching when he comes. I tell you the truth, he will dress himself to serve, will have them recline at the table and will come and wait on them. It will be good for those servants whose master finds them ready, even if he comes in the second or third watch of the night." *Luke 12:35-38*

MY CHALLENGE: *Simply—to be ready! To be ready in service to the* L*ORD*, *to do what He calls me to do, to go where He calls me to go and to be what He'd have me to be. Again—be ready!*

My eyes are ever ready, LORD,
To see where You will lead,
To walk the path You have for me.
I'll walk it straight indeed.

My ears are ever ready LORD,
To hear that gentle sound,
Which brings to me encouragement
And willingness unbound.

My heart is ever ready, LORD,
To trust You and obey;
For I desire to please Your heart,
Be one with You today.

My feet are ever ready, LORD,
To spread the Gospel news,
To take Your love throughout the land,
Wherever You may choose.

My lips are ever ready, LORD,
To witness to the lost,
And help them see Your only way
And fire of Pentecost.

My body's ever ready, LORD,
To fill my promised vow,
To go in service with You, LORD.
Yes, I am ready now.

CM

PRAYER AND PRAISE: L*ORD, as I follow You, I know I must be ready all the time. I know readiness includes being immersed in Your Word, prepared with plenty of prayer, and attuned to Your voice. Make me ready,* L*ORD! Amen!*

Week 9 ✦ Day 3 Theme: Follow Him Feb 28

FOLLOW AFTER HIM

HIS WORD: "The fear of the Lord is the beginning of wisdom;
all who follow his precepts have good understanding.
To him belongs eternal praise."
Psalm 111:10

*MY CHALLENGE: To follow Him without fear,
but only with the fear of the Lord,
which is an awesome respect for Him!
As a believer, the only fear I should
experience is the fear of the Lord.*

We need not fear to follow Him,
His Light cast on our road,
That we would see each step to take,
Without a heavy load.

We need not fear a future time,
To cause anxiety,
But keep our vision sharp on Him,
To follow clingingly.

There is no other such as He,
Who leads us through the strife,
Then brings us out the other side,
To grant a better life.

It is our choice to follow Him,
Through light or through the dim,
To go where He would have us go,
To follow after Him.

CM

PRAYER AND PRAISE: Lord, that is a real challenge for us human beings—that is, to have a healthy fear of You and, at the same time, not to have fear and trembling of earthly matters.
Help me, Lord, to keep this in mind and in practice,
as I follow You each day.
Praise Your Name!

Week 9 ❖ Day 4   Theme: Follow Him   Feb 29

LET NOT YOUR HEART BE TROUBLED

HIS WORD: "Do not let your hearts be troubled.
Trust in God; trust also in me."
John 14:1

MY CHALLENGE: To trust in Him completely, as I follow Him.
That's it! As I follow Him, my heart need not be troubled,
and the more I follow Him and trust in Him, the less troubled my heart will be!
Trust in Him completely and be completely at peace.

The message He brings for all of us to learn
Is simple and yet profound.
"Let not your heart be troubled, trust in Me,"
Are the words He did expound.

As we follow His Word and trust in Him,
He will set our hearts at rest.
We know that He will provide all our need
And give us the very best.

Let us all rejoice in the victory
Of surrender to His will,
To have given up our lives to follow,
Wherever He leads until.

I must abide in His will all the time,
Trusting Him implicitly,
As I follow Him on this path of faith
And grow to maturity.

10 7.10 7

PRAYER AND PRAISE: LORD, I confess that I so often pray to trust in You
and then find myself being troubled by something in my life that
shouldn't bother me at all.
Thank You for helping me to grow in You, that I would trust more in You
and less in worldly things and people.

Week 9 ❖ Day 5   Theme: Follow Him   Mar 1

I WOULD FOLLOW

HIS WORD: "May the God who gives endurance and encouragement give you a spirit of unity among yourselves as you follow Christ Jesus, so that with one heart and mouth you may glorify the God and Father of our Lord Jesus Christ."
Romans 15: 5-6

MY CHALLENGE: *To follow Him with His endurance and encouragement, and, at the same time, without my intervention of flesh. That is a true challenge—daily!*

Is Jesus calling, have you heard,
To "Come and follow Me"?
He is the Truth, the Life and Way,
God's Son in Trinity.

In worldly terms, we need not know
The facts in all of this.
That's why we need to trust Him so
And live in blessed bliss.

Why is it, my dear Lord Jesus,
The flesh is all so weak,
Yet willing in the spirit and
To mount the greatest peak?

I crucify this flesh of mine
And give Your Spirit reign,
That I would follow after You,
Eternity to gain.

CM

PRAYER AND PRAISE: *Thank You, Lord, for helping me to understand the importance of following You in the Spirit and not in the flesh. So often I think I'm following You by doing a lot of good works, but I know that to truly follow You, I must first be in the Spirit, worshipping You and listening for Your voice. I am one of Your sheep. I know Your voice. Oh, how much more determined I must be to listen and to hear! Thank You, Lord Jesus.*

Week 9 ❖ Day 6   Theme: Follow Him   Mar 2

COME, FOLLOW ME

HIS WORD: "As Jesus walked beside the Sea of Galilee, he saw Simon and his brother Andrew casting a net into the lake, for they were fishermen. 'Come, follow me,' Jesus said, 'and I will make you fishers of men.' At once they left their nets and followed him."
Mark 1:16-18

MY CHALLENGE: To obey Him <u>at once</u>! To obey Him now!
I have an amazing ability to drag my feet.
The fishermen were obedient, and I should I be the same.

To My Waiting Child:

As I called to the chosen men,
To come and follow Me,
They left their fishing nets behind,
To follow obediently.

I know it's not the normal thing,
To follow such a way.
But they had submitted their all,
To walk with Me each day.

I chose them for a special task.
I knew how it would end.
They gave their lives for the Gospel
And walked with Me as Friend.

I turned their loss and tragedy
From defeat to victory.
Their work with Me will e'er be known
Throughout all history.

And now, My child, please look to me,
For you I have a plan.
I plead with you to follow Me,
As one of special clan.

I'll give you everything you need,
To follow in My Way.
So do not hesitate, my child.
Come, follow Me this day.

Your Loving Dad

CM

PRAYER AND PRAISE: Lord, my desire is to obey instantly. But I confess I so often drop the ball and drag my feet. Lord, I need You to help me listen,
help me hear and understand and
help me to respond in a moment.
I allow You to do in me whatever is necessary to do just that.
Thank You, Lord.

Week 9 ❖ Day 7   Theme: Follow Him   Mar 3

10

HIS PEACE

As you trod on God's Path of Peace,

To follow Him every day,

May God Himself, the God of peace,

Make you holy all the way.

I ABIDE IN YOUR PEACE

HIS WORD: "The mind of sinful man is death, but the mind controlled by the Spirit is life and peace."
Romans 8:6

"Aim for perfection, listen to my appeal, be of one mind, live in peace. And the God of love and peace will be with you."
2 Corinthians 13:11bc

MY CHALLENGE: To allow myself to be controlled by the Holy Spirit that I may live in love and peace.

To My Peace-Giving Lord:

It is my decision, my Lord,
To abide in Your Peace,
To put aside all worry and fret
And make my cares to cease.

The frenzy of frantic thinking,
With impatience and fear,
I leave at the foot of the cross,
Where drops the fearful tear.

I place my faith in You, my God,
And faith You do impart.
Faith is knowing You will provide
Your Peace into my heart.

I live today as one with You.
This joy shall never cease;
For that is my decision, Lord,
Abiding in Your Peace!

Your Expectant Child

CM

PRAYER AND PRAISE: Lord, I appeal to You: Help me to learn to allow my mind to be controlled by Your Spirit, thereby shutting out the wrongful thought, and enabling me to hear Your voice loud and clear, that I may continually experience Your peace. Thank You, Jesus!

Week 10 ❖ Day 1   Theme: His Peace   Mar 4

PEACE AND CONTENTMENT

HIS WORD: "Turn from evil and do good; seek peace and pursue it."
Psalm 34:14

"May the God of hope fill you with all joy and peace as you trust in him,
so that you may overflow with hope by the power of the Holy Spirit."
Romans 15:13
(Also see Romans 8:6)

MY CHALLENGE: *To learn to turn away from wrongful ways and thinking,
and turn to my God of Hope, trusting completely in Him,
to experience His mighty, powerful peace.*

Practicing patience produces His peace.
Fretting just tears your life apart.
While practicing patience and contentment
   Produces quietness of heart.

When life isn't the way you want it to be,
And it seems to be filled with strife,
Just accept it for the way it may be.
Let LORD Jesus control your life.

To achieve pure contentment in your soul,
Accept all that may come your way.
Whether it be good or bad in your eyes,
Receive it with joy every day.

For God is still in control of this world.
All things are still under His Hand.
Just trust that He will bring the best for you.
Faith in Him is your holy stand.

Peace and Contentment are goals to achieve.
In your life, give Him full consent.
Surrender all matters disturbing you.
Enjoy His peace and contentment.

10 8.10 8

PRAYER AND PRAISE: *LORD, I thank You for showing me that the more I
practice patience and trust in You, the greater peace I will have in You.
Thank You, LORD, as I give myself wholly to You
and experience Your contentment and peace. What a joy! Amen!*

Week 10 ❖ Day 2   Theme: His Peace   Mar 5

LET HIS PEACE RULE

HIS WORD: "Let the peace of Christ rule in your hearts, since as members of one body you were called to peace. And be thankful."
Colossians 3:15

MY CHALLENGE: *To let the peace of Christ rule in my heart! That's it, so simple to state, but difficult to do, when I let the worries and problems of this world rob me of His peace. LET His Peace Rule!*

Let His peace rule in you today.
Let nothing interfere,
That you may live in contentment,
With nothing left to fear.

For He will meet your every need,
If you but trust Him to,
As you obey His Word for you,
His leading to pursue.

It matters not what be your past
And all the things you've done.
Just come to Him, confess your sins.
A new life has begun.

Then pray to Him and ask Him in,
To take control of you;
For if you give your all to Him,
You'll find His loving rule.

He cleanses us from head to toe.
New creature we behold.
He's changes us from our past life,
And forms us in His mold.

I know not how He does it all,
To sainthood from a fool.
I only know that our God reigns.
Today let His peace rule.

CM

PRAYER AND PRAISE: Lord, That is what I desire,
that is what I need, that is what I pray for.
Letting Your peace rule in my heart and life would be a great advancement in
my spiritual walk with You. Therefore, I take that step today.
I am Yours, and You are mine. I open up my heart fully to be filled
with Your Peace. Thank You, My God of Peace.

Week 10 ❖ Day 3   Theme: His Peace   Mar 6

AN INNER PEACE

HIS WORD: "For He himself is our peace, who has made the two one and has destroyed the barrier, the dividing wall of hostility, by abolishing in his flesh the law with its commandments and regulations. His purpose was to create in himself one new man out of the two, thus making peace, and in this one body to reconcile both of them to God through the cross, by which he put to death their hostility. He came and preached peace to you who were far away and peace to those who were near. For through him we both have access to the Father by one Spirit."
Ephesians 2:14-18 (Also see Proverbs 14:30)

MY CHALLENGE: *To experience that inner peace that only Jesus can give, as I become one with Him. It is far different from the peace the world offers, which is simply political peace. The peace that Christ gives is that inner peace that brings contentment, regardless what the world is doing.*

Do you enjoy an inner peace
That nothing can disturb,
A peace that goes so deep within
It's nothing but superb?

Do you desire a closer walk,
That He'd be better known,
To live a life that can be lived
With peace from Him alone?

You know it's only from the Lord,
As you have cast aside
All worldly cares and its desires,
And let Him be your Guide.

As you submit your all to Him,
The things of world decrease.
You sense His Presence greater now,
Enjoy His inner peace.

CM

PRAYER AND PRAISE: *Lord, How grateful I am to You for Your inner peace. As your child, help me to offer this peace to those in the world. I thank You for empowering me to do just that. I can only do it because of Your power and inner peace. Thank You, my Lord.*

Week 10 ❖ Day 4   Theme: His Peace   Mar 7

PEACE IN HIS LIGHT

HIS WORD: "... because of the tender mercy of our God, by which the rising sun will come to us from heaven to shine on those living in darkness and in the shadow of death, to guide our feet into the path of peace."
Luke 1:78-79

"Glory to God in the highest,
and on earth peace to men on whom his favor rests."
Luke 2:14

MY CHALLENGE: *To daily walk that path of inner peace, as mentioned of yesterday. My glorious God bestows His peace and favor on all His believers.*

His precious peace comes breaking through
In darkest time of night.
At the time I felt most alone
'Twas then I saw His light.

It was then I understood Him,
Why He had waited long,
Preparing my heart to serve Him,
To hear His heav'nly song.

I wonder why there's ever doubt,
That He's working with me,
To grow me to be more like Him,
A trusted devotee.

He has my best in His concern,
Working behind the scene.
Quietly He makes all things around
Conform to His will unseen.

I thank Him now for His result
And light to understand.
Amazing is His work in me.
'Twas more than I had planned.

There is no need to lose my hope,
Through darkest time of night.
His precious peace comes breaking through
To bask me in His light.

CM

PRAYER AND PRAISE: *My gracious* LORD, *Your peace within is a light for my soul that carries me through trials in life that I would have trouble bearing alone. Oh yes, how I wish I had a thousand tongues to thank and praise You for the peace that only You can give. Thank You,* LORD!

Week 10 ❖ Day 5   Theme: His Peace   **Mar 8**

HE GIVES HIS PEACE

HIS WORD: "Peace I leave with you; my peace I give you.
I do not give to you as the world gives.
Do not let your hearts be troubled and do not be afraid."
John 14:27

"The Lord gives strength to his people;
the Lord blesses his people with peace."
Psalm 29:11

MY CHALLENGE: *To do just what Jesus said and not let my heart be troubled nor afraid, but, instead, to receive His blessings of peace.*

Let us thank Him for His Presence,
His peace within our hearts;
For they are gifts He gives to us.
We know they'll ne'er depart.

The words of His that comfort brings,
"My peace I leave with you;
I do not give as the world gives,
My Peace I give to you."

"Do not let your hearts be troubled,
And do not be afraid."
Now receive the gifts of His peace.
The price for it is paid.

Receive that which He promised you.
With it He will renew.
In walk of life recall His words,
"My Peace I give to you."

CM

PRAYER AND PRAISE: *Yes, my Lord, You promised it, and I receive it. Therefore, I thank You for Your promises, Your Presence and Your Power that brings me that peace that passes all understanding. Amen!*

Week 10 ❖ Day 6 Theme: His Peace Mar 9

THE GIFT OF PERFECT PEACE

HIS WORD: "Do not be anxious about anything, but in everything, by prayer and petition, with thanksgiving, present your requests to God. And the peace of God, which transcends all understanding, will guard your hearts and your minds in Christ Jesus."
Philippians 4:6-7

MY CHALLENGE: *To keep my eyes on the abundance of His peace and to remain assured that His peace will reside in my heart, as I open my heart to His control and guidance.*

To My Peace-Loving Child:

Waste not your time on earthly goals,
Like chasing after wind;
But look to what I've promised you.
My Word I won't rescind.

I AM the LORD of time and space,
It's all in my control;
Hold fast to peace I've given you,
This is your Godly goal.

Give no place to the enemy,
To steal, kill and destroy;
I've given you authority,
To overcome with joy.

So take My Name and use it, child,
As though it were your own;
For that, in fact, is just the case.
That's why I've made it known.

I'll give you everything you need,
To follow after Me,
And do the things I ask of you,
To be completely free.

Abundance will My portion be,
My joys will never cease,
To give you all you need for life,
My gift of perfect peace.

Your Peace-Giving Father

CM

PRAYER AND PRAISE: LORD, I truly am grateful for Your peace. Your peace not only lives within me, You ARE my peace. My prayer, my LORD, is that I may share this peace of Yours I experience. May it pour out onto others, and be a true witness for You.
Thank You, My LORD.

Week 10 ❖ Day 7   Theme: His Peace   Mar 10

11

HIS PLAN

God has a special plan for us,

To follow in His way,

To save the lost and heal the sick,

And daily seek and pray.

FULFILL YOUR PLAN

HIS WORD: "Then I heard the voice of the LORD saying,
'Whom shall I send? And who will go for us?'
And I said, 'Here am I. Send me!'"
Isaiah 6:8

MY CHALLENGE: *To answer His call to follow His plan.
I need to seek it. I need to seek direction.
I need to seek fulfillment. I need to seek Him.
All in order that I will follow His plan for me.*

To My Fulfilling Father:

*You know the future from the past,
Beginning from the end;
For You had planned it long ago,
For Jesus to descend.*

*You have a plan for each of us,
To live our life anew,
That we'd be one in family,
To follow after You.*

*How can I ever know Your plan
Your future holds for me,
The truth of which I need not know,
But trust implicitly?*

*We thank You, Jesus, for Your care,
To use us as You can,
To be a vessel in Your hand,
That we'd fulfill your plan.*

Your Seeking Child
CM

PRAYER AND PRAISE: *LORD, It is my desire to follow the plan
You have for my life.
Therefore I submit to Your Lordship, seek Your direction,
and stand on Your Word, that I may fulfill Your plan for me.
Thank You, LORD!*

Week 11 ❖ Day 1   Theme: His Plan   **Mar 11**

HIS PLAN (Part 1 of 3)

HIS WORD: "'For I know the plans I have for you,' declares the LORD."
Jeremiah 29:11a

MY CHALLENGE: *It is to know His plans, since I have answered His call and have decided to follow His plan. After all, can my plans be better and greater than His? I will follow His plan!*

Lord Jesus, I honor Your Great Plan!

Is there an interruption in
Your walk of life today?
It saps you of your energy,
You hurt along the way?

Now take this opportunity
To look to Him, our King.
Let this be a gentle prompting
To pray for everything.

Just talk it out with Him at once,
Then listen for His voice.
He knows what is ahead for you,
But you must make the choice.

Be joyful in the midst of pain
Of heart or soul or mind.
Now leave your problems with the LORD.
Then peace of heart you'll find.

Lord Jesus, I honor Your Great Plan!

CM

PRAYER AND PRAISE: *My LORD Jesus, I'm not completely sure of Your plans for me. But as You lead me, I'll follow You, and I know, in that way, I will be in Your plans for me. Thank You, Jesus!*

Week 11 ❖ Day 2   Theme: His Plan   Mar 12

HIS PLAN (Part 2 of 3)

HIS WORD: "—plans to prosper you and not to harm you"
Jeremiah 29:11b

MY CHALLENGE: To know that in the LORD's plan for me, He has my best interests at heart, as He brings me success—His success— in all I do for Him.

Lord Jesus, I honor Your Great Plan!

If you will take all setbacks, then
Turn them to acts of praise,
You'll find the most amazing thing:
He turns your nights to days.

The sun comes breaking through the clouds.
You see, His loving Hand
Has worked the very best for you.
And now You understand

That He had planned the very best
For you along the way.
E'en though there were diversities,
He knew the final play.

That's why we trust Him at all times,
No matter what the need.
We put ourselves into His care,
To let Him take the lead.

Lord Jesus, I honor Your Great Plan!
CM

PRAYER AND PRAISE: Dear God, help me to remember to keep my eyes on Your plans and not on mine. I thank You now for empowering me to fulfill Your plans and, down the road, to see Your success take place. Amen!

Week 11 ❖ Day 3   Theme: His Plan   Mar 13

HIS PLAN (Part 3 of 3)

HIS WORD: "—plans to give you hope and a future."
Jeremiah 29:11c
(Also see Philippians 3:7-9)

MY CHALLENGE: *To know that in His plan of things, He is my hope, He is my future, and, in fact, He is my plan!*

Lord Jesus, I honor Your Great Plan!

It takes a lot of practice, child,
So start with little things,
To give Him thanks for all that comes.
His joy then intervenes.

Accept the losses in your life
As part of His great plan,
To mold you into His design
He planned since time began.

My LORD, I give myself to You,
A living sacrifice,
To use me as You will, my God.
I'll gladly pay the price.

For I am Yours, and You are mine.
I do surrender all.
This grants me freedom in this life,
Regardless what befalls.

LORD Jesus, I honor Your Great Plan!

CM

PRAYER AND PRAISE: *Okay, LORD, I confess that often I make plans, and try to fulfill them before seeking You. Then I have the audacity to ask You to bless my plans! My commitment to You, LORD, is to seek You and Your plan first and then to get on board with You. That way, I am guaranteed success in whatever the venture may be, because it is Yours! So be it!*

Week 11 ❖ Day 4   Theme: His Plan   Mar 14

THE MARVELOUS PLAN OF GOD

HIS WORD: *"The plan seemed good to Pharaoh and to all his officials. So Pharaoh asked them, 'Can we find anyone like this man, one in whom is the spirit of God?' Then Pharaoh said to Joseph, 'Since God has made all this known to you, there is no one so discerning and wise as you. You shall be in charge of my palace, and all my people are to submit to your orders. Only with respect to the throne will I be greater than you.'"*
Genesis 41:37-40

MY CHALLENGE: *To trust in God to fulfill His plan, even when I can't see the purpose in the present, and I can't see victory in the future. I have to trust Him to the point of knowing that regardless of what takes place, the future is in His hands. For His plan is a marvelous plan, whether I can see it or not.*

The marvelous plan of God on earth
We cannot comprehend;
For we cannot go beyond ourselves,
To see around the bend.

As Joseph spent his years in jail,
Not knowing what would come,
He praised His God above for all,
For all to overcome.

God used him as a pawn in life,
To bring about His plan,
And save His people from their plight,
And bring them to new land.

We, too, know not what is ahead,
The plan God has for us.
That's why we must give all to Him.
His way we are to trust.

We rejoice in all things today,
As we travel this sod,
Knowing we are a part of it,
The marvelous plan of God!

CM

PRAYER AND PRAISE: *Thank You, LORD, for gathering faith to persevere in your plan, even though we can't see it. We're to be like Joseph and trust You in all circumstances at all times. I can't see into the future, but I know You are there. And that is good enough for Me. Thank You, LORD!*

Week 11 ❖ Day 5   Theme: His Plan   Mar 15

MY BEST PLANS

HIS WORD: "Then Job replied to the LORD;
'I know that you can do all things;
no plan of yours can be thwarted.'"
Job 42:1-2

MY CHALLENGE: *To know, beyond a shadow of a doubt,
that the LORD's plans will not change and I cannot change them.
They will not be thwarted.*

The best plans I've had in this life
Don't measure up to goals,
That I had once formulated,
For riches to control.

I thought I had it figured out,
To live a life of ease,
Have everything I ever need,
And do as I well please.

My world around me crumbled in,
My goals came crashing down.
There was no way to carry on,
Wearing a self-made crown.

'Twas then I saw a better plan,
Revealed from heaven's gates.
LORD Jesus gave His life for me,
To live a better fate.

And so I gave my life to Him.
He saved me from my sin.
I opened up my heart to Him.
He now lives there within.

My plans are now completely changed.
I look to Him to lead,
To follow plans He has for me,
My best plans gone indeed.

CM

PRAYER AND PRAISE: *LORD, it is with great joy I bow before You and
thank You in prayer that Your plans for me—or anyone else—
cannot be changed—by anyone else.
It is us humans who need to change our plans to be in line with Yours.
So that's my prayer, LORD. Help me to relinquish all my efforts and goals,
to be submitted to Your plans. Thank You, my LORD!*

Week 11 ❖ Day 6   Theme: His Plan   Mar 16

MY GREAT PLAN

HIS WORD: "In His heart a man plans his course,
but the LORD determines his steps."
Proverbs 16:9

MY CHALLENGE: *To know the LORD determines my steps, regardless of what plan I may devise. Therefore it behooves me to follow Him as He leads—that is—His course for me.*

To My Beloved Child:

Can you understand My heartache,
When people choose not Me,
But rather turn to other gods,
As worthless as can be?

There are gods of fame and fortune
And money to pursue.
There're gods of power and success,
And the gods of self-rule.

But I have such a better plan,
I offer unto all:
Take up your cross and follow Me
And listen for My call.

My arms are waiting to hold you.
Lay head upon my breast.
I want to love and comfort you
And give eternal rest.

My plan for all has been the same,
But some hear not my plea.
Turn your face to My saving grace,
And set your spirit free.

I love you, child, with all My heart.
You're in my Holy Clan.
You have given your life to Me.
Now follow My Great Plan!

Your Loving Dad

CM

PRAYER AND PRAISE: *I Thank You, Father, that I'm in Your family. I'm a loving child, and You have determine my steps, in spite of the courses I plan. May Your plans for me become mine to know and follow. Thank You, my LORD!*

12
NEED

Your Father knows just what you need,

Before you even ask.

Therefore you need to trust in Him,

No matter what the task.

MY NEEDINESS

HIS WORD: "His divine power has given us everything we need for life and godliness through our knowledge of him who called us by his own glory and goodness. Through these he has given us his very great and precious promises, so that through them you may participate in the divine nature and escape the corruption in the world caused by evil desires."
2 Peter 1:3-4

MY CHALLENGE: *To <u>know</u> my needs, especially my spiritual needs, and to acknowledge and pray for them.*

To My Beloved Lord:

I thank You for my neediness.
It causes me to pray,
Trust fully in Your Sovereignty,
To guide me every day.

It matters not my present need,
For it teaches me much,
To lean on Your pure love for me,
As leaning on a crutch.

You know that which is best for me,
To help me grow in You,
To learn new lessons every day,
On path I'm to pursue.

I know that I have tendencies
To "go my way," I confess.
I give You thanks for everything,
Including neediness.

Your Needy Child
CM

PRAYER AND PRAISE: *Dear Lord, I lay my needs at Your feet. The burden is too heavy for me to carry any longer. I give up. I give them to You. Thank You, Lord, for Your ensuing peace of heart and comfort of soul, as I have given them to You.*
Amen!

Week 12 ❖ Day 1   Theme: His Need   Mar 18

HE SUPPLIES MY EVERY NEED

HIS WORD: "Now He Who supplies seed to the sower and bread for food will also supply and increase your store of seed and will enlarge the harvest of your righteousness. You will be made rich in every way so that you can be generous on every occasion, and through us your generosity will result in thanksgiving to God."
2 Corinthians 9:10-11

MY CHALLENGE: *To <u>know</u> and trust Him to supply my every need. He said He would. And He will! I know I can count on it!*

Turn my blunders into blessings,
My heartaches into hope.
Turn my crying into comfort,
In order I may cope.

Turn my sadness into smiling,
My misery to delight.
Turn my weeping into laughter,
My weakness into might.

Turn my problems into pleasures,
My pity into praise.
Turn my eyes to Your great mercy,
To set my heart ablaze.

Turn my sorrow into rapture,
Your Spirit to enjoy.
Turn my roadblocks into highways,
To run my race with joy.

Turn my hurting into healing,
My blindness into sight.
Turn my grieving into gladness,
My darkness into light.

Turn my eyes to You, my Savior.
Give answer, as I plead;
For it's You I must remember
Supplies my every need.

CM

PRAYER AND PRAISE: *Thank You, LORD, for the comfort You bring in assuring me of the promise that You will supply my need. I confess I need to look to Your supply and not to my own. Thank You, Jesus!*

Week 12 ❖ Day 2   Theme: His Need   **Mar 19**

NEED

HIS WORD: "So do not worry, saying, 'What shall we eat?' or 'What shall we drink?' or 'What shall we wear?' For the pagans run after all these things, and your heavenly Father knows that you need them."
Matthew 6:31-32

MY CHALLENGE: *To face any need without worry, knowing my Savior will meet my need. What a glorious comfort and peace this brings!*

There is a basic human need
That cannot be denied,
That every human ever born
Has needed higher guide.

That desire that's born within us,
Supreme power to receive,
Created many religions,
In someone to believe.

God was known at the beginning,
With Adam and with Eve;
But then, as they caved in to sin,
Began to disbelieve.

They did not trust their only God,
To follow Him alone;
But, rather, believed the devil,
To sit on human throne.

Jesus came to redeem the world,
To show God's only way.
T'would lead them to eternal life,
And save them for that Day.

Therefore as we look out on life
And follow in His lead,
We look to Him, our Higher Power,
That basic human need.

CM

PRAYER AND PRAISE: *My God and my LORD, what a blessing You are! What a comfort You bring to me. I can only praise You and give You the honor and the glory! Thank You, LORD, for meeting my needs! For You are my Higher Guide. You are my Supreme Power. You are my God. You are my Higher Power that supplies my basic human needs. Amen!*

Week 12 ✦ Day 3   Theme: His Need   **Mar 20**

THE NEED OF A SAVIOR

HIS WORD: "Let us then approach the throne of grace with confidence,
so that we may receive mercy and find grace
to help us in our time of need."
Hebrews 4:16

MY CHALLENGE: To continually approach His throne of grace with
confidence, for I certainly have need of my Savior,
while, at the same time, my Savior meets my needs.

We have the need of a Savior,
To take our sins away,
To give us hope eternally,
Forever and a day.

We cannot do it by ourselves.
There is no way at all.
To live our life independent,
We're headed for a fall.

We may think that we're in control
All phases of our lives.
We're master of our destiny.
We'll find ways to survive.

When in fact it's not true at all
That fate is in our hands.
We're not an island to ourselves,
To do as we command.

Thank God we have a Savior Friend,
Who knows our every need.
Is it a task to trust in Him,
To forego all our greed?

His Name is Jesus; He's our LORD.
From our sins we've been freed.
One thing on which we can depend:
Our Savior fills our need.

CM

PRAYER AND PRAISE:
*All praises to my glorious King,
Are words that I must sing;
For as I look to You for all,
It's You I'm trusting in.
Amen!*

Week 12 ❖ Day 4   Theme: His Need   Mar 21

JESUS FILLS OUR NEED

HIS WORD: "And my God will meet all your needs according to his glorious riches in Christ Jesus."
Philippians 4:19
(Also see 2 Corinthians 8:13-15)

MY CHALLENGE: That no matter where I am in Christ, He is ready to meet my needs out of His glorious riches. I look to Him.

I heard the call of worldly ways.
The promises were great,
To only on myself depend,
And worry not my fate.

I tried so many different things
To satisfy my life;
But found myself deeply immersed
In bondage and in strife.

I walked the way of selfish pride,
To satisfy my greed,
But found myself in bondage then.
I needed to be freed.

I got so low, nowhere to look,
So lifted up my eyes.
Then called out to our Savior LORD,
To come and hear my cries.

I found there is One you can trust
To hear your sorry plea,
And bring new life to hungry souls,
Who desire to be free.

This is the truth for all to see,
As you give up your greed.
To learn this lesson we should learn,
Our Jesus fills our need.

CM

PRAYER AND PRAISE: My Jesus, You have proved it over and over again.
You have met my needs when I fully trusted in You.
The world drained me; You filled me.
I pray, LORD, to continually look up to You and down on the world.
My LORD and my God, how blessed I am!
Amen!

Week 12 ♦ Day 5   Theme: Need   Mar 22

TAKE IT TO JESUS

HIS WORD: "And when you pray, do not keep on babbling like pagans, for they think they will be heard because of their many words. Do not be like them, for your Father knows what you need before you ask him."
Matthew 6:7-8

MY CHALLENGE: *To take all my needs to Him! He knows my needs, but in my needs, I am to approach Him and ask!*

Have you taken your need to Jesus,
Knowing His promises true?
Have you laid down your life to trust Him,
As He gave His life for you?

This is something you're to think about,
When trials have you tightly bound:
Turn to the best Friend you've ever had.
His advice is always sound.

What kind of man would give up himself,
As a living sacrifice,
And give up the golden heavn'ly life,
Came and paid the highest price?

We cannot blame it on the Romans,
As they nailed Him to that tree.
Nor can we blame Jewish rulers then,
Who accused illegally.

The blame can go to only one thing,
To the sins of man alone.
He took the beating and shed His blood,
That our sins would be atoned.

Just how great can be our gratitude,
As before His throne we bow,
And leave before Him our sin-filled past!
Take it all to Jesus now.

97.97

PRAYER AND PRAISE: Jesus, I bring to You my prayer requests now.
They are: _____
Thank You, LORD, for answered prayer.
Amen!

Week 12 ❖ Day 6   Theme: Need   Mar 23

I WILL SUPPLY INDEED

HIS WORD: "And do not set your heart on what you will eat or drink; do not worry about it. For the pagan world runs after all such things, and your Father knows that you need them. But seek his kingdom, and these things will be given to you as well."
Luke 12:29-31

MY CHALLENGE: *To seek the King of all kings, and for His bountiful supply.*

To My Needy Child:
You have heard the adage of old,
Said as though it were true,
"You have not because you ask not."
What is it you will do?

In many proverbs we offer
Sound like beautiful gems;
But most leave out the God factor,
Of what is best for them.

What is it you want, My dear child?
Are you rushing for time?
What is best for your life today?
Is it your will or Mine?

That is a choice you have to make,
A daily guide to live,
That if you want the best of all,
Follow My directive.

For it gives Me a great pleasure
To fill My child with joy,
To see your smiling, laughing face,
My promises employ.

I invite you to ask, dear child,
For all your earthly needs.
Your desires, in line with My heart,
I will supply indeed.

Your Giving God
CM

PRAYER AND PRAISE:
Yes, my Giving LORD, I ask You,
in praise, for all my needs;
for You're the great God over all,
and You will supply indeed.

Week 12 ❖ Day 7   Theme: Need   Mar 24

13

SERVE

Let us serve Him because we love Him,

And serve Him without fear.

Always serve Him with a whole heart,

And to His Word adhere.

MY LORD

HIS WORD: "Jesus called them together and said, 'You know that the rulers of the Gentiles lord it over them, and their high officials exercise authority over them. Not so with you. Instead, whoever wants to become great among you must be your servant, and whoever wants to be first must be your slave—just as the Son of Man did not come to be served, but to serve, and to give his life as a ransom for many.'"
Matthew 20:25-28

MY CHALLENGE: *Simply—to serve! To serve Him in whatever capacity He calls me to serve.*

To My Living LORD:

You've called me to Your service, LORD,
To walk in step with You.
You've given everything I need,
To step out and pursue.

My LORD, I bask in Your Presence,
To walk in Your great care.
Your Presence is ever with me,
Your life with all to share.

My LORD, I breathe Your Power in.
It fills to overflow,
That Your commission be fulfilled,
As to the world I go.

My LORD, I bathe in Your great Peace,
That gives me comfort grand.
I rest in Your great love for me.
My life is in Your hands,

My LORD, I bow to Your Passion,
To love with all my heart,
And fill the needs of those revealed,
Your Good News to impart.

I know You've given me a charge,
To wield Your saving sword,
The honor of my serving You,
For You're my Living LORD.

Your Serving Child
CM

PRAYER AND PRAISE: *I thank You, LORD, for empowering me for Your service. There is no greater honor than to serve You. I pray to be a faithful servant and child of Yours, as I step out in faith. Thank You, Jesus!*

Week 13 ❖ Day 1   Theme: Serve   Mar 25

FILL US AS WE GO

HIS WORD: "So, my brothers, you also died to the law through the body of Christ, that you might belong to another, to him who was raised from the dead, in order that we might bear fruit to God. For when we were controlled by the sinful nature, the sinful passions aroused by the law were at work in our bodies so that we bore fruit for death. But now, by dying to what once bound us, we have been released from the law so that we serve in the new way of the Spirit, and not in the old way of the written code."
Romans 7:4-6

MY CHALLENGE: *To serve in the way of the Spirit, putting aside the old way of the law.*

God can't use an empty vessel.
There is no other way.
As Jesus filled the jars with wine,
His Spirit fills today.

One must be filled with His Spirit
And also with His Word,
Have great desire and willingness,
To do what He's preferred.

It matters not the destiny
We planned as though our own;
For His Master plan is greater
Than any we have known.

He requires we submit to Him
Our lives and everything,
Allowing Him to fill our hearts,
For He's our loving King.

So fill us, Lord, fill us today.
Fill us to overflow,
That we would be Your vessel full,
To serve You as we go.

CM

PRAYER AND PRAISE: *My prayer to You, my* LORD, *is to fill me with Your Holy Spirit to overflowing, that I may serve You in the way of the Spirit, as You have asked.*
In fact, my prayer is that You would fill me every day, that I may serve You to the best of my ability, as I follow You.
Amen!

Week 13 ❖ Day 2   Theme: Serve   Mar 26

DARE TO BE

HIS WORD: "No servant can serve two masters. Either he will hate the one and love the other, or he will be devoted to the one and despise the other. You cannot serve both God and Money."
Luke 16:13

"Serve wholeheartedly, as if you were serving the Lord, not men, because you know that the Lord will reward everyone for whatever good he does, whether he is slave or free."
Ephesians 6:7

MY CHALLENGE: *To serve my Lord wholeheartedly as my one true Master, as I dare to be what He's called me to be.*

Dare to be what God called you to be.
He knows what is best for you.
Fear not what the future may bring you,
For He will carry you through.

He has made promise to all His own,
That in them He would abide.
He will bring about His will for them,
As they stay close by His side.

We can take risks, as we toil for Him,
In spite of our many flaws.
We step out in faith, trusting in Him,
Giving our lives for His cause.

As you go about your daily tasks,
Know you have this guarantee:
He will empower you for all His work,
To be what You dare to be.

97.97

PRAYER AND PRAISE: *Thank You, Lord, for opportunities to serve You wholeheartedly, as You empower me to serve You. I pray to be the persistent worker in Your field that You've called me to be. Yes, Lord, I dare to be what You've called me to be. In the precious Name of Jesus!*

Week 13 ♦ Day 3   Theme: Serve   Mar 27

STEADFAST IN OUR FAITH

HIS WORD: "Last night an angel of the God whose I am and whom I serve stood beside me and said, 'Do not be afraid, Paul. You must stand trial before Caesar; and God has graciously given you the lives of all who sail with you.'" *Acts 27:23-24*

"And the God of all grace, who called you to his eternal glory in Christ, after you have suffered a little while, will himself restore you and make you strong, firm and steadfast." *1 Peter 5:10*

MY CHALLENGE: *To hold steadfast in my faith in the face of trials, knowing that by God's grace, He will be with me.*

We must be steadfast in our faith,
Not wavering to and fro,
To be what Christ would have us be,
In service as we go.

To be a beacon light for Him,
Revealing His true way,
That other's lost in storms of life
Might see His light today.

Our steadiness and our firm grip,
On steering through the strife,
Give hope to others all around
To receive the Christ of life.

It's a responsibility
We have in serving Christ,
To keep His light shining through us,
To show His sacrifice.

For as the lost are convicted,
With feelings of remorse,
It's then that Christ can use you, child,
To help them change their course.

So as we serve our risen LORD,
Be an enthusiast,
To see the lost won to our LORD,
In faith to be steadfast.

CM

PRAYER AND PRAISE: *LORD, I confess, steadfastness is of great concern to me. I sometimes wonder if I'll hold steadfast when things get extremely tough; when I'm greatly challenged in my faith, and when many things are going wrong. I ask You, LORD, keep me filled, as I follow You.*

Week 13 ❖ Day 4   Theme: Serve   **Mar 28**

A GOOD HELPMATE

HIS WORD: "It was he who gave some to be apostles, some to be prophets, some to be evangelists, and some to be pastors and teachers, to prepare God's people for works of service, so that the body of Christ may be built up until we all reach unity in the faith and in the knowledge of the Son of God and become mature, attaining to the whole measure of the fullness of Christ."
Ephesians 4:11-13

MY CHALLENGE: *To be prepared for service to my LORD, in whatever capacity He may call me.*

He worked His trade as carpenter,
Beginning as a lad.
As Jesus grew and plied His trade,
He learned it from His dad.

He taught Him how to work the wood,
To build and to create,
In how to use the tools of trade,
To be a good helpmate.

And so it is with us, His child,
As in our faith we grow,
That we would learn it from our Dad,
To gain all we should know.

The Holy Spirit teaches us
To build and to create,
In how to use the tools of trade,
And be a good helpmate.

CM

PRAYER AND PRAISE: *Teach me, LORD, whatever I need to learn, to be of service to You. Yes, to be a good helpmate. I know You'll furnish the tools; I just need to be ready with the skills needed to serve You in the best possible way. Praise Your Holy Name!*

Week 13 ♦ Day 5   Theme: Serve   Mar 29

SERVING HIM

HIS WORD: "Therefore I glory in Christ Jesus in my service to God."
Romans 15:17

MY CHALLENGE: *To glory in Christ Jesus in my service to God.
That's it!*

The light of His Presence	As His extended hands,
Shining on me,	Reaching to all,
Giving me peace of mind,	Serving Him faithfully,
With joy unspeakable,	Sharing His giving heart,
Full of glory,	Bringing His love,
Leaving the world behind.	For all the world to see.
I look to His guidance,	I give myself to Him
Teaching to me,	Once and for all,
Words, Holy and profound,	A living sacrifice.
That I might follow Him,	What more could He have done?
His steps Divine,	He gave His all
Until I'm heaven bound.	And paid the final price.
Until I'm on my way	Therefore my lips will e'er
To heaven's gate,	Proclaim His love,
There's work for me to do.	To set the world aflame.
His Holy Spirit fills	My goal is firmly set.
With power within,	Forever on
Continuing to renew.	I'll praise His Holy Name!

10 6.10 6

PRAYER AND PRAISE: *My LORD Jesus, how great it is to serve You
and to glory in You!
I pray to be the best praising servant I can possibly be.
I pray to experience more of Your glory!
In Your precious Name!*

Week 13 ❖ Day 6   Theme: Serve   Mar 30

SERVE ME

HIS WORD: "Then he called the crowd to him along with his disciples and said: 'If anyone would come after me, he must deny himself and take up his cross and follow me. For whoever wants to save his life will lose it, but whoever loses his life for me and for the gospel will save it.'"
Mark 8:34-35

"Be dressed ready for service and keep your lamps burning, like men waiting for their master to return from a wedding banquet, so that when he comes and knocks they can immediately open the door for him."
Luke 12:35-36

MY CHALLENGE: *To look to Him, to learn from Him, to lean on Him, looking to serve Him at His will, in His way, while waiting for His glorious return.*

To My Serving Child:

Put all behind as you begin
To give yourself today.
Pass on to others My true love.
Serve Me in this, My way.

For as you serve the needs of those
I place upon your heart,
You serve Me as a child of Mine.
My love hence you impart.

You know not where I'm taking you.
On Me you must rely.
Put self below all other cares.
Your needs I will supply.

For this I called you forth, My child,
In service to fulfill.
Take up your cross and follow Me,
To serve Me as I will.

Your Ever-Caring Dad

CM

PRAYER AND PRAISE: *And so, L*ORD*, we come to the last day of this segment, reflecting on my service to You. However, L*ORD*, I pray this is just a beginning of serving You in a new, fresh and dynamic way. I give myself to You now to use me in any way You see fit. Glory to God!*

Week 13 ♦ Day 7   Theme: Serve   Mar 31

14

GRATITUDE FOR RESURRECTION

The bodily resurrection

Of Jesus Christ, our Lord;

The greatest miracle of all time,

His love to us outpoured.

YOUR RESURRECTION POWER

HIS WORD: "I want to know Christ and the power of his resurrection and the fellowship of sharing in his sufferings, becoming like him in his death, and so somehow to attain to the resurrection from the dead."
Philippians 3:10-11

MY CHALLENGE: *To know the power of His resurrection! It is this power that saves me, revives me, changes me, empowers me, (and much more) and will eventually lead me home to be with Him forever.*

My All-powerful LORD:

The power of Your resurrection,
I know must live in us;
For You have given us Your Spirit,
Just as at Pentecost.

That power that raised You up, my LORD,
Also resides in me.
I thank You for Your gracious gift,
The gift that set me free.

Freedom in the Spirit of God,
Not a license to sin;
But power to go and serve my LORD,
To bring glory to Him.

I have a new language to use,
One that praises Your Name,
And lifts You up to heavenly throne.
Your glory I proclaim!

So as Your power resides in me
And gives me victory,
I step out in boldness and love,
To share Your saving story.

That's what You have empowered me for,
The message of the hour,
To share with all who will receive
Your Resurrection Power.

Your Victorious Child

CM

PRAYER AND PRAISE: LORD, I know that's why You are different from all other gods, for You are truly the only God. The power of Your resurrection proves that! Thank You, LORD, that You have given me this same power to live my life for Your glory. Amen!

Week 14 ♦ Day 1 Theme: Gratitude for Resurrection **April 1**

THE SACRIFICE OF GRATITUDE

HIS WORD: "Through Jesus, therefore, let us continually offer to God a sacrifice of praise—the fruit of lips that confess his name. And do not forget to do good and to share with others, for with such sacrifices God is pleased."
Hebrews 13:15-16

MY CHALLENGE: *To praise my LORD continually.*
I do this by confessing His Name, doing good for others and sharing with others.

The sacrifice of gratitude
Gives pleasure to our LORD,
And brings to us the peace and joy
Of heavenly reward.

When we're in doubt or things go wrong,
Bad news has come this day,
Burst out with songs of praise to Him.
His peace will come your way.

To sing a song of praise to Him
With gusto in our song,
Will bring the enemy defeat,
And keeps us all day long.

We start our day and end our day,
With hymns of joyful praise,
Then sense His Presence filling us,
Our hearts become ablaze.

Our praise to Him brings victory,
In comfort of our soul.
We lay all things down at His feet
And give Him full control.

We thank You, LORD, for Your great care,
In all our earthly needs.
We give to You our gratitude,
For You're our God indeed.

CM

PRAYER AND PRAISE: *LORD, I praise You, but I confess it is never enough. I know there are many times when I should be praising Your Name, and I'm not. Help me, LORD, to remember to do it, and then just to do it! You are my LORD and God, and I praise You!*

Week 14 ❖ Day 2   Theme: Gratitude for Resurrection   **April 2**

MORE THAN ENOUGH

HIS WORD: "Now to him who is able to do immeasurably more than all we ask or imagine, according to his power that is at work within us, to him be glory in the church and in Christ Jesus throughout all generations, for ever and ever! Amen." *Ephesians 3:20-21*
Also see 2 Peter 1:3 and Philippians 4:19

MY CHALLENGE: To give Him my gratitude because I know that He IS more than enough!
I know He will supply all my needs and more too!

To answer all your prayerful needs,
Is your god a powder-puff?
Or do you need our living God,
For He is more than enough!

My God will supply all your needs,
Unlimited His supply.
His gracious heart will pour it out,
In an answer to your cry.

Worry not that He will hear you.
He knows everything you need.
Just take it all to Him in prayer,
As the planting of a seed.

Then water it with love for God.
With Him you have concurred.
Surrender all your life to Him,
And obey His Holy Word.

We know not what the future holds,
Nor know when He may fulfill.
We only know that He is God.
We trust Him for all until.

Therefore we put all in His hands,
With a Godly attitude.
This is how we must live our lives
And show Him our gratitude.

87.87

PRAYER AND PRAISE: My Jesus, I do give You my gratitude for
Your bountiful provision,
Your promises true and Your wonderful heart.
I place all in Your hands—even me—all of me!
Amen!

Week 14 ◆ Day 3   Theme: Gratitude for Resurrection   **April 3**

PLEASE YOUR HEART

HIS WORD: "So we make it our goal to please him, whether we are at home in the body or away from it."
2 Corinthians 5:9

MY CHALLENGE: *To please Him! Yes, simply to please Him. No more—no less. That is my challenge. Am I up to it?*

My Lord Jesus, Savior and Friend,
I want to please Your heart,
To be all You would have me be,
With Your joy to impart.

In this world, I am a stranger.
My thoughts are not in line
With the worldly way of thinking,
With actions so unkind.

It gives me great pleasure to know
Your heart is pleased today,
By my Godly thoughts and actions,
To follow in Your Way.

I'll give You glory and honor,
Till that day I depart.
There is no greater task on earth,
With joy to please Your Heart!

Therefore You have my gratitude,
In all things said and done;
For all the blessings that You give,
All through Your Loving Son.

To know You are my King of kings,
And You'll never depart
Gives comfort and peace to my soul.
I pray to please Your Heart!

CM

PRAYER AND PRAISE: *My God in heaven, Help me to stop more often and count the ways I could please Your heart, then go ahead and do it! I confess: I like to be pleased and am anxious to give that pleasure right back to the person who gave it to me. And so it is in our relationship! That's why I need to be more aware of pleasing Your heart, in all ways, every day. That's my goal. Thank You, Lord!*

Week 14 ♦ Day 4   Theme: Gratitude for Resurrection   **April 4**

GRATITUDE FOR RESURRECTION

HIS WORD: "Jesus said to her, 'I am the resurrection and the life. He who believes in me will live, even though he dies; and whoever lives and believes in me will never die. Do you believe this?'"
John 11:25-26

MY CHALLENGE: To believe—really believe—that He is the resurrection and the life. His bodily resurrection is central to my faith. Without His bodily resurrection I would have nothing but a dead religion. There are plenty of those in the world. But, praise to Him, I have a risen LORD!

Words can't express the gratitude,
The miracle You gave.
Through power of our Almighty God,
You rose up from the grave.

The greatest enemy of life
Was death forevermore;
But You overcame all of that
And opened heaven's door.

What joy there is we can express,
In shouting out our praise;
For You had conquered death and sin
And saved us from our ways.

There is no other we can praise,
Who's done it all for us.
We know there is no other God
Sheds light on our darkness.

That greatest miracle of all,
His rising from the grave,
Has given proof for all to see
He's here to heal and save.

We're grateful, LORD, for what You've done,
The promises You've made.
We have eternal life with You,
Because of price You paid.

CM

PRAYER AND PRAISE: LORD, as Your disciple said, "I believe, but help my unbelief." I know I believe in Your resurrection, but I also know many times I don't act or talk like it.
I pray to be such a believer that I will show gratitude for Your resurrection in all I say and do—all the time. Thank You, LORD Jesus!

Week 14 ❖ Day 5   Theme: Gratitude for Resurrection   April 5

HE IS RISEN

HIS WORD: "He is not here; he has risen!
Remember how he told you, while he was still with you in Galilee:
'The Son of Man must be delivered into the hands of sinful men,
be crucified and on the third day be raised again.'
Then they remembered his words."
Luke 24:6-8

MY CHALLENGE: *To wholeheartedly believe in His bodily resurrection
and to know that His resurrection power lives within each believer.
To be able to understand this, then express: "WOW! That is awesome!"*

"He is risen" are the greatest words
That ever could be spoken.
The greatest miracle of all,
The grip of sin was broken.

The resurrection of our Christ,
Produced by God's great act,
Gave hope of our eternity,
An undeniable fact.

That power that raised Him from the dead
And wrought the victory
He gives to us in full measure,
To serve Him properly.

There is no other power on earth
That raises from the dead,
Or saves and heals and delivers,
With earthly passions shed.

That power comes in the same way,
To share Him with the lost.
'Twill fall on us and fill us up,
That fire of Pentecost.

So it is on the road of faith,
Resurrection pow'r we need.
For we will always be assured,
He is risen indeed.

CM

PRAYER AND PRAISE: L*ORD*, help me to continue to increase my comprehension
of Your resurrection power and the fact that Your power is living in me.
Therefore I'm capable of doing a lot more than I'm doing, because of it.
So I pray for Your illumination and revelation to help me utilize
Your power in ever-increasing ways. Thank You, L*ORD*!

Week 14 ♦ Day 6   Theme: Gratitude for Resurrection   **April 6**

RESURRECTION POWER

HIS WORD: "The angel said to the women, 'Do not be afraid, for I know that you are looking for Jesus, who was crucified. He is not here; he has risen, just as he said. Come and see the place where he lay. Then go quickly and tell his disciples: "He has risen from the dead and is going ahead of you into Galilee. There you will see him." Now I have told you.'"
Matthew 28:5-7

MY CHALLENGE: To hear my LORD speaking His resurrection power to me. I have received it. I must remain aware of it, take advantage of it and use it.

To My Beloved Child:

I gave My life for you to live,
The sacrifice for all.
For truth I rose up from the grave,
To overcome the fall.

In the Bible My truth is found.
I breathed its every word.
You can depend upon its truth,
Waiting to be captured.

My written Word is there for you,
Takes precedence over all.
It rules supreme o'er all the earth.
All must obey its call.

My death and My resurrection,
The heartbeat of your faith.
So you must never waiver, child,
But look unto My face.

You have My resurrection power.
At Pentecost the same,
When I filled all the believers,
To go and preach My Name.

So take that power I gave to you,
To preach and heal the sick,
Deliver all the evilness,
Now dare to be drastic.

Your Loving Dad

CM

PRAYER AND PRAISE: Yes, my LORD and my God, empower me with Your resurrection power to be at Your work, doing Your will and going Your way. There is no greater privilege than this—no greater honor. I give myself to You, to be used by You today, with and through Your resurrection power! Amen!

Week 14 ❖ Day 7   Theme: Gratitude for Resurrection   April 7

15

PRAYER

Prayer gets us in touch with our LORD,

As we submit to Him,

To spend time in His devotion,

Our Holy Elohim.

CLOSET OF PRAYER

HIS WORD: "But when you pray, go into your room, close the door and pray to your Father, who is unseen. Then your Father, who sees what is done in secret, will reward you."
Matthew 6:6

MY CHALLENGE: To be in secluded prayer. Whatever my "prayer closet" is or wherever it may be, I must go there to spend time in seclusion with my God.

My Listening Lord:

The prayer closet is my hiding place,
Away from all worldly sounds,
To bring me closer to You, my Lord,
And sense Your Presence surround.

I cannot help but seek Your embrace
And to hear Your gentle voice.
To know that I have full assurance
Is cause for me to rejoice.

As I kneel in this closet of mine,
I will put all else aside,
Then focus on Your Holy Presence,
And with You alone abide.

I hear not but this heartbeat of mine,
At this time I do declare.
As I pray and am focused on You,
Here in my closet of prayer.

Your Praying Child
87.87

PRAYER AND PRAISE: I must confess, Father, that many times when I have gotten secluded with You in prayer, I felt uneasy. But every time I confessed and repented, I felt the release, and the returning back to You. Thank You, Lord, for being with me and helping me to learn to enjoy our secluded times together. Amen!

Week 15 ✦ Day 1   Theme: Prayer   April 8

ATTITUDE OF PRAYER

HIS WORD: "Devote yourselves to prayer, being watchful and thankful."
Colossians 4:2

MY CHALLENGE: *To be <u>devoted</u> to prayer: That IS the right attitude!*

Be in an attitude of prayer,
In everything you do.
Let your focus be on His life,
To light the path for you.

We know that prayer is nothing more
Than personal dialogue,
As friend with Friend, meeting as one,
Until the epilogue.

We learn to listen to His voice,
In quiet times alone,
To receive word He has for us,
And make it clearly known.

That is what prayer is all about,
As one-on-one we share,
That we would be constantly in
An attitude of prayer.

CM

PRAYER AND PRAISE: *My God, as I come to You in prayer,
I must confess that so often I don't have the right attitude.
Too many times I don't feel like praying.
I know. I know. I need to faith it, not feel it.
Therefore I promise, with Your help,
to put aside all negative thinking and to look at prayer
as a very positive action to take.
In the Name of Jesus,
Amen!*

Week 15 ❖ Day 2   Theme: Prayer   April 9

YOUR PLACE OF PRAYER

HIS WORD: "On the Sabbath we went outside the city gate to the river, where we expected to find a place of prayer."
Acts 16:13a

MY CHALLENGE: *To find a suitable place of prayer, a place that is quiet, without interruption, and where I can be comfortable to get quiet before my LORD.*

As you enter your place of prayer,
Be still and know He's there.
And close the world behind you, child,
Your needs with Jesus share.

He knows your needs before you do,
But now confess to Him,
All things in life that shouldn't be,
To clear your heart of sin.

Give praise to Your Father above,
And thank Him for His power,
To keep you in His love embrace,
And blessings every hour.

Give praise to Him for everything.
You talk with Him until,
Then as you leave your place of prayer,
His Will you will fulfill.

CM

PRAYER AND PRAISE: LORD, I come to You in the quietness of this space, to quiet my mind and spirit, to be at one with You. I want to hear Your voice and sense Your love and care for me, as I give myself into Your loving care.
Thank You, my Jesus.
So be it!

Week 15 ✦ Day 3 Theme: Prayer **April 10**

MY SECRET SOLITUDE

HIS WORD: "At daybreak Jesus went out to a solitary place. The people were looking for him and when they came to where he was, they tried to keep him from leaving them."
Luke 4:42

MY CHALLENGE: To make solitude with my Savior a first priority. How well I'm able to do this and how often is indicative of my maturity in Him.

It is in my secret solitude
I withdraw from all around,
And I take my time with Him alone,
Put aside all worldly sound.

For I know I must repel all thoughts
That bring road blocks with this time,
And to focus on His Presence here,
An experience sublime.

All the noise outside this solitude
Will all fade to quietness.
It is then I know tranquility,
All to feel His sweet caress.

So as often as I crawl away,
To devour His Holy food,
As I give myself to be alone,
In my secret solitude.

97.97

PRAYER AND PRAISE: I thank You, LORD, for allowing me to discover that we can be in secret solitude, even in a busy, noisy place. Not ideal, but possible. However I cherish our times together in the quiet solitude of being alone with You, and all the world without.
Thank You, My Jesus.

Week 15 ✦ Day 4   Theme: Prayer   April 11

EXALTED PRAYER

HIS WORD: "They raise their voices, they shout for joy;
from the west they acclaim the LORD's majesty.
Therefore in the east give glory to the LORD;
exalt the name of the LORD, the God of Israel,
in the islands of the sea.
From the ends of the earth we hear singing;
'Glory to the Righteous One.'"
Isaiah 24:14-16a

MY CHALLENGE: *To incorporate His Word and praise into my prayers.
That is, to pray His Word back to Him. What a joy!*

To take God's printed Word we have
And pray it back to Him
Is Exalted Prayer at its very best,
A good way to begin.

For as we take His printed Word
And use it in our prayer,
We're speaking it right back to Him.
We are a truth conveyor.

If prayers are dead and need some life,
Assured that they are heard,
Know you'll touch the heart of God
By praying back His Word.

Then as we lift His Name on high,
To give Him honor and praise,
We do the thing that's asked of us
And pray it in His way.

"My God, You love so very much,
You gave Your only Son."
From John 3:16 I've learned
Eternal life I've won.

Then, so it is, as we do this,
Appropriate His Word,
To pray it back to Him and then,
We're blessedly assured.

CM

PRAYER AND PRAISE: LORD, Your written Word is precious to me,
and as I exalt You in prayer, I pray it back to You.
May it bring You honor, glory and praise!
I thank You now for Your Word that guides me,
gives me strength and inspires me to follow You. Amen!

Week 15 ❖ Day 5   Theme: Prayer   April 12

ANSWERED PRAYER

HIS WORD: "Elijah was a man just like us.
He prayed earnestly that it would not rain,
and it did not rain on the land for three and a half years.
Again he prayed, and the heavens gave rain,
and the earth produced its crops."
James 5:17-18

MY CHALLENGE: *To know my prayers are powerful!
He will not go against His will for us,
therefore we need to be careful what we pray.
But, I need to know that my prayers are
heard by Him and will be heeded.*

*Before the rise of sun,
The day has just begun,
With time spent in my closet of prayer,
All to Him I submit,
Many things I admit,
And everything with Him I will share.*

*Then, as I bend my knee,
And make my needed plea,
I release all my needs to His care.
And, in the interim,
As I focus on Him,
At His feet, I leave it all there.*

*I thank Him for these hours
And for His mighty power,
In fighting a spiritual warfare,
For victory has been won,
With my LORD one on one,
With time in my closet of prayer.*

668.668

PRAYER AND PRAISE: *I praise You, my LORD, for answered prayer.
I know the answer may not come today or even tomorrow,
but You have heard it, have taken it to heart and are working on it.
Thank You, Jesus!*

Week 15 ❖ Day 6   Theme: Prayer   April 13

EXALT MY WORD

HIS WORD: "Exalt the Lord our God and worship at his footstool; he is holy." *Psalm 99:5*

"Exalt the Lord our God and worship at his holy mountain, for the Lord our God is holy." *Psalm 99:9*

MY CHALLENGE: *To exalt God's Word—His Name is Jesus— and to do so continually. Yes, He IS God's Word!*

To My Praying Child:

There is no other name on earth,
On which you can rely.
The only name by which you're saved
And truly satisfy.

And so it is, My beloved child,
As you lift up My Name,
I bring to you the best I have,
And set your heart aflame.

Now take My Word unto yourself
And pray it every day.
You'll find that doors will open wide,
When praying in this way.

Do not fear what others may think
Or what their words imply.
Just take My words and pray them, child.
On them you can rely.

You give your Father's heart a thrill,
To hear His words prayed back.
When your trust is always in Me,
You'll never have a lack.

Now lift My Name above all else,
That you have ever heard.
Give Me the honor and the praise,
As you exalt My Word.

Your Listening Dad

CM

PRAYER AND PRAISE: *I thank You for the reminder, Lord, for in my busy life I often forget to praise and lift up Your Name. I thank You for Your Word and I lift Your Name on high. As one has said before me: "O, for a thousand tongues to sing Your praise!" Amen and Amen!*

Week 15 ❖ Day 7   Theme: Prayer   April 14

16

HIS PRESENCE

His Presence was a promise made,

Became reality,

When He rose up from out of death,

To be our victory.

I BASK IN YOUR PRESENCE

HIS WORD: "This then is how we know that we belong to the truth, and how we set our hearts at rest in his presence whenever our hearts condemn us. For God is greater than our hearts, and he knows everything."
1 John 3:19-20

MY CHALLENGE: *To set my heart at rest in His Presence, that is, to bask in His Presence as I would bask in the sun, and as I do, I find my heart is at rest in Him.*

To My Living Lord:

I bask in Your Holy Presence.
I bask while You set me free.
I look to Your Presence to guide me,
Until Your Face I will see.

My task, to draw closer to You.
My task is to love You so.
I open the heart of my life.
You set my spirit aglow.

I ask You to keep me covered.
I ask to fill me also,
My life with Your Holy Spirit,
To walk Your path as I grow.

Now, as I trust You completely,
Now, as I've made it my task
To follow you implicitly,
It's in Your Presence I bask!

Your Loving Child
87.87

PRAYER AND PRAISE: *It is my prayer, dear Lord, to experience this rest in Your Presence, by basking there in increasing measure each day. I know that's the best possible place to be—in Your Presence, with Your protection, with Your praise on my lips. May it be so, always.*
So be it!

Week 16 ♦ Day 1 Theme: His Presence April 15

YOUR HOLY PRESENCE

HIS WORD: "In my integrity you uphold me
and set me in your presence forever."
Psalm 41:12

MY CHALLENGE: To know that I know that I know—
I am in His Holy Presence, now and forevermore.

I belong to You, and I seek Your face,
Longing to draw closer to You.
I quiet myself in Your Presence now,
As I hear Your voice breaking through.

I pray for protection and discernment,
To live out my life in Your care.
I will not worry or be defeated.
My life shall be a life of prayer.

It matters not what tomorrow may bring,
Living out a day at a time.
I trust in Your care, You lead me each day,
To walk with You, the world behind.

With You as my Lord on the road of life,
Helping me trod the hills and dales,
With my ups and downs all placed in Your hands,
Your Holy Presence I inhale.

10 8.10 8

PRAYER AND PRAISE: All I can do is praise You at this time, knowing that
I am in Your Holy Presence. Nothing can change that.
I praise You with tongues unknown,
I praise You with my own;
I praise You with all of my heart,
I praise You on Your throne.
I'm in Your Presence forever and ever.

Week 16 ❖ Day 2   Theme: His Presence   April 16

PEACE IN HIS PRESENCE

HIS WORD: "Let the peace of Christ rule in your hearts, since as members of one body you were called to peace. And be thankful."
Colossians 3:15

MY CHALLENGE: *To let the peace of Christ rule in my heart! Now, that is a true challenge, if I will but look at my own life and the many times I lack His peace and His Presence in me.*

There's peace in His Presence desired by all,
Just waiting for everyone.
It can be obtained as one turns to God
And worships His only Son.

All coming to Him, confessing their sin,
Giving their life and their all,
Receive new life in the family of God,
And heed His glorious call.

Then, as we embrace our new walk of life,
Developing in His lead,
We grow, as we walk in learning each day,
To trust Him for all our need.

All gold is refined as dross is removed,
By heat of the furnace fired.
The dross is removed, as it bubbles up,
To leave the gold purified.

On our road of faith, that's how it will be.
Though it may look perilous,
We focus our eyes and follow His path,
While living His life in us.

Therefore we expect to go through some heat,
To purify us from sin,
That all the dross be removed from our lives,
He cleanses us from within.

10 7.10 7

PRAYER AND PRAISE: *Yes, my LORD, I confess I have lacked Your peace and Presence, simply because I haven't sought it. I do now. Fill me with Your Peace in Your Presence at this time. Thank You.
And so it is!*

Week 16 ✦ Day 3   Theme: His Presence   April 17

THE MYSTERY OF GOD

HIS WORD: "Blessed are those who have learned to acclaim you, who walk in the light of your presence, O LORD."
Psalm 89:15

MY CHALLENGE: *To know and live the fact that the light of His Presence lives in me, and therefore I am blessed!*

The mystery of God above,
Is that He lives within.
A love so great, He gave His life
That I would be His kin.

How can it be a God so big
Created all you see,
Yet He has the ability
To also live in me?

My earthly mind can't fathom this,
To fully understand,
Creator of the universe
Is leading by His hand.

But this I know I trust in Him,
His promises are true.
It matters not I know not all.
My faith will see me through.

Therefore I can relax in Him,
Enjoy His company,
To talk with Him as friend to friend,
In perfect harmony.

I give Him thanks for His great love.
My future has been sealed.
Now I look forward to that time
His mystery is revealed.

CM

PRAYER AND PRAISE: *My Jesus, I confess, this is a mystery as to how the light of Your Presence lives within us, guides us, assures us, teaches us, protects us, and reveals to us Your heart of love. All I can say is: Thank You, Jesus!*

Week 16 ❖ Day 4   Theme: His Presence   April 18

HIS AWESOME PRESENCE

HIS WORD: "Surely you have granted him eternal blessings
and made him glad with the joy of your presence.
For the king trusts in the LORD;
through the unfailing love of the Most High
he will not be shaken."
Psalm 21:6-7

MY CHALLENGE: *To discover the awesomeness of His joy
while in His Presence.
That joy cannot be fully described nor fully appreciated,
because it is far beyond the human realm of reality.
All I can do is relax and relish it.*

When words won't come to you,
It's time to go to Him.
Spend time in His awesome Presence,
As one in lovely hymn.

Seek Him for who He is,
God of eternity.
Know that He wants the best for you,
To be in harmony.

Praise Him for His goodness.
Give Him acknowledgment,
It matters not amount of time,
Thankful every moment.

Soak up His Holy Presence.
Be still before His throne.
Cast aside all worldly thinking.
Focus on Him alone.

We give to You our lives.
Your words have set us free.
You're the only One we look to,
Submitting totally.

It's now I bow in prayer,
In true humility,
To come and seek Your Presence, LORD,
When word's won't come to me.

SM

PRAYER AND PRAISE: *Yes, My LORD, Your Presence is awesome. We see Your Presence in every salvation, every healing and every deliverance that takes place. We see it in Your beautiful nature, and we see it shining through other people. LORD, I pray to be a light beam of your Presence to others as I serve You this day. Amen!*

Week 16 ❖ Day 5   Theme: His Presence   April 19

YOUR PRESENCE

HIS WORD: "It is written: 'I believe; therefore I have spoken.' With that same spirit of faith we also believe and therefore speak, because we know that the one who raised the LORD Jesus from the dead will also raise us with Jesus and present us with you in his presence."
2 Corinthians 4:13-14

MY CHALLENGE: *To be prepared to be presented to the LORD in His very Presence at the time I am raised to Him. What a glorious thought! And then to know that His very Presence resides in me continually, until the time I meet Him face to face.*

Aware of Your Presence in Me,
I humble self to You,
To use me as You would, my LORD,
That I'd be tried and true.

It grieves me so when people seek
Pleasures of worldly ways,
And not give thought to You, our LORD,
Nor what You'd have to say.

How can it be, with all Your grace,
Your mercy, peace and love,
Revealed to us through creation,
Brought from heaven above?

LORD, I pray for all who will seek
Salvation by Your Grace,
Then move on to maturity,
To grow at their own pace.

We cannot hurry the process
Or shorten length of time,
But simply enjoy Your Presence,
Throughout our whole lifetime.

You guide me through my daily life,
To freshen and renew.
Thank You for Your Presence within,
That fills my life with You.

CM

PRAYER AND PRAISE: *My LORD, I pray that I may continually experience Your very Presence in ever greater ways, to the extent that I am trusting in You, leaning on You and praying to You in every situation. In the precious Name of Jesus.*

Week 16 ♦ Day 6   Theme: His Presence   **April 20**

MY PRESENCE

HIS WORD: "You have made known to me the path of life;
you will fill me with joy in your presence,
with eternal pleasures at your right hand."
Psalm 16:11

MY CHALLENGE: To be in His Presence at all times.
The LORD has eternal pleasures at His right hand,
as He fills me with joy.

To My Seeking Child:

You have read about My Presence,
My written Word to you,
From the very day of creation,
And every day on through.

You have known about My Presence,
From new birth until now.
You were filled with My Holy Spirit
And made your holy vow.

You have sensed My Holy Presence,
When My good Name you raised,
As you surrendered all to Me
And gave Me all your praise.

You have seen My Godly Presence,
Shared with you from My own,
As they gave of themselves to you,
To make My Word be known.

You have yearned for loving Presence,
Of Mine to comfort you,
In times when you were hurting so,
And didn't know what to do.

You sought by seeking My Presence,
Because you were afraid.
I gave you everything you need,
When asking for My aid.

As you continue to seek Me,
Forsaking common sense,
I give you more of Me this day,
My loving, Holy Presence.

And so, My child, as we go on,
Your destiny pursue,
Continue in joy of My Presence,
In guidance I give you.

Your Fulfilling Father

CM

PRAYER AND PRAISE: *The joy of Your Presence is the greatest joy of all. Greater than any worldly joy! So, I thank You, LORD, for the joy of Your Presence with me and in me, as I go about my daily tasks. There is none other who can give such joy, for there is no other Presence as Yours.*

Week 16 ❖ Day 7   Theme: His Presence   **April 21**

17

SUBMISSION

As we submit unto the L<small>ORD</small>

And follow in His way,

His blessings are poured upon us,

To give new life each day.

WE BOW TO YOU

HIS WORD: "Submit to God and be at peace with him;
in this way prosperity will come to you."
Job 22:21

MY CHALLENGE: *To submit to Him in order to have peace with Him.
There can be no peace with Him without submission.
Therefore, Lord, I submit to You.*

To My Precious Lord:

I bow to You, my precious Lord,
Quiet my busy mind,
To take these moments just with You
And leave my world behind.

There is no other here on earth
Who takes my sin away,
Fills me with Your Holy Spirit,
Gives power for each day.

It's You I need to grant me peace,
Tranquility so sweet.
That's why I must spend time with You,
While bowing at Your feet.

Take me and use me as You will.
I'll serve in one accord.
That is my prayer request today.
I bow to You, my Lord.

From Your Submitted Child

CM

PRAYER AND PRAISE: *Yes, Lord, I've discovered that the
more I surrender to You, the greater the peace I experience.
Submission, trust and peace go hand in hand.
Thank You for Your peace, my Lord, as I submit to You.
Amen!*

Week 17 ❖ Day 1   Theme: Submission   April 22

I SURRENDER MY ALL

HIS WORD: "But he said to me, 'My grace is sufficient for you, for my power is made perfect in weakness.' Therefore I will boast all the more gladly about my weaknesses, so that Christ's power may rest on me."
2 Corinthians 12:9

MY CHALLENGE: *To know that, in the surrender of my life to Him, I need not be concerned because His grace is sufficient, and the power of Christ rests on me. Praise the LORD!*

I have so many shortcomings,
That make me feel so small.
I wonder if I'll ever learn
To walk above a crawl.

My lack in my abilities,
I wonder why it's so;
But when I look to You, my LORD,
I live above my woes.

Your grace is sufficient for me.
I relish that is true.
Your Word has placed it on my heart,
In all things look to You.

Therefore I surrender my all,
My future and my past.
And give it all to You until
I'm home with You at last.

CM

PRAYER AND PRAISE: *I confess, my LORD, that I feel weak in so many things at so many times. And yet I know Your Word and Your promise give me the assurance that, as I surrender all to You, I need not worry, because Your grace is sufficient. Thank You, Jesus!
Amen!*

Week 17 ✦ Day 2   Theme: Submission   April 23

SURRENDER

HIS WORD: "Submit yourselves, then, to God.
Resist the devil, and he will flee from you.
Come near to God and he will come near to you."
James 4:7-8a

MY CHALLENGE: To submit to God. It IS a challenge for me
because of my human pride. But at the same time I have
a desire to draw near to Him. I know, I know, submission to Him is the key.

To surrender is to win the victory,
Not like the way of the world;
For their way is to crush, conquer and destroy,
Raising their banners unfurled.

Surrender is to bring true pleasure in life,
A pleasure Holy and pure,
That you would rejoice far above worldly ways,
Your eternal life assured.

Surrender your desires and your needs to Me,
Then see My mercy unfold;
For I love to see My children follow Me,
To give them pleasures untold.

Surrender your entire life to My Spirit.
Yield all your trials to Me,
That together, as we trod this path of life,
We'll rejoice in victory.

11 7.11 7

PRAYER AND PRAISE: I thank You, my God, for Your understanding,
because You know I have a struggle surrendering everything to You.
I ask You now to help me grow in this aspect.
Help me to surrender every part of my life to You,
for Your way is the victorious way.
Thank You, my God.

Week 17 ♦ Day 3   Theme: Submission   April 24

LAY IT ALL AT HIS FEET

HIS WORD: "One of them, when he saw he was healed, came back, praising God in a loud voice. He threw himself at Jesus' feet and thanked him—and he was a Samaritan."
Luke 17:15-16

MY CHALLENGE: *To kneel at the feet of Jesus, in submission to Him. Have you tried praising God in a loud voice, alone, in your prayer time? Don't knock it, if you haven't tried it.*

Chance takes a back seat to God's love.
Destiny is forged by Him.
Whatever may come your way today,
Don't think it just a whim.

God is still in the driver's seat,
Everything in control.
He does it all for His purpose,
His design and His goal.

We are to leave it all to Him,
And let Him have the reins,
To accomplish all the things in life,
That bring a final gain.

This is not a fatalist attitude,
Nor one that brings dismay,
But one of simple trust in Him.
So let Him guide your way.

He knows the future from the past,
He knows what's up today.
He wants the very best for you,
So follow in His Way.

You will never be discouraged
And never see defeat;
For victory, place your life in His.
Lay all down at His feet.

CM

PRAYER AND PRAISE: *My loving God, I give myself to You today, as I kneel before You, at Your feet, and lay everything right there. All my concerns, worries, troubles, trials, failures and defeats I leave them there, for You have promised to carry my burdens. Thank You, my LORD!*

Week 17 ♦ Day 4   Theme: Submission   **April 25**

MY PRECIOUS JESUS

HIS WORD: "Therefore God exalted him to the highest place
and gave him the name that is above every name,
that at the name of Jesus every knee should bow,
in heaven and on earth and under the earth,
and every tongue confess that Jesus Christ is LORD,
to the glory of God the Father."

Philippians 2:9-11

MY CHALLENGE: *To know the many various Names of our LORD Jesus,
the One to whom I submit my will and desires.
It is in this submission that I come to appreciate His
Holy Name and the part He plays in my life
and in the function of the whole earth.
That's my precious Jesus!*

Jesus, You are:

My Advocate,
My Wonderful Counselor,
My Creator,
My LORD Almighty,
My Deliverer,
My Everlasting Father,
My Friend,
My Glorious One,
My Holy One of Israel,
My Soon and Coming King,
My Great Light,
My Sanctuary,
My Messiah,
My Way,

My Truth,
My Life,
My Returning King,
My Judge,
My Great Forgiver,
My Refuge,
My Everlasting Joy,
My Prince of Peace,
My Sacrificial Substitute,
My Way of Holiness,
My Strength,
My One and Only,
My Precious JESUS!

IRR.

PRAYER AND PRAISE: *I confess, LORD Jesus, that the greater understanding
I gain of all these Names that have been attributed to You,
the greater understanding I have of You!
There is no other who can fulfill all of these Names.
Therefore I submit to You and to Your will for my life.
Amen!*

Week 17 ✦ Day 5   Theme: Submission   April 26

IN MY PRAYER TIME, O LORD

MY CHALLENGE: *To soar, to seek, to serve, to submit.*

I SOAR WITH YOU AS I PRAISE YOU
"Those who hope in the LORD will renew their strength.
They will soar on wings like eagles;
They will run and not grow weary,
They will walk and not be faint."
Isaiah 40:31

I SEEK YOU WITH ALL MY HEART
"You will call upon me and come and pray to me,
and I will listen to you.
You will seek me and find me when you
seek me with all your heart.
I will be found by you."
Jeremiah 29:12-14a

I SERVE YOU WITH ALL FAITHFULNESS
"Be sure to fear the LORD
and serve him faithfully with all your heart;
Consider what great things he has done for you."
1 Samuel 12:24

I SUBMIT TO YOUR LORDSHIP
"Submit yourselves, then, to God.
Resist the devil, and he will flee from you.
Come near to God and he will come near to you.
Humble yourselves before the LORD,
and He will lift you up."
James 4:7-8a, 10

IRR.

PRAYER AND PRAISE: *LORD, each one of these is a challenge to fulfill. But I pray to grow in my faith to the point of meeting the challenge of each. Thank You for Your power in me to do so. Amen!*

Week 17 ❖ Day 6   Theme: Submission   **April 27**

I AM YOUR GOD

HIS WORD: "Moreover, we have all had human fathers who disciplined us and we respected them for it. How much more should we submit to the Father of our spirits and live! Our fathers disciplined us for a little while as they thought best; but God disciplines us for our good, that we may share in his holiness. No discipline seems pleasant at the time, but painful. Later on, however, it produces a harvest of righteousness and peace for those who have been trained by it."
Hebrews 12:9-11

MY CHALLENGE: *To submit to the discipline of my heavenly Father. I do this for the sake of my own spiritual growth, and that I will produce a harvest of righteousness and peace.*

To My Precious Child:

My child, My child, My precious one,
If only you could know
The depths of Love I have for you.
Would set your heart aglow.

Please do not fret and worry so.
Trust in My tender care.
Open the eyes of your spirit,
For you're My loving heir.

Others may hurt and take your joy.
For this they have no right.
Take back your joy and carry on.
Then victory's in sight.

Reach out to Me, My loving child,
I know what's best today.
I love you more than you can know.
I'll lead you all the way.

So follow as I lead you on,
New ventures to behold.
Together we'll fulfill My cause.
Nothing will I withhold.

I AM your shield and all your strength,
I'm everything you need.
Let us joy in the victory,
I AM your God indeed.

Your Ever-Loving God

CM

PRAYER AND PRAISE: *As Your loving child, I reach out to take Your hand, to hold on tight and hear Your voice, guiding me through these steps of life. I thank You that my submission to You is growing each day, and each day I am feeling new power to overcome obstacles in life. Thank You, my Father God.*

Week 17 ❖ Day 7   Theme: Submission   April 28

18

RIGHTEOUSNESS

Right living with God a privilege,

To obey is our joy,

To talk with Him as friend to Friend,

And be His viceroy.

ROBE OF RIGHTEOUSNESS

HIS WORD: "I delight greatly in the LORD;
my soul rejoices in my God.
For he has clothed me with garments of salvation
and arrayed me in a robe of righteousness,
as a bridegroom adorns his head like a priest,
and as a bride adorns herself with her jewels."
Isaiah 61:10

MY CHALLENGE: To comprehend the delight and joy of wearing
the Robe of Righteousness Christ has given me!
I can't earn it, I can't buy it and nor can I bargain for it.
His salvation and robe are free for the asking!

To My Beloved LORD:

My garments of salvation, LORD
And robes of righteousness,
Given by You alone, my God,
To clothe me and to bless.

I cannot earn these garments fine,
For I can only give
My life to You a loving gift,
For You that I may live.

These acts of righteousness I give,
Fine linen bright and clean.
Brings glory to You alone, my God.
To praise is my routine.

I give my life and all for You
And persevere as Job,
To clothe myself with Christ above,
A joy to wear Your robe.

From Your Loving Child
CM

PRAYER AND PRAISE: I can only praise You with all my heart, LORD,
giving You thanks for the most beautiful gift of the righteousness robe.
The gift of salvation and righteousness are far greater than my words can express.
Praise Your Holy Name!

Week 18 ❖ Day 1   Theme: Righteousness   April 29

OUR BEAUTIFUL ROBE

HIS WORD: *"You are all sons of God through faith in Christ Jesus,*
for all of you who were baptized into Christ
have clothed yourselves with Christ."
Galatians 3:26-27

MY CHALLENGE: *To allow Christ to clothe me completely with Himself.*
I am washed in the water of baptism and clothed with His Majesty.
Can it get any better than that?

What will we wear to the party?
Clothes that will be nicest of all,
That will reveal prosperity,
Leaving people standing in awe.

Those worldly concerns are very real,
As we want to shine above all;
But this earthly pride will not last,
For our pride goes before a fall!

The clothes that we should be seeking
Are never made by mortal men,
But clothing only Christ will give,
To those whom He has forgiven.

He is our Robe of Righteousness,
For believers around the globe.
As we're clothed with the loving Christ,
Know He is our Beautiful Robe.

LM

PRAYER AND PRAISE: *I praise You for Your having clothed me*
with Yourself and Your righteousness. It humbles me.
I bow to Your Presence and to Your gift of righteousness.
Thank You, my LORD.

Week 18 ♦ Day 2   Theme: Righteousness   **April 30**

WE'RE ROYAL FAMILY

HIS WORD: "But you are a chosen people,
a royal priesthood, a holy nation, a people belonging to God,
That you may declare the praises of him who called you out of darkness
into his wonderful light."
1 Peter 2:9

MY CHALLENGE: *To take my rightful place as a person belonging to God.
I have been chosen, I am in the royal priesthood and
I belong to Him. Therefore I declare His praises.*

It thrills our hearts to be a part
Of the Royal Family.
To share with all His Royal call,
Much joy there is to be.

We cannot see all there's to be,
Nor what the future holds.
We trust His grace and walk His pace,
As partners in His fold.

We work as one till all is done,
To all His life is preached,
To do His plan to very end,
Until His goals are reached.

His message true, it comes to you,
The world is blind to see.
Those who believe with joy receive
Salvation that is free.

He's paid the fare so we can wear
His robes of righteousness.
To Him, our praise, His anthem raise.
His glory we profess.

Now that we're part, we'll ne'er depart,
For all eternity.
His praise we sing for He is King.
We're Royal Family!

CM (446.446)

PRAYER AND PRAISE: LORD, why is it I so often don't act like I'm a part of Your family, when I know that I am! I am a king's kid, living in Your Kingdom now! I ask You, LORD, to keep me reminded of that fact, that my life may reflect Your glory and the fact that I am a member of the royal family. Thank you, my Jesus. Amen!

Week 18 ❖ Day 3   Theme: Righteousness   May 1

WEAR HIS RIGHTEOUS ROBE

HIS WORD: "Then one of the elders asked me,
'These in white robes—who are they, and where did they come from?'
I answered, 'Sir, you know.' And he said,
'These are they who have come out of the great tribulation;
they have washed their robes and made them white in the blood of the Lamb.'"
Revelation 7:13-14

MY CHALLENGE: *To know He is my righteousness and that, even though I may go through many struggles here in this life, there is, waiting for me, His robe of righteousness, when I see Him face to face.*

If you could hold Him in your arms
And whisper in His ear,
Then tell Him anything you want,
What is it He would hear?

Would your words be something special
Or asking some desire?
Would you give Him your glorious praise
That sets His heart afire?

For now we have His blessedness,
To share around the globe,
As we look forward to that day
We wear His righteous robe.

Our words of love will ne'er run out,
Eternally proclaim,
All that which He has done for us.
Spread forth His Mighty Name.

The mounting pressures of this world
Would you with me forsake.
To trust Him with absolute trust,
And then His Peace partake?

That Day is coming down the road.
His glory we'll behold.
Then, when we see Him face to face,
We'll wear His righteous robe.

CM

PRAYER AND PRAISE: *Lord, I can do nothing but praise You at this time, for You have paid the ultimate price that I would be set free, be made righteous, and then to have the privilege of wearing Your robe of righteousness when I gaze at You beyond this life.*

Week 18 ❖ Day 4   Theme: Righteousness   May 2

MADE PERFECT FOREVER

HIS WORD: "Since that time he waits for his enemies to be made his footstool, because by one sacrifice he has made perfect forever those who are being made holy."
Hebrews 10:13-14

MY CHALLENGE: *To accept the fact that I have been made perfect forever. I am being made holy, thanks to that shed blood of Christ Jesus. He is my sacrifice for sin, and therefore my sins are forgiven and gone forever.*

Jesus did for us the most wonderful thing:
He made us perfect forever.
His sacrifice on the cross of Calvary,
It was our salvation answer.

He is, for us, unconditional Love.
It is difficult to fathom,
That He could love us to such an extent
He'd give Himself as a ransom.

His love so great He forgave all our sins,
By shedding His blood for all time.
We need not plead for forgiveness from Him;
He's forgiven for our lifetime.

When He gave His life for your sins and mine,
It was a one-time sacrifice.
We were set free from the burden of sin,
Because He paid the total price.

We now rejoice in our freedom of life;
Our sins are gone forevermore,
All sins of the past, the future and now,
Far beyond the most distant shore.

We thank You, LORD, for this new way of life,
That sets us apart from the rest;
For You have made us perfect forever,
In You, we are thoroughly blessed.

10 8.10 8

PRAYER AND PRAISE: *My LORD, I admit I don't fully understand all that You have done, through Your sacrifice, to bring me righteousness. I only know I am learning more every day and growing in You. I thank You daily for this and for the gift of righteousness. Amen!*

Week 18 ❖ Day 5   Theme: Righteousness   May 3

RIGHTEOUSNESS

HIS WORD: "Blessed are the peacemakers,
for they will be called sons of God."
Matthew 5:9

"Peacemakers who sow in peace
raise a harvest of righteousness."
James 3:18

MY CHALLENGE: *To raise a harvest of righteousness,
as a peacemaker of the L*ORD*.*

*The wisdom that comes from heaven
Is pure and gives release.
The seed whose fruit is righteousness
Will reap harvests of peace.*

*We cannot make ourselves righteous,
By doing some good works.
We cannot earn, in any way,
The right to heavenly perks.*

*Righteousness can never be earned.
A gift, it's given free,
If we'll believe His sacrifice,
Shed blood on Calvary.*

*He bore our sins in His body,
That we'd be truly blessed,
That we would die to all our sins
And live for righteousness.*

Receive Him as Savior and L*ORD*.
*Then walk with Him each day
In personal relationship.
Come, follow in His Way.*

CM

PRAYER AND PRAISE: L*ORD, help me to continually be a peacemaker of
Yours and to live to reap a harvest of righteousness.
Amen!*

Week 18 ❖ Day 6   Theme: Righteousness   **May 4**

A LIFE OF RIGHTEOUSNESS

HIS WORD: "He himself bore our sins in his body on the tree, so that we might die to sins and live for righteousness; by his wounds you have been healed."
1 Peter 2:24

MY CHALLENGE: To die to sins and live for righteousness! It's that simple, and yet it doesn't seem simple in living it out in everyday life. But I must know that I know that by His wounds I have been forgiven forever and have been healed.

To My Righteous Child:

My child, will you please look to Me
And to My righteous act;
For I have given you My all.
Accept this real-life fact.

It's not a story told of old.
It's real for you today.
The blood I shed on calvary
Forgave you for always.

I gave My righteousness to you,
As you trust alone in Me.
You have not gained it on your own,
A gift from Calvary.

So take this gift and use it, child,
With others, as you share.
Recall I AM Your righteousness;
You're My extended care.

As you touch others with My love,
In words and with your deeds,
You're acting out the gift I gave,
To give out of your needs.

For you have heard it all from Me.
To this, you have confessed.
Therefore you're living My lifestyle,
A life of righteousness.

Your Giving God

CM

PRAYER AND PRAISE: Yes, my LORD, I'm living a life of righteousness because of You, and only because of You.
How grateful I am! Praise Your Holy Name!
What a blessing to be the loving child of an ever-loving heavenly Father!
I bow in thanksgiving, gratitude and ever-giving praise to You!
So be it!

Week 18 ✦ Day 7   Theme: Righteousness   May 5

19

HEAVEN BOUND

What a glorious confidence we have,

To know we're heaven bound,

When our time on earth is over,

A new life to have found.

SHOUTING VICTORY

HIS WORD: "Then I heard a loud voice in heaven say: 'Now have come the salvation and the power and the kingdom of our God, and the authority of his Christ. For the accuser of our brothers, who accuses them before our God day and night, has been hurled down. They overcame him by the blood of the Lamb and by the word of their testimony; they did not love their lives so much as to shrink from death.'"

Revelation 12:10-11

MY CHALLENGE: *To be ready to shout the victory!*
I wait for His return to earth, for He'll surely come again.
I look forward to His coming and to His glorious reign.

To My Coming Jesus:

Right now it's unrealistic,
In fact seems mighty strange,
That this old world will come to end
And make a total change.

That's the way You say it will be.
We know Your Word is true.
We trust Your written prophecy.
Therefore we follow You.

We know not when You'll come again,
When this will all take place,
A time that changes history,
And see You face to face.

We thank You, LORD, for all You'll do
At time You will descend,
Your Kingdom of Peace to bring us
And bring world's sin to end.

Oh, what a joy that will be ours,
Unspeakable in its scope,
As we see Your glorious coming,
And see our Blessed Hope.

For You will come to reign o'er earth
And bring this all about.
We won't contain our happiness,
The victory we will shout.

Your Waiting Child
CM

PRAYER AND PRAISE: LORD, the more we contemplate Your return, the greater excitement we sense. Therefore I pray to be ready to shout victory with all the other saints. What a glorious day that will be!
I give You praise every day for being a part of this.
I look forward with great hope and to Your poured-out bliss. Amen!

Week 19 ❖ Day 1   Theme: Heaven Bound   **May 6**

BELIEVERS DELIGHT

HIS WORD: "The seventh angel sounded his trumpet, and there were loud voices in heaven, which said:
'The kingdom of the world has become the kingdom of our LORD and of his Christ, and he will reign for ever and ever.'"
Revelation 11:15

MY CHALLENGE: *To stand firm, keep watch and be ready. That trumpet will surely sound. He will surely come! As a believer, I will surely experience delight!*

Stand firm, keep watch and be ready.
Keep eyes focused on Him.
When you hear that shout of victory,
You'll see Him coming in.

I know not when that hour will be,
Nor do I know the day;
But I am ready for Him to come
And Him to have His way.

He'll part the stars and split the sky,
Then give a victory shout.
He's come to reign forever more.
That's what it's all about.

It will not be a pretty scene,
For those who don't believe;
For they will be gathered in,
Their judgement to receive.

For as He's ruling on this earth,
As King of kings proclaimed,
He'll bring His judgement on this world.
Then all will know His Name!

When the LORD has kept His promise,
Returned and made things right,
Then all believers will rejoice.
That scene is their delight.

CM

PRAYER AND PRAISE: *LORD, help us to learn to praise You all the more while here on earth, that we'll be better prepared to praise You with welcome shouts when You return. I pray to be ready. I praise You for helping me. Thanks to You, we have the victory!*

Week 19 ❖ Day 2   Theme: Heaven Bound   May 7

FACE TO FACE

HIS WORD: "Now we see but a poor reflection as in a mirror;
then we shall see face to face. Now I know in part;
then I shall know fully, even as I am fully known."
1 Corinthians 13:12

"No longer will there be any curse. The throne of God and of the Lamb
will be in the city, and his servants will serve him.
They will see his face, and his name will be on their foreheads."
Revelation 22:3-4

MY CHALLENGE: *To keep watch for the signs of the times, in my
anticipation and preparation to see Him face to face.
I must remember that the returning Jesus is my Blessed Hope.*

Face to face is my strong desire,
When from this life I will retire.

I trust You, my Lord, in every way,
Searching for Your Way through this day.

I look to You in all my strife,
In all the aspects of my life.

I feel as though life's been a chase.
Now guide me through at quiet pace.

I depend on You this very hour,
To fill me with Your mighty power.

Following the Word You have decreed,
Looking to You for all my needs.

My thanks for Your transforming Grace,
That saves me from this worldly race.

The trials of life so burdensome,
Your blessings to me have overcome.

When heaven's gates are open wide,
And You call in Your glorious bride.

You'll bring me to Your dwelling place;
We'll see each other face to face.

8 8

PRAYER AND PRAISE: LORD, *as I keep watch for all the signs of the times,
and have the certainty of Your return, I am blessed to have that assurance that
I'll see You face to face. Thank You, LORD!*

Week 19 ❖ Day 3   Theme: Heaven Bound   May 8

STREETS OF PUREST GOLD

HIS WORD: "The wall was made of jasper, and the city of pure gold, as pure as glass.
The twelve gates were twelve pearls, each gate made of a single pearl.
The great street of the city was of pure gold, like transparent glass."
Revelation 21:18, 21

MY CHALLENGE: *To catch a glimpse of the glory of heaven awaiting. God is creating a city of pure gold that has beauty far beyond my ability to understand here on earth.
All I can do is be ready and look forward, with anticipation to that great day!*

There is no need to fret the strife,
Nor look back to the past.
He holds our future in His hands,
His victory won at last.

No matter what our dreams may be,
Nor what the prophecy.
The LORD is sure to return again
To end our history.

He has been our truth and our life,
As claimed in His own Word,
To bring about the golden time.
In that, we are assured.

We cannot see the overall,
The picture He can see.
Therefore we trust His loving care,
To bring the victory.

While here on earth we bide our time,
In serving Him until
That hour He says, "My child, come home,
Your work has been fulfilled."

As we see the lights of Glory,
It's beauty can't be told.
We see our home is waiting there
On streets of purest gold.

CM

PRAYER AND PRAISE: *LORD, I can do nothing but praise You at this time, for enabling me to catch a glimpse of Your glory and the beauty that awaits us.
Oh, that I would have more tongues to praise You,
more time to lift up Your Name, more talent to use the words and more tears to shed for Your beauty.
Amen!*

WAITING FOR HIS NOD

HIS WORD: "Behold, I am coming soon!
Blessed is he who keeps the words of the prophecy in this book.
Blessed are those who wash their robes, that they may have the right to
the tree of life and may go through the gates into the city."
Revelation 22:7,14

MY CHALLENGE: *To wait, in great anticipation, for that Day
of His return to earth to reign and rule.
I'm not to be so heavenly bent that I'm no earthly good.
I need to look forward while, at the same time, carrying out my
Godly duties, while I'm still here.*

I've got a home that's there for me,
When time on earth is through,
A home that God has built Himself,
Somewhere beyond the blue.

While serving in my place on earth,
I try to see it all.
It's far beyond my vision now,
But waiting for His call.

The LORD will call me home one day.
I'm ready for the flight.
Then heaven's gates will open wide.
'Twill be a glorious sight.

With gates of pearl and golden streets,
And ne'er the night shall fall.
The LORD Himself will greet me there,
In answer to His call.

In meantime, there is work to do,
To follow His commands,
To be in service to the King,
As His extended hands.

My thanks to Him, my LORD and God,
While treading on this sod.
I'm looking forward to my home,
While waiting for His nod.

CM

PRAYER AND PRAISE: LORD, *I confess that Your return is so exciting that it can consume my thoughts and time. Help me to keep my focus on You while, at the same time, keeping my feet on earth to serve You. Thank You, Jesus!*

Week 19 ♦ Day 5   Theme: Heaven Bound   May 10

PATIENTLY WE WAIT

HIS WORD: "It (the grace of God) teaches us to say 'No' to ungodliness and worldly passions, and to live self-controlled, upright and godly lives in this present age, while we wait for the blessed hope—the glorious appearing of our great God and Savior, Jesus Christ, who gave himself for us to redeem us from all wickedness and to purify for himself a people that are his very own, eager to do what is good."
Titus 2:12-14

MY CHALLENGE: *It is simply this: To wait patiently, to stand firm, keep watch and be ready.*

Patiently we wait for His call,
As we anticipate
To hear that voice break through the sky.
It's time to celebrate.

Wide is the gate, broad is the road
That many trod in vain.
They have not seen the truth in Him,
Eternal life to gain.

But small the gate, narrow the road
Leads to life eternal.
Only a few choose the right course,
Receive life supernal.

That Name has been worshiped throughout,
O'er two millennium.
Will come in Person once again,
For all His Christendom.

When He breaks through that eastern sky,
'Twill be a glorious sight,
As He returns in all His glory,
In all His Golden Light.

Oh, what a great day that will be,
The Day we graduate.
We look forward to His return,
As patiently we wait.

CM

PRAYER AND PRAISE: LORD, I confess that many times I am not patient. But this I know: when it comes to Your return, I must wait patiently. Thank You, LORD, for Your great power in my life to do just that. So be it!

Week 19 ♦ Day 6   Theme: Heaven Bound   May 11

A HOME PREPARED

HIS WORD: "In my Father's house are many rooms; if it were not so, I would have told you. I am going there to prepare a place for you. And if I go and prepare a place for you, I will come back and take you to be with me that you also may be where I am."
John 14:2-3

MY CHALLENGE: *To be heaven bound and have the glorious assurance of that fact. That means coming to salvation in Christ, if I haven't already, being filled with His Holy Spirit and growing in Him. This gives me that glorious assurance, as I look forward to being heaven bound.*

To My Anticipating Child:

I have a home prepared for you,
Just waiting on My shelf.
I know your likes and your desires,
More than you know yourself.

When that time comes, I call you home,
To your heavn'ly abode.
I'll take it from its resting place
And see your joy explode!

For it will be more beautiful
Than anything you've dreamed.
Your dreams are based on earthly sight,
While Mine for now unseen.

You cannot imagine the sight,
From perspective of earth,
The beauty of My heavenlies
I designed from its birth.

By faith, you must accept the fact,
The promise of My Word,
That when you leave that earth of Mine,
See My Glory unheard.

Be sure to walk My narrow road,
Keeping My Way in view;
For this road leads on to heaven,
A home prepared for you.

Your Carpenter Dad

CM

PRAYER AND PRAISE: *Jesus, today I again confess You as my Savor and receive You as LORD of my life. I thank You, Jesus, my LORD, for bearing my sins and setting me free in order that I would be heaven bound. Amen!*

Week 19 ♦ Day 7　　　Theme: Heaven Bound　　　May 12

20

FEAR NOT

"Fear not for I am with you,"

The Master said to me.

"Let not your heart be troubled,

For I have set you free."

FEAR NOT

HIS WORD: "But now, this is what the LORD says—he who created you,
O Jacob, he who formed you, O Israel:
'Fear not, for I have redeemed you;
I have summoned you by name; you are mine.'"
Isaiah 43:1

MY CHALLENGE: *To fear not! Do not fear! Fear not!
With the LORD, this is absolute truth. I am to live it!*

My Comforting LORD:

I listen, LORD, to what You've said,
For You created me:
"Fear not, for I have redeemed you,
My Word has set you free."

"Now hear My call, I've summoned you
By name. I claim you're Mine.
So look to Me and Me alone,
For you are My design."

"When passing through the waters deep,
I'll always be with you.
When passing through the rivers wide,
They'll not sweep over you."

"When walking through the fires of life,
You will not be consumed.
My arms are wrapped around you, child.
Recall I AM your Groom."

"I love you more than you can know.
You're precious in My sight.
Be not afraid, I AM with you.
I AM your Holy Light!"

And so, my LORD, I've heard Your Word.
It makes me to rejoice;
For I'm with You forevermore.
I've made that precious choice.

Your Comforted Child

CM

PRAYER AND PRAISE: *Yes, my LORD, You are my Holy Light.
You light my way so that I need not fear, as I trust in You for all things,
at all times, in all circumstances.
LORD, I know the promises of Your Word to not fear. I pray You would help
me at those times I slip and have doubt and fear.
I know You are with me and will answer. Therefore I am committed to not fear.
Thank You, Jesus!*

Week 20 ✦ Day 1   Theme: Fear Not   **May 13**

DO NOT FEAR

HIS WORD: "So do not fear, for I am with you;
do not be dismayed, for I am your God.
I will strengthen you and help you;
I will uphold you with my righteous right hand.
For I am the LORD, your God,
who takes hold of your right hand and says to you,
Do not fear; I will help you.
Isaiah 41:10,13

MY CHALLENGE: To <u>know</u> that He is the Great I AM and, therefore, there is absolutely no need to fear. He is my God. He strengthens me. He upholds me. He is with me. He assures me that I need not fear. Could He make it any more plain?

Do not fear, for I AM with you,
And do not be dismayed.
I will strengthen you and help you,
My Righteousness displayed.

You know I AM the LORD, your God.
I take you by the hand.
I say to you, You're not to fear.
My child, heed My command.

For worry saps you of your strength.
It leaves you weak and pale.
I give to you My promises,
For they will never fail.

Rejoice in Me, your LORD and God.
Give me your listening ear;
For I'm the Holy One, your God.
You never need to fear.

CM

PRAYER AND PRAISE: Dear LORD, my prayer is like a two-sided coin.
On the one side, I pray to have a greater fear of You, my LORD;
To know You better and to follow You more closely.
On the other side, I pray to have less fear of the world and its offerings.
There is no need for me to fear the things of the world while, at the same time, trusting You, my LORD, and Your great promises and provisions.
Thank You, Jesus!

Week 20 ❖ Day 2   Theme: Fear Not   May 14

YOUR WALK ALONE #1

HIS WORD: "But those who hope in the Lord
will renew their strength.
They will soar on wings like eagles;
they will run and not grow weary,
They will walk and not be faint."
Isaiah 40:31

MY CHALLENGE: *To maintain my hope in the Lord.
I will not fear in the midst of adversity. Adversity can sometimes be overwhelming.
But I have an overcoming God!*

When the loss of a loved one leaves you alone
Your hopes and dreams forever lost,
You cry and you scream and ask a thousand times,
Can I bear the emotional cost?

The pathway of loneliness seems without end,
Many stumbling blocks to endure.
Though family and friends surround you with their love,
Your walk alone is still obscure.

The nighttimes reflect the darkness of the soul.
As heart-sinking feelings prevail,
You lecture yourself that you must move along,
Plodding the pathway of travail.

With life's clouds of darkness hanging overhead,
Discouragement is all you know.
You suddenly remember your God above.
A beam of light comes breaking through.

11 8.11 8

PRAYER AND PRAISE: *Yes, my Lord. Let Your beam of light break through
to me today, as I put my hope in You. I pray to be renewed in strength, able
to run and walk without growing weary and faint. I look to You and You alone,
as I spend this time alone with You.*

Week 20 ❖ Day 3 Theme: Fear Not **May 15**

YOUR WALK ALONE #2

HIS WORD: "When you pass through the waters, I will be with you; and when you pass through the rivers, they will not sweep over you. When you walk through the fire, you will not be burned; The flames will not set you ablaze. For I am the LORD, your God."
Isaiah 43:2-3a

MY CHALLENGE: *To hold on tight to Him as I pass through my struggles. Remember: "This, too, shall pass." So, whatever I may be going through, I'll stay close to Him, as He leads me through to the other side, always remembering He is the God who is with me.*

You cry to the Lord and cast all at His feet,
Begging for strength is your demand;
You're trying to break through the ceiling of brass,
And somehow reach to grasp His hand.

You find He is there at the deepest of need,
He fills you with His love and grace;
It's possible you had not reached Him before,
Sorrow had smothered His embrace.

Though the hurt remains, you perceive there is hope,
To gather strength needed for life.
With the Lord by your side and leading the way,
You must cast upon Him your strife.

As you begin to pray and praise His Holy Name
And claim Him as your Cornerstone,
You find that your path of life takes on new hope,
He's with you on your walk alone.
Yes, He'll always be with you on your walk alone.

11 8.11 8

PRAYER AND PRAISE: *I come now to praise You, LORD Jesus, as You are leading me through the quagmire of my life, help me see Your light. Thank You, Jesus!*

Week 20 ◆ Day 4 Theme: Fear Not **May 16**

FEAR OF THE LORD

HIS WORD: "He (the angel) said in a loud voice, 'Fear God and give him glory, because the hour of his judgment has come. Worship him who made the heavens, the earth, the sea and the springs of water.'"
Revelation 14:7

MY CHALLENGE: *To fear God and give Him the glory! Not to fear the things and the people of the world, and to worship my Creator.*

Always be zealous for the fear of the Lord.
*Do not let your heart be led astray.
There's surely a hope in the future for you.
Give your heart and your mind to His Way.*

*Fear God in your life and give glory to Him.
Be strong in your faith to walk His Way;
Then, His peace will be yours, deep down in your soul,
And His contentment in you will stay.*

*He commands we fear not the ways of the world,
But put everything under His care;
And if we are to fear anything at all,
Fear Him, as you meet with Him in prayer.*

11.9.11.9

PRAYER AND PRAISE: *I pray that You would help me become more zealous for You. Let my fear of You increase and my fear of the world decrease, to the point I am trusting only in You. I have to pray this repeatedly,* Lord, *but I'll not give up because I know You will never give up on me. To fear the* Lord *is awesome! Amen!*

Week 20 ✦ Day 5   Theme: Fear Not   **May 17**

IN HIM WE LIVE AND MOVE

HIS WORD: "God did this so that men would seek him and perhaps reach out for him and find him, through he is not far from each one of us. 'For in him we live and move and have our being.' As some of your own poets have said, 'We are his offspring.'"
Acts 17:27-28

MY CHALLENGE: To reach out and find God, in Whom I am to live and move and have my being.

In Him we move and have our being.
We seek Him, reaching out.
As we are offspring of our God,
We should never have a doubt.

To have a fear of the future,
When gazing down ahead,
Projecting yourself mentally,
Will bring you naught but dread.

You need not worry down the road,
For Jesus has a plan,
To make your life a fruitful one,
Together Hand in hand.

Sit quietly with your Savior,
His voice of love will soothe.
He gives to us His love embrace.
In Him we live and move.

CM

PRAYER AND PRAISE: Thank You, Jesus! For it is because of You, only You, that I can live and move in freedom without fear of worldly things. My fear of You is a Godly fear that gives me my life and movement today. In Jesus' Name, Amen!

Week 20 ❖ Day 6   Theme: Fear Not   May 18

I AM YOUR HOPE

HIS WORD: "May the God of hope fill you with all joy and peace as you trust in him, so that you may overflow with hope by the power of the Holy Spirit."
Romans 15:13

"But even if you should suffer for what is right, you are blessed. 'Do not fear what they fear; do not be frightened.' But in your hearts set apart Christ as LORD. Always be prepared to give an answer to everyone who asks you to give the reason for the hope that you have. But do this with gentleness and respect."
1 Peter 3:14-16

MY CHALLENGE: *To keep my hope in the God I fear. He is the great I AM, the Father of all. I am His child.*

To My Trusting Child:

Fear not, dear one, I am with you
And never shall I leave.
I want to share My Peace with you.
Be ready to receive.

I AM your God of hope, My child.
I fill you with My joy.
As you trust in Me day by day,
My Peace you will enjoy.

With Holy Spirit power in you,
That fills to overflow,
I have so very much for you,
In helping you to grow.

So put your hope in Me, dear one.
I will not let you down;
For you mean all the world to me.
I'm waiting with a crown.

It matters not what trials you're in.
With all things you can cope.
Cast all your cares on Me today.
In Me, you have your hope.

That's why, regardless depth of pit,
I'm your solution here.
Just rise to me, above all else.
You never need to fear.

Your Caring Father
CM

PRAYER AND PRAISE: *Dear Father God, I confess that as I have contemplated the "Fear of the LORD" these last few days, I have come to a more loving, awesome fear of You and less the fear of the world. I thank You, my God!*

Week 20 ✧ Day 7 Theme: Fear Not **May 19**

21

LISTEN TO HIS VOICE

Let's stop and listen to His voice,

Hear what He has to say;

For His soothing words will guide us

Through all our futile fray.

HELP ME TO LISTEN

HIS WORD: "Here I am! I stand at the door and knock.
If anyone hears my voice and opens the door,
I will come in and eat with him, and he with me."
Revelation 3:20

MY CHALLENGE: *Again, to hear His voice!
When He knocks on the door of my heart,
will I hear His voice and answer Him?*

My All-Knowing God:

> Lord, **help me to listen**
> To Your voice everyday.
> Help me to understand it all,
> To follow in Your way.
>
> I sense, so many times,
> My hearing is not good.
> My mind races on other things,
> To not do what it should.
>
> I know You must be speaking,
> So dull though be my ear.
> I want to hear Your every word
> And hear them loud and clear.
>
> And now, as I hear You,
> Breaking through the din,
> I listen close to every word
> And soak it up within.
>
> As I learn to listen
> And hear You from the start,
> I bow down now and thank You, Lord,
> For speaking to my heart.
>
> I cast aside all else,
> Make You my only choice.
> Therefore, I give myself to You
> And listen for Your voice.

Your Listening Child
SM

PRAYER AND PRAISE: *My Lord, You lead me, You guide me, You speak to my heart and encourage me. I thank You for helping me to learn to listen to Your voice, by first quieting myself before You. Thank You, Jesus!*

Week 21 ♦ Day 1   Theme: Listen to His Voice   **May 20**

LISTEN FOR THE PROMPTING

HIS WORD: "The watchman opens the gate for him, and the sheep listen to his voice. He calls his own sheep by name and leads them out. When he has brought out all his own, he goes on ahead of them, and his sheep follow him because they know his voice."
John 10:3-4

MY CHALLENGE: *To follow my Shepherd's voice.*
I hear Him. I heed Him. I honor Him.

Our ears can be dulled so easily
By worldly sounds that roar,
That will divert our attention
From hearing our Savior.

Are you listening for the prompting
The Spirit in your heart?
That still small voice that whispers soft,
His wisdom to impart?

A small directive it could be
Or be a gentle nudge,
To reach out to another hand,
To guide them as they trudge.

The LORD may bring across your path
One needing a loving touch.
He's guiding you, as His own hands,
For them, to be a crutch.

Each moment, as you listen close,
Keep open wide your ears;
For He is guiding you, His child,
So you should never fear.

That still, small voice comes quietly,
To be His helping hand,
To fill His purpose in this world,
And to fulfill His plan.

CM

PRAYER AND PRAISE: *Okay, LORD Jesus, I'm listening. I confess to You that the noises of the world are so loud I have trouble hearing Your still, small voice. Your promise is that we will hear. My problem is that I feel dense. My promise is that I will do whatever is necessary to be still and hear Your voice. I grant You permission to do whatever is necessary in my life that I will learn to listen to Your still, small voice.*
Amen!

Week 21 ◆ Day 2   Theme: Listen to His Voice   **May 21**

THE FOURTH WATCH OF THE NIGHT

HIS WORD: "During the fourth watch of the night Jesus went out to them, walking on the lake. When the disciples saw him walking on the lake, they were terrified. 'It's a ghost,' they said, and cried out in fear. But Jesus immediately said to them: 'Take courage! It is I. Don't be afraid.'"
Matthew 14:25-27

MY CHALLENGE: *To be aware of this special time of early morning, and keep my eyes open to whatever Jesus may want to show me. It may not be walking on a lake, but maybe it could be one of my own pet projects in which I'm sinking. Whatever, I am to keep aware when waking up during this special fourth watch of the night.*

During the fourth watch of the night,
They're very precious hours.
All the world around is quiet.
Your Word we can devour.

These special hours we cherish.
It is a holy time,
Communing with You, our Savior,
Hours that are sublime.

For, Jesus, it is You alone,
During these quiet hours,
That we can hear Your voice so clear.
We're open to devour.

The pre-dawn hours of three to six
Give opportunity
To receive Your inspiration
And creativity.

In darkness of these early hours,
We thought we couldn't do,
There's found a blessing to behold,
In spending time with You;

It's during these times of reflection,
Before the morning light,
We're open to receive Your Word,
The fourth watch of the night.

CM

PRAYER AND PRAISE: *My LORD Jesus, I dare to pray that You would show me something special during a fourth watch of the night. My request is that You wake me at your pleasure, and then help me to immediately understand it is of You, so that I will arise to commune with You. In great anticipation I will wait to hear Your voice share something very special. Thank You, my LORD.*

Week 21 ❖ Day 3 Theme: Listen to His Voice   **May 22**

* Note from author: The vast majority of the rhymes in this book were written during a fourth watch of the night.

HEAR HIS CALL

HIS WORD: With this in mind, we constantly pray for you, that our God may count you worthy of his calling, and that by his power he may fulfill every good purpose of yours and every act prompted by your faith.
We pray this so that the name of our LORD Jesus may be glorified in you, and you in him, according to the grace of our God and the LORD Jesus Christ.
2 Thessalonians 1:11-12

*MY CHALLENGE: To hear His calling on my life,
and to fulfill it in accordance with His purpose and
by His power, in order that the LORD Jesus may be glorified in me.*

Be alert when He calls you to action,
Ready to fill His call.
Worry not what others may do or say.
Fret not, for God's your All!

When His gentle voice calls, will you hear Him,
Your answer to entreat,
In obedience to His perfect will for you,
To make your life complete.

He's always ready to speak to your heart,
Addressing your burden,
By putting aside all interruptions,
If ready to listen.

Where e'er you are, be alert to His voice.
Listen to Him always.
You can be sure His call will come to you.
Then give Him all the praise.

10 6.10 6

PRAYER AND PRAISE: LORD, that's what I pray for—to hear Your calling on my life—that I will know, for an absolute certainty, I am hearing You and following the way You would have me travel.
Thank You, my LORD Jesus!

Week 21 ✦ Day 4   Theme: Listen to His Voice   May 23

LISTEN TO HIS VOICE

HIS WORD: "My sheep listen to my voice; I know them, and they follow me. I give them eternal life, and they shall never perish; no one can snatch them out of my hand. My Father, who has given them to me, is greater than all; no one can snatch them out of my Father's hand. I and the Father are one."
John 10:27-30

MY CHALLENGE: *To listen to the Shepherd's voice.*
I am a sheep of His pasture. He knows me. I follow Him.
He protects me. His Name is Jesus!

If we do not stop to listen
To what He has to say;
Is it because we're afraid to hear
Of our own wrongful way?

If we really want answered prayer
And know His will for us,
Shouldn't we put Him first and then
Give to Him all our trust?

If we desire to know the truth
And pay the higher price,
Can we not listen to His voice,
And follow His advice?

If we want to hear Him speak to us,
It's we must make the choice.
We are to set all else aside
And listen to His voice.

CM

PRAYER AND PRAISE: *My Shepherd of shepherds, my mighty LORD of lords. I stop now and listen for Your voice. I am still and listening. I am quiet before You. Speak now. Your servant waits.*

Week 21 ♦ Day 5 Theme: Listen to His Voice **May 24**

LISTEN

HIS WORD: "After the earthquake came a fire, but the LORD was not in the fire. And after the fire came a gentle whisper. When Elijah heard it, he pulled his cloak over his face and went out and stood at the mouth of the cave."
1 Kings 19:12-13

MY CHALLENGE: To hear His gentle whisper whenever He speaks to me. Whenever He speaks to me, the difficulty is to shut out the outside noises, concentrate on that gentle whisper deep within, and know that it is the LORD.

Shhh! Shhh! Be quiet and listen.
His voice speaking to you.
His words are quiet and gentle.
Now hear them coming through.

Listen before the world comes in,
Disturbing inner peace,
Demanding your attention now,
All other things to cease.

But this is not the way of the LORD.
Your eye should be on Him,
Your ear attentive to His voice,
The world's sounds to be dim.

It's that first loving voice you hear,
With tone of His pure love.
It brings to you His word today,
By power of Holy Dove.

So take that loving voice you hear.
His word will edify.
If in line with His written Word,
You need not reason why.

His word to you is precious, child.
It brings you great rewards.
So listen to the King of kings.
He is our LORD of Lords.

CM

PRAYER AND PRAISE: LORD, as I bow before You and pray, I acknowledge that it is my desire to hear Your voice. At the same time, I acknowledge that I need to know Your written Word, which is most important. So, as I study Your Word, help me to absorb and understand it. Thank You, Jesus!

Week 21 ♦ Day 6   Theme: Listen to His Voice   May 25

STORMIN' HEAVEN

HIS WORD: "Do not merely listen to the word, and so deceive yourselves. Do what it says. Anyone who listens to the word but does not do what it says is like a man who looks at his face in a mirror and, after looking at himself, goes away and immediately forgets what he looks like. But the man who looks intently into the perfect law that gives freedom, and continues to do this, not forgetting what he has heard, but doing it—
he will be blessed in what he does."
James 1:22-25

MY CHALLENGE: *To persevere.*
Persevere in "stormin' heaven" to hear His voice and follow His Word.

My Pleading Child:

When stormin' heaven till answer comes through,
Your persistence is the key.
Keep up the stormin'; don't ever take leave,
Keeping up your mighty plea.

You then hear My voice coming through to you.
Listen closely to My word;
For My voice guides and assures of My love,
As you follow Me onward.

It builds up your faith as you persevere,
Finding you are drawing near.
Then break through that brass ceiling overhead.
Now things are becoming clear.

You're flooded and filled with wonderful joy,
The warmth of My Presence here.
You sense My glory like never before,
While stormin' heaven's frontier.

Your Appreciative Father
10 7.10 7

PRAYER AND PRAISE: *I pray for a heart that has the will to do whatever is necessary to persevere in seeking Your will, i.e. in "stormin' heaven" to hear and heed Your word for me to follow. Thank You, my LORD!*

Week 21 ❖ Day 7   Theme: Listen to His Voice   May 26

22

HELP FROM THE LORD

I lift my eyes unto my Lord,

For He has given new birth.

My help comes from the Lord, my God,

Maker of heaven and earth.

HELP ME, HOLY SPIRIT

HIS WORD: "Guard the good deposit that was entrusted to you—guard it with the help of the Holy Spirit who lives in us."
2 Timothy 1:14

MY CHALLENGE: To be led by the Holy Spirit in all I do and say.
To listen, learn and be led by Him.

My Precious Holy Spirit:

Help me, Holy Spirit,
To walk Your way today,
To listen to Your voice today,
The words You have to say.

Your yoke I take on me,
To follow after You.
To go in the direction, LORD,
You'd have me to pursue.

Oft I have a problem,
To hear Your gentle voice;
For worldly sounds are all around,
In trying to make a choice.

I want to follow You,
Obeying at all times.
Help me, precious Holy Spirit,
To walk Your path Divine.

I'm thankful for the times
I hear Your voice break through,
It makes me wonder why, at times,
You love me as You do.

You're patient and you're kind,
To guide me all the way,
If I will but listen to You,
To walk Your path today.

For nothing is so grand
As to walk in Your Will,
To have You guide me in my steps,
Knowing You will until.

As I close my request,
With desire to commit,
My prayer will always be to You,
Help me, Holy Spirit.

Your Listening Child
SM

PRAYER AND PRAISE: Thank You, my beloved LORD, for sending the
Holy Spirit, my Comforter and Guide.
My helpmate, my counselor, always by my side.
You live within me and fill me up, to overflow with power
to serve You, my God, You're the only God to worship. Amen!

Week 22 ♦ Day 1   Theme: Help from the LORD   **May 27**

HELP ME! HELP ME, MY LORD! PART #1

HIS WORD: "The LORD is with me; I will not be afraid. What can man do to me?"
Psalm 118:6
(Also quoted in the New Testament: Hebrews 13:6)

MY CHALLENGE: To look to Him and not to anyone else, including ourselves. He is the One with the answers. He is the One with the power. He is the One to Whom I am to turn in every need.

Help me! Help me! Help me, my LORD!
Please help me to contend.
I am accused of doing wrong.
My honor I defend.

I stand before You innocent.
No wrong have I conceived.
I want restored my purity,
That others not perceive.

They think I am who I am not.
They know not what's inside.
I've got to shout and make it known.
In You, I've got my pride.

The LORD spoke clearly to my heart,
"You fear for naught, dear one.
Do not worry, for I am here,
And we will overcome."

CM

PRAYER AND PRAISE: LORD, That is my prayer today. Help me! Help me! Help me! I confess my pride has been hurt, when it shouldn't matter at all when I'm trusting in You. I'm so terribly human, LORD, when I know I should be trusting completely in You. I thank You now as I give myself wholly to You.
Amen!

Week 22 ❖ Day 2   Theme: Help from the LORD   May 28

HELP ME! HELP ME, MY LORD! Part #2

HIS WORD: "The LORD is with me; he is my helper.
I will look in triumph on my enemies."
Psalm 118:7
(Also quoted in the New Testament: Hebrews 13:6)

MY CHALLENGE: *To look to Him <u>and</u> to the promises in His Word.
I'll trust Him and His Word to fulfill every need and meet every challenge.*

"You're not as trusting as you think.
Remember, I know all.
I will spare you the agony
Of memories to recall."

"Be that as it may, my dear child.
Rest in My blissful peace;
For I have things in My control,
And I will handle this."

Therefore let go of hanging on
To things of little worth.
Do not look to human advice,
And things that stem from earth."

"Always stand on My promises.
They'll keep you to the end.
Never waiver, nor turn aside.
Remember, you're My friend."

"Throughout your life, let's live as one.
We'll be in one accord.
I'll always hear you when you call,
'Help me! Help me, my LORD!'"

CM

PRAYER AND PRAISE: *Thank You, LORD! I come to You now with praise!
I do know You help me, as You have done so many times.
The evidence is overwhelming.
I know not why I doubted when I should have trusted.
I now look to You for the fulfillment of Your promises
and thank You for being my LORD and Savior.
To You be the glory!*

Week 22 ♦ Day 3   Theme: Help from the LORD   May 29

MY HELP COMES FROM THE LORD

HIS WORD: "I lift up my eyes to the hills—where does my help come from? My help comes from the LORD, the Maker of heaven and earth."
Psalm 121:1,2

MY CHALLENGE: To <u>know</u> that my help comes from the LORD! I may seek help from others, but it's to Him I should always go first. It's on Him I am to rely. It's Him in whom I am to trust.

Be not afraid, nor be distraught.
Don't wallow in despair.
Please look to Me in troubled times,
For I AM always there.

I wait for you to look My Way
And walk the path with Me,
To know My loving Presence, child,
And from your troubles flee.

My heart does ache to hold you close,
To have you place your trust
In One who wants to carry you,
And bring you what is just.

Now, open up your life to Me.
Take up My mighty Sword.
Then learn from it, so you can say,
"My help comes from the LORD."

CM

PRAYER AND PRAISE: LORD, I confess that I usually look to others first for my help. And I should know better. Help me, LORD, to put You first in all aspects of my life. I am to lean my head upon Your breast, just as that precious disciple did at the Last Supper, symbolic of my trusting in You for all my help. Yes, for <u>all</u> my help. Thank You, my LORD Jesus!

Week 22 ❖ Day 4   Theme: Help from the LORD   May 30

THE ONLY WAY IS YOU!

HIS WORD: "In my distress I called to the LORD;
I cried to my God for help.
From his temple he heard my voice;
my cry came before him, into his ears."
Psalm 18:6

MY CHALLENGE: To remember to cry out to Him for help
and then to remember that He does hear me!
His answer will come in His perfect timing for me.

You've come to the end of your rope,
And you realize your need.
You go to Him in confession
And plant a prayerful seed.

Oh, LORD, I know not where to turn.
I know not what to do;
But I make this my confession now,
My answer, LORD, is You!

I've tried it long to go my way,
In just the way I'd planned;
But I give up and come to You,
To follow Your command.

I now know my independence
Brought this calamity;
But as I now surrender all,
You'll bring the victory.

Your victory is not the same
As the world understands;
But rather it is giving self,
To hold on to your hand.

Your will to follow is the way
To faithfully pursue,
And look to You for all my help,
For the only way is You!

CM

PRAYER AND PRAISE: LORD, I'm supposed to be a grown-up child of Yours, and yet there are times when I feel the need to cry out to You for help. But then again, I'll always be Your child, and I'll always need Your help. Therefore I'll always have opportunity to cry out to You.
What a privilege! What an honor! What a joy!

JESUS, HELP ME

HIS WORD: "The woman came and knelt before him. 'Lord, help me!' she said. He replied, 'It is not right to take the children's bread and toss it to their dogs.' 'Yes, Lord,' she said, 'but even the dogs eat the crumbs that fall from their masters' table.' Then Jesus answered, 'Woman, you have great faith! Your request is granted.' And her daughter was healed from that very hour."
Matthew 15:25-28

MY CHALLENGE: *To have no fear to cry out to my Lord Jesus at all times for my needs. The one thing that holds me back is pride. I must put that aside, cry out to Him, and know that He hears and listens to every cry from my heart.*

"Jesus, help me!" is my loud cry,
When evil strikes at me,
When tempting rises to control,
And bring defeat to be.

There is no other Name on earth
That has the power of this,
When uttered in His truth and love,
Will give you victory's bliss.

For that Name is above all names.
As "Jesus" we cry out,
All demons flee and Satan bows.
There is no greater clout.

So, as a child of the Most High,
Take glory in that Name,
That you have taken on yourself,
Forever to proclaim.

As you grow stronger day by day,
The road of faith you walk,
You know you have authority,
To use His Name in talk.

When you invoke that powerful Name,
You have the victory.
Now do it all in love and grace.
"Jesus, help me!" is the key.

CM

PRAYER AND PRAISE: *Thank You, my Lord Jesus, for every opportunity to come to You. Not just those times I need help, but other times too, when I come to You just to thank and praise Your Holy Name! It's in Your precious Name I pray.*

Week 22 ❖ Day 6   Theme: Help from the Lord   **Jun 1**

TURN PROBLEMS INTO PEACE

HIS WORD: "For I am the LORD, your God, who takes hold of your right hand and says to you, Do not fear; I will help you. Do not be afraid, O worm Jacob, O little Israel, for I myself will help you, declares the LORD, your Redeemer, the Holy One of Israel."
Isaiah 41:13-14

MY CHALLENGE: *To put my problems into His hands and, thereby, receive His Peace. I must remember: His peace is that inner peace that passes all understanding and comforts me in the midst of turmoil.*

To My Beloved Child:

First seek Me, LORD God Almighty,
In decisions you make.
Ask first before taking action,
What is best for your sake.

Regardless what it may entail,
Be it small or be it great,
Or it may seem unimportant,
And you don't want to wait,

That's just the time you'll go it wrong
And rush into the night,
To make choices without asking,
When I have shed no light.

When you're faced with a choice to make,
There's no need to hurry.
Just take your time and come to Me.
Then you'll never worry.

You know that I will lead you straight.
I know what's best for you.
Bring all your decisions to Me.
I'll guide you what to do.

In that way you will do it right,
In giving full release,
By placing all into My Hands,
You'll rest in perfect Peace.

Your Loving Dad

CM

PRAYER AND PRAISE: *Thank You, my loving Father, for taking me by the hand so that I need not fear the many things I have feared. I rest now, Your Peace within my heart. Thank You!*

Week 22 ❖ Day 7   Theme: Help from the LORD   **Jun 2**

23

HEALING/MIRACLES

He is the miracle worker

And the healer of all.

He brings salvation to the ones

Who on His Name they call.

EMPOWERED BY HIM

HIS WORD: "On one occasion, while he was eating with them, he gave them this command: 'Do not leave Jerusalem, but wait for the gift my Father promised, which you have heard me speak about. For John baptized with water, but in a few days you will be baptized with the Holy Spirit.'
'But you will receive power when the Holy Spirit comes on you; and you will be my witnesses in Jerusalem, and in all Judea and Samaria, and to the ends of the earth.'"
Acts 1:4-5, 8

MY CHALLENGE: *To be baptized with His Holy Spirit, with the power to follow Him, obey Him and serve Him as His present-day disciple.*

My Living Lord:

Fill me with Your Holy Spirit,
To be empowered by You,
To follow You in all Your ways,
Your mission to pursue.

As Your extended hands, I pray,
With love to touch someone,
That they'd receive Your saving grace,
And to Your Kingdom won.

Oh, what it means to be empowered,
To work out in Your field.
Then, with Your Word, to save and heal,
And bring a mighty yield.

It matters not what it may cost.
You'll give me all I need,
To walk the road laid out for me.
I walk by faith indeed.

I need it for my daily walk.
Please fill me, is my plea,
That I would work all You have planned,
To do Your will for me.

You will not leave me all alone,
Your mission to pursue.
You fill me with Your Holy Spirit,
To be empowered by You.

Your Loving Child
CM

PRAYER AND PRAISE: *Yes, my Lord, fill me to overflowing with the power of Your Holy Spirit, that I will hear You and follow Your every direction and fulfill the purpose You have for me on earth. Thank You for this gift of the Holy Spirit, to better serve You, in cooperation with other born-again, Spirit-filled Christians. Thank You, Jesus!*

Week 23 ❖ Day 1   Theme: Healing/Miracles   **Jun 3**

JESUS, THE GREAT "I AM"

HIS WORD: "Martha answered, 'I know he will rise again in the resurrection at the last day.'
Jesus said to her, 'I am the resurrection and the life. He who believes in me will live, even though he dies; and whoever lives and believes in me will never die. Do you believe this?'"
John 11:24-26

MY CHALLENGE: *To believe this most important fact and most remarkable of miracles: that is, that Jesus is the Resurrection and the Life. There is no other. Never has been and never will be.*

Our Jesus is the great I AM,
The Master of the world.
He is the Way, the Truth and Life.
His banner we unfurl.

He'll always be the Great I AM,
Creator of mankind,
The Resurrection and the Life,
The Healer of the blind.

He saves the lost and heals the sick,
Delivers from evil force.
He draws the people by His love.
He's our Divine resource.

So, thank You, Lord, for who You are,
The Son of God, His Lamb.
We bow to You and give our all.
You are the Great I AM!

CM

PRAYER AND PRAISE: *I confess, my Lord, You are the Resurrection and Life; You are the Healer and Miracle Worker. You are the great I AM! Therefore I commit all to You and to Your care.
I submit to You my needs of body, soul, spirit and finances.
Thank You, my Lord Jesus!*

Week 23 ❖ Day 2   Theme: Healing/Miracles   **Jun 4**

NEED A MIRACLE?

HIS WORD: "You are the God, who performs miracles;
you display your power among the peoples."
Psalm 77:14

"Believe me when I say that I am in the Father and the Father is in me;
or at least believe on the evidence of the miracles themselves."
John 14:11

MY CHALLENGE: *To believe in Jesus and the evidence of His miracles.
He still performs miracles today. They have never ceased.
What a joy it is to be in the family of this Miracle Worker!*

When we get tired of living life,
The world is in a spin.
Our life's been drained of energy.
We need a boost within.

Take mind in hand, turn it around,
To focus on the LORD.
Then we will see with clarity
His love to us outpoured.

For as His hand begins to move
And lifts us to His throne,
He gives embrace of love and joy,
And makes His grace be known.

His Presence penetrates our lives,
Fills to capacity.
Our situation that seemed lost
Is now a victory.

We take this time to honor You
And fill it all with praise.
We lift Your banner up on high.
Your Holy Name we raise.

We thank You, LORD; all praise to You.
We've learned it once again:
As we give up all things to You,
The miracles begin.

CM

PRAYER AND PRAISE: *First, my LORD, I praise You for Who You are!
Secondly, I praise You for Your miracle working power even today.
Thirdly, I praise You for the miracles to come,
for come they will, like the world has never seen before,
as we move on into the end of time. Thank You, Jesus!*

A TOUCH OF HEALING

HIS WORD: "When she heard about Jesus, she came up behind him in the crowd and touched his cloak, because she thought, 'If I just touch his clothes, I will be healed.' Immediately her bleeding stopped and she felt in her body that she was freed from her suffering."

Mark 5:27-29 See verses 25-34

MY CHALLENGE: To have the faith of this woman—"If I just touch." That has been the great challenge down through the ages and is yet today the same challenge for me. "If I just touch—"

The woman was sick for twelve years,
A constant bleeding disease.
She had been to many doctors.
None could satisfy her pleas.

Then she heard about this Jesus
And saw Him in a big crowd.
So she came up behind Him there.
Just to touch Him she had vowed.

She felt if she could just touch Him,
Without His being aware,
So she reached out and touched His cloak.
She was healed right then and there.

She knew she'd been healed by His power,
Without a verbal appeal.
Her suffering had come to an end.
She had been totally healed.

The power had gone out from Jesus.
He knew someone had received.
She fell at His feet in fear, trembling,
Told Him what she had achieved.

Jesus, in love and compassion,
Had given her life a new lease.
"Daughter, your faith has made you well,
You are healed go forth in peace."

87.87

PRAYER AND PRAISE: LORD Jesus, it was recorded in scripture that the father said to You: "I do believe; help me overcome my unbelief!" *(Mark 9:24)* That's the way I feel, my LORD! I need a stronger faith, a more dynamic faith, a faith that will move mountains.
I thank You now for moving me in that direction and providing everything I need to accomplish just that. Amen!

Week 23 ❖ Day 4   Theme: Healing/Miracles   **Jun 6**

BY FAITH IN HIS NAME

HIS WORD: "By faith in the name of Jesus, this man whom you see and know was made strong. It is Jesus' name and the faith that comes through him that has given this complete healing to him, as you can all see."
Acts 3:16

MY CHALLENGE: *To have faith in that Name, a healing faith, a saving faith, a wonderful faith that sustains and carries me through this life.*

It's faith in that Name of Jesus,
That healing comes to be.
No other name has that power,
To face adversity.

That Name that is above all names
Should be first in our lives,
If we are to live productively,
Till that time He arrives.

Wonderful faith that comes through Him,
Brings us to His healing,
And, as we share Him with others,
Makes His life appealing.

That Name will save us from our sins,
To set completely free.
It's faith in that Name of Jesus
That brings us liberty.

CM

PRAYER AND PRAISE: L ORD, I know, from Your Word, what faith means, what it does and how important it is. Now, L ORD, be with me as I step out in faith, even though it feels more like a leap. Thank You, Jesus!

Week 23 ❖ Day 5   Theme: Healing/Miracles   Jun 7

THE GREATEST MIRACLES

HIS WORD: "Do not believe me unless I do what my Father does. But if I do it, even though you do not believe me, believe the miracles, that you may know and understand that the Father is in me, and I in the Father."
John 10:37-38

MY CHALLENGE: A two-fold challenge: 1) To believe the miracles of the Bible, and 2) To know and understand that Jesus and Father are One.

The greatest miracles of all time,
Can be reduced to three.
They're two in the life of the Lord
And one for you and me.

The virgin birth of our Lord God,
Brought from heaven to earth
By the Holy Spirit Himself,
A miracle in birth.

It had never happened before
And never will again.
This was the Great Shepherd of God,
To bring us to His Pen.

The resurrection of our Lord,
From depths of death He came,
To lead the way for all of us,
Salvation to proclaim.

The promise of resurrection
Gives us hope indeed,
For our eternal life with Him,
A miracle indeed.

How can a man be born again?
Once asked the Pharisee.
"Eternal life belongs to him,
When he believes in Me."

There is nothing that can equal
The miracle of new birth,
Save His birth and resurrection,
The greatest things on earth.

CM

PRAYER AND PRAISE: My Lord, how is it possible to give You enough thanks and glory for Your resurrection, Your miracles, Your healing power and Your saving grace? To You be the glory forever! Amen!

Week 23 ❖ Day 6   Theme: Healing/Miracles   Jun 8

I MAKE YOUR LIFE ANEW

HIS WORD: Be joyful always; pray continually; give thanks in all circumstances, for this is God's will for you in Christ Jesus. *1 Thessalonians 5:16-18*

MY CHALLENGE: *To praise and give thanks to Him even in times of hurting and pain. It is now and will continue to be one of the greatest challenges in my faith walk. I am His beloved child and I must believe that He will bring the very best for me out of my present circumstances.*

To My Hurting Child:

You say you have received bad news,
I sense your aching heart;
What is bad news to you My child,
Is good news from the start.

Your sickness is eating away,
At your strength and your will;
Just quiet your soul before Me,
Look to Me and be still.

I know the big picture is Mine,
You see only a little bit;
That's why trust is so important,
To My Way please submit.

I have your best interest at heart,
I've not forsaken you;
I reach out to embrace you child,
My love for you is true.

Believe My healing Hand is out,
Restoring through and through;
Receive My healing touch for you,
To make your life anew.

Now as you praise My Holy Name,
To give thanks as you should;
Let us relax in victory,
As bad news turns to good.

Your Healing Dad
CM

PRAYER AND PRAISE: L*ORD* Jesus, I'm learning to give You thanks in all circumstances, even though it is so very difficult at times. Thank You for Your patience as I put my trust in You regardless of that which is going on around me. You're patient. I'm trying. You're teaching. I'm learning. You're touching. I'm healing. You're filling. I'm receiving. I am Your loving child. You are my loving Dad. Thank You for everything!

Week 23 ❖ Day 7   Theme: Healing/Miracles   Jun 9

24

GIVING

Our giving is a way of life.

Lord Jesus showed the way

To give ourselves for others' sake,

And to our Lord obey.

A LIVING SACRIFICE

HIS WORD: "Therefore, I urge you, brothers, in view of God's mercy, to offer your bodies as living sacrifices, holy and pleasing to God—this is your spiritual act of worship. Do not conform any longer to the pattern of this world, but be transformed by the renewing of your mind. Then you will be able to test and approve what God's will is
—his good, pleasing and perfect will."
Romans 12:1-2

MY CHALLENGE: *To be transformed by the renewing of my mind, that I would comprehend the full extent of offering my body as a living sacrifice, which is a spiritual act of worship.*

My Beloved LORD:

I pray to be a living sacrifice,
Holy and acceptable to You,
Submitted completely unto Your will,
To share with others Your good news.

I want to be what You'd have me to be,
To do what You'd have me to do,
To go wherever You want me to go,
Your will for my life to pursue.

To be Your extended hands, reaching out,
To give my life to Your full reign,
Obedience to be in automatic mode,
Living in Your Holy Domain.

Whatever's holy and acceptable to You,
I accept Your word of advice.
Therefore I give myself to You, my LORD,
As a living true sacrifice.

Your Loving Child
10 8.10 8

PRAYER AND PRAISE: My LORD, I confess that the patterns of this world have a very strong pull, and I know I need to resist that, turn from it, and be transformed by the renewing of my mind. Therefore, that is my prayer—
my earnest prayer—that I would look to You and You alone,
that my faith would reflect my spiritual act of worship. I give myself to You,
totally, wholly, to mold me and make me
according to Your will, not mine. Thank You, LORD!
Amen!

Week 24 ❖ Day 1   Theme: Giving   Jun 10

GIVING IS A WAY OF LIFE

HIS WORD: "Remember this: Whoever sows sparingly will also reap sparingly, and whoever sows generously will also reap generously. Each man should give what he has decided in his heart to give, not reluctantly or under compulsion, for God loves a cheerful giver."
2 Corinthians 9:6-7

MY CHALLENGE: *To give until it helps, to give with a good, positive attitude, to give in complete trust in Him.*

Our giving is a way of life,
To follow His own lead,
To give our lives for others' sake,
To give our all indeed.

Our giving may be limited.
Resources are so small.
It matters not exact amounts,
But percentage overall.

I give myself a sacrifice,
A living one at that,
To serve my LORD in every way,
In my own habitat.

He may not call to foreign shore,
A mission to embrace,
But asks of us to give our all
Right here in our own place.

Our service is a way to give,
As His extended hands,
To do what He would have us do
And follow His commands.

We have this life to live on earth,
And as we go on living,
There's one thing we must ask ourselves:
How is it with our giving?

CM

PRAYER AND PRAISE: LORD, I pray that my giving, in every facet of my life, would be joyful, without regret, generous, without remorse, and regular—without interruption.
May I be the cheerful giver You bless!
Thank You, LORD!

Week 24 ❖ Day 2   Theme: Giving   Jun 11

HELPING HANDS

HIS WORD: "And we urge you, brothers, warn those who are idle, encourage the timid, help the weak, be patient with everyone. Make sure that nobody pays back wrong for wrong, but always try to be kind to each other and to everyone else."
1 Thessalonians 5:14-15

MY CHALLENGE: *To have my "helping hand" ready to do just that—to reach out wherever needed, whenever I can, with whatever I have to give.*

Focus on the needs of others.
Be His extended hands.
Reach out and touch others in His Name,
That they would understand.

He is the Savior of mankind.
He came to set us free.
He took the stripes upon Himself,
Gave life abundantly.

There's healing in His love for us,
Deliverance from all sin.
We're free to walk this earth of His,
In victory as we win.

It's not that we'll have no more trials
Or struggles in our life.
It's just that we will look to Him
And trust Him through all strife.

So keep your eyes focused on Him,
Your ears to hear His voice,
With hearts all warmed with His pure love,
All willing to rejoice.

In light of this, there is His plea,
To answer His demands.
Let's fulfill the Great Commission,
Reach out with helping hands.

CM

PRAYER AND PRAISE: L ORD, I pray to be Your extended hand reaching out to others, as You so lead. The need is far greater than I can meet alone, but as You lead, I will give to meet it.
Thank You, my L ORD!

Theme: Giving

GIVE ALL YOU CAN

HIS WORD: "Give and it will be given to you. A good measure, pressed down, shaken together and running over, will be poured into your lap. For with the measure you use, it will be measured to you."
Luke 6:38

MY CHALLENGE: *To give all I can, in accordance with God's Word. It is also a challenge to realize that this verse is talking about every aspect of my life and not just monetary giving.*

Give all you can to charity.
Make it a blessed act,
That you may bless a needy cause,
With holding nothing back.

The LORD will bless you mightily,
For giving in His Name.
As His extended hands on earth,
Bring honor to the same.

It matters not status on earth,
How well known you may be,
Nor what kind of auto you drive,
Or high in society.

Some people give their best impress,
By making a great show,
With expensive clothes and jewelry,
That everyone will know.

What matters most to our LORD God
Is helping to supply
The many needs and hurts around.
So to His Word comply.

It is so blessed to give out,
From that which God has giv'n.
We know that He will never fail
To give us His provision.

CM

PRAYER AND PRAISE: LORD, I know that the giving of ourselves in all aspects, is a way of submitting to Your way and Your will. Therefore, my LORD, I give myself to You now, submitting to Your Lordship, to give in accordance with all that You would ask.
Thank You for Your blessing, in the precious Name of Jesus!

Week 24 ❖ Day 4   Theme: Giving   Jun 13

GIVING IN HIS WILL

HIS WORD: "Therefore, my dear brothers, stand firm. Let nothing move you. Always give yourselves fully to the work of the Lord, because you know that your labor in the Lord is not in vain."
1 Corinthians 15:58

MY CHALLENGE: *To give myself fully to the Lord and to His work. There is no greater honor, no greater privilege and no greater work I could do.*

Our giving is a way of life,
As we walk the Christian way,
To fulfill the great commandment
And obey His Word each day.

When we think of the price He paid,
To set us completely free,
And then He filled us with His Spirit,
With Him to walk obediently.

He set for us the way of life,
To follow His perfect way,
That we would fill His will for us,
And do it without delay.

As we give our service to Him,
And give our thanksgiving song,
We give Him our tithes and offerings;
For to Him it all belongs.

CM

PRAYER AND PRAISE: *Thank You, Lord, as you continually teach me Your way of giving myself for the sake of others, doing it all in Your Name. I thank You for the continued strength, energy and motivation to keep on. So be it, my Lord!*

Week 24 ❖ Day 5   Theme: Giving   Jun 14

GIVING HIM PRAISES TODAY

HIS WORD: "Through Jesus, therefore, let us continually offer to God a sacrifice of praise—the fruit of lips that confess his name."
Hebrews 13:15

MY CHALLENGE: To offer Him praise continually, making this a sacrifice I am privileged to give.

Don't ponder the problems you have,
But practice His presence and pray.
Hold on to His promises true,
By giving Him praises today.

There is nothing greater to give
Than praise unto His Holy Name;
For as we give it unto Him,
It's in His honor we proclaim.

We thank You, LORD, for You're our God.
To obey is our one request,
To lift Your Name up gloriously,
And serve you as we give our best.

We're ofttimes burdened down with cares.
We look to You, our only way,
To do what You've asked us to do,
By giving You our praise today.

LM

PRAYER AND PRAISE: LORD, help me to remember that Your Word says a lot more about praise than it does about prayer. I confess, I need to praise You much more than I do. In fact, Your Word says we are to <u>continually</u> offer You praise. Thank You for that reminder, and today I give You all the praise!

Week 24 ❖ Day 6   Theme: Giving   Jun 15

THE ART OF GIVING

HIS WORD: "You yourselves know that these hands of mine have supplied my own needs and the needs of my companions. In everything I did, I showed you that by this kind of hard work we must help the weak, remembering the words the Lord Jesus Himself said: 'It is more blessed to give than to receive.'"
Acts 20:34-35

MY CHALLENGE: *To give beyond my comfort zone and into His zone, of outpoured blessings.*

To My Giving Child:

The act of giving is an art.
My children must learn this,
That as they learn to act on it,
I send my heavn'ly bliss.

Your joy comes from My Holy source,
Stems from your giving gift;
For joy and giving are as one.
Together they uplift.

I fill you with all joy and peace,
As you remember Me,
And look to Me as your true Source,
Brought from the heavenlies.

The art of giving brings you joy
The world cannot conceive,
A joy that springs from My own well,
That they cannot perceive.

But you, My child, have endless source.
Drink to your heart's content.
Fill up until you overflow.
It's Holy nourishment.

You can't outgive the Lord, your God,
When giving from the heart.
My joy is yours, when you have learned
That giving is an art.

Your Loving Father

CM

PRAYER AND PRAISE: *Thank You, my Father, that as I continue to grow in You, I will continue to learn to give more of myself in all aspects. I know, in my mind, that the more I give, the greater blessings received. Help me, Lord, to also get this down into my heart. Amen!*

Week 24 ❖ Day 7   Theme: Giving   Jun 16

25

HE IS MY VICTORY

The victory in our LORD Jesus

Was won by Him alone.

He won it all upon the cross,

Now sits upon the throne.

TO WALK IN VICTORY

HIS WORD: "This is love for God: to obey his commands. And his commands are not burdensome, for everyone born of God overcomes the world. This is the victory that has overcome the world, even our faith. Who is it that overcomes the world? Only he who believes that Jesus is the Son of God."

1 John 5:3-5

MY CHALLENGE: To walk in the kind of victory that overcomes the world. That kind of victory is none other than my faith, total faith in Christ Jesus.

To My Victorious Jesus:

I came to You in my distress,
Confessing all my sin,
And gave up everything to You.
Your Spirit entered in.

Now You are mine, and I am Yours.
No one can take it from me.
You have declared it in Your Word.
You've made this guarantee.

To follow in Your Way for me,
To do all You command,
I need Your power to carry on,
To take a solid stand.

Baptize me in Your Holy Spirit.
Fill me to overflow.
All spiritual gifts now are mine,
Wherever I may go.

I want to draw closer to You
And feel Your Presence near,
That I may clearly hear Your voice,
With nothing else to fear.

With Your love and Holy Spirit,
You have empowered me,
To meet the challenges of life,
And walk in victory.

Your Loving Follower

CM

PRAYER AND PRAISE: I pray, LORD, to walk in victorious faith every day, by the power of Your Holy Spirit, in my submission to You and my belief in You as Almighty God. I ask for Your daily help and guidance to achieve and maintain this victorious walk. Thank You, LORD!

Week 25 ❖ Day 1   Theme: He is My Victory   **Jun 17**

A LIFE OF VICTORY

HIS WORD: "I do not trust in my bow, my sword does not bring me victory; but you give us victory over our enemies, you put our adversaries to shame. In God we make our boast all day long, and we will praise your name forever."
Psalm 44:6-8

MY CHALLENGE: *To remember that it is God Who brings the victory, and not anything of earth. It's to Him I look and in Him I put my trust.*

When you're at the end of your rope,
You wonder what is next.
Should you let go or hang on tight,
For life seems so complex.

Then give it up unto His care.
Quit clinging to that rope.
Just fall into the arms of Jesus.
He is your only Hope!

When you've let go of everything,
To fully trust this day,
You'll find there is great freedom then,
To walk His pilgrim way.

There is no need to fret the past,
Nor future time indeed.
Just walk the present, go with Him.
He will supply your need.

Be not discouraged, nor be wrought;
For He has paid the price,
To give you life of victory.
Praise is your sacrifice.

So that is what we do each day:
We lift His Name on high.
We give ourselves to Him and say,
Now use me; here am I.

CM

PRAYER AND PRAISE: Lord, I confess that too often I have a fear of failure and, therefore, do not move ahead in faith. Forgive me now. You are my Victory, and in this fact I will move ahead on that path You have laid out for me. I will move ahead, even though I can't see the end. In fact, I can't see much beyond the next few steps. But that's Okay. Victory is mine! I need not fear! I have faith! You are my Victory!

Week 25 ❖ Day 2   Theme: He is My Victory   Jun 18

WALK IN VICTORY

HIS WORD: "But thanks be to God!
He gives us the victory through our Lord Jesus Christ."
1 Corinthians 15:57

MY CHALLENGE: *To walk in victory!
I have it, so why not walk and talk like it?*

We know not what's ahead.
We know it has been said,
Trust Him for all.
We'll never fall,
For Jesus is our Head.

Others, gone before me,
Have followed You I see.
Lord, give us strength,
To go the length,
To walk in victory.

In God we learn to trust.
To serve Him is a must.
We make our mark
As we embark,
Support that which is just,

Thank God for helping me
To be all I can be,
To walk His way
And never stray,
To walk in victory.

SM (or 66446)

PRAYER AND PRAISE: That's just it, Lord! I need Your help! I know by Your Word I have the victory. I know that's Your promise. I know I'm to walk in it. Then why do I often feel like I fail to follow what You've promised?
I praise You now because You have given these promises to me, and my part is simply to appropriate Your Word and promises and move ahead, knowing that the victory is already won!
I thank You, Lord, for that assurance.
I praise You for that power.
Amen!

Week 25 ❖ Day 3   Theme: He is My Victory   Jun 19

JESUS, OUR VICTORY

HIS WORD: "The Lord is my strength and my song;
he has become my salvation.
Shouts of joy and victory resound in the tents of the righteous:
the Lord's right hand has done mighty things!"
Psalm 118:14-15

MY CHALLENGE: *To rejoice in the mighty things He has done!
He wrought my victory on the cross and paid the ransom price.*

Jesus went to extreme measures,
To save us from our sin.
He left His Father and came down,
A babe in Bethlehem.

He grew as any human child,
With parents in control.
He learned proper ways in life,
Accepted His giv'n role.

When He became fully mature,
Embarked on ministry,
To give His life once and for all,
To set all captives free.

He paid the most horrible price,
On the cross of Calvary,
Crucified and buried in the tomb,
But rose to victory!

That's why we all rejoice today
And celebrate His birth.
That Babe is the King of all kings
And Lord o'er all the earth.

Lay down your life; lift up your voice;
Proclaim His Majesty.
He is the Way, the Truth and Life.
Jesus, our Victory.

CM

PRAYER AND PRAISE: *My Lord, that is my deep desire: that is to
lay down my life and proclaim Your Majesty, by lifting my voice
in proclaiming Your life and victory. There is no other to proclaim.
There is no other who paid the ransom price.
There is no other who created.
Therefore, again today, I give myself to You and celebrate victory!*

Week 25 ❖ Day 4   Theme: He is My Victory   Jun 20

THE GREATER THE VICTORY

HIS WORD: "The horse is made ready for the day of battle, but victory rests with the LORD."
Proverbs 21:31

MY CHALLENGE: *To rest in His victory.*
It matters not what is swirling around me at any given time.
All that matters is to rest in Him, rest in His victory.
He did it for us, so why shouldn't we?

Are you lulled into the stupor
Of self-sufficiency?
Do you think it's all up to you,
To live victoriously?

Is your success dependent on
The measures of your wealth,
Your peace in life provided by
Your great financial health?

Where do we put our trust in life?
Is it in all we own?
Or can, in honesty, we say,
We trust in Him alone?

That is so difficult for us,
As humans on this earth,
To hand it all over to Him
And give our faith new birth.

But as we exercise the plan
God has for us in life,
We look to Him for all our needs
And live above the strife.

For He is our full sufficiency.
He cares for you and me.
The more we give ourselves to Him,
The greater the victory!

CM

PRAYER AND PRAISE: *I confess, my Jesus, You are more than sufficient!*
Worry is such a waste of time. Fretting is futile to my faith.
It need not be, when I rest in You—in Your victory.
And so my promise is this: From now on, I will do just that!
So be it!

Week 25 ❖ Day 5   Theme: He is My Victory   Jun 21

VICTORY OVER ALL

HIS WORD: "You give me your shield of victory,
and your right hand sustains me;
you stoop down to make me great."
Psalm 18:35

"In addition to all this, take up the shield of faith,
with which you can extinguish all the flaming arrows of the evil one."
Ephesians 6:16

MY CHALLENGE: *To take up my shield of faith, to receive His shield of victory.*

God has a calling on your life.
Never, never retreat.
He'll give you everything you need.
You'll never see defeat.

As you keep on trusting in Him
And follow in His Way,
You'll find the most amazing thing,
His strength for you each day.

So as you go on in His will,
Just shout the victory call.
Pay no attention to others.
It's victory over all.

He guides and leads through every turn.
Fear not to grow weary.
Now follow in His leading you,
To bring you victory.

So make the determination
Not ever to retreat;
For He'll bless the work of your hand,
Gives victory, not defeat.

And so the most amazing thing,
When you consider all:
That when you give your life to Him,
He gives victory o'er all.

CM

PRAYER AND PRAISE: L*ord*, I confess. When I think about the alternative to Your victory, there is only one choice to make! And thank You, my God, I have made that choice—and it is You! Thank You for the victory! Amen!

Week 25 ❖ Day 6   Theme: He is My Victory   Jun 22

ENJOY THE VICTORY

HIS WORD: "Blessed are those who have learned to acclaim you, who walk in the light of your presence, O LORD."
Psalm 89:15

"He holds victory in store for the upright, he is a shield to those whose walk is blameless, for he guards the course of the just and protects the way of his faithful ones."
Proverbs 2:7-8

MY CHALLENGE: *To enjoy the victory! Regardless of all the negative things that may be going on in my life, I am to enjoy His victory!*

To My Hopeful Child:

So you have suffered ridicule,
For this entire season.
They will not listen to your voice,
Accused without reason.

They laugh and mock and bring false charge,
So wise they think they be;
But do not forget, My dear child,
They did the same to Me!

Walk in the Light of My Presence.
Then fear won't have it's way.
I overcame fear on the cross,
That you'd have peace this day.

Their minds are set like pure, hard stone.
They cannot hear My voice.
Though hard I try to change their hearts,
Now they have made the choice.

I say pray for your enemies.
Release them unto Me.
It's a difficult thing to do,
But lets your heart be free.

It is this you must exercise,
Keeping your eyes on Me:
Though walking the path of ridicule,
Enjoy the victory!

Your Caring Jesus

CM

PRAYER AND PRAISE: *Thank You, my Jesus! I can no nothing but praise You —for who You are, for what You've done and for the victory You have wrought for me. Praise Your Holy Name!*

Week 25 v Day 7   Theme: He is My Victory   **Jun 23**

26

FORGIVE/PARDON

"Forgive and you shall be forgiven,"

Are words to us He gave,

To live a life of forgiveness,

To follow in His way.

TO MY LORD

HIS WORD: "Praise the LORD, O my soul, and forget not all his benefits—who forgives all your sins and heals all your diseases, who redeems your life from the pit and crowns you with love and compassion."
Psalm 103:2-4

MY CHALLENGE: *To know I am on the forgiven side of the cross. In Old Testament times, an animal sacrifice was needed once a year. However, since the cross of Christ, His resurrection and the coming of the Holy Spirit, I have been forgiven.*

My Dear LORD:

I know that if I'm born again,
I'm perfect in Your sight.
Your Word tells me; I know it's true;
I try to do what's right.

But there are many times, my LORD,
I cannot comprehend,
Comparing actuality,
With Word that You have penned.

I know I'm not to go by feelings,
But go by faith instead,
To cast aside all doubt there is,
And trust in my Godhead.

That's why I need You so, my LORD,
To make it through each day.
Though You may see me as perfect,
I struggle on the way.

One thing I ask of You, my LORD,
Is help me understand
That Your forgiveness, once for all,
Made perfect by Your hand.

Your forgiveness to me is free.
It cost me not a cent.
I thank You, LORD, for Your great gift,
As now I'm heaven bent.

Your Loving Child
CM

PRAYER AND PRAISE: *Yes, my LORD, I am beginning to comprehend that You have <u>already</u> forgiven me and have set me free. Therefore, when I sin, I confess it, repent of it and praise You for the forgiveness You wrought for me on the cross. Thank You, my LORD Jesus!*

Week 26 ❖ Day 1   Theme: Forgive/Pardon   **Jun 24**

FORGIVEN ETERNALLY

HIS WORD: "I write to you, dear children, because your sins have been forgiven on account of his name."
1 John 2:12

MY CHALLENGE: To accept the fact that I have been forgiven on account of His Name!

From birth to the last breath we take,
We've our life to go through.
We're not here by choice or by chance.
It's by God's plan is true.

As we live this life He's given us,
How is it we can dream
Of things that really shouldn't be,
That are of such extreme?

We need to throw ourselves on Him,
His mercy to attain,
And ask forgiveness for our thoughts,
Before they cause some pain.

He is our God who has forgiven
Our sins upon the cross.
He shed His blood and gave His life
That we not suffer loss.

Therefore we have opportunity
To look to Jesus, our LORD,
To recognize His authority
And be in one accord.

We thank You now, our LORD and God,
For we have been set free.
From birth to last of breath we take,
Forgiven eternally.

CM

PRAYER AND PRAISE: LORD Jesus, How can I thank You enough for paying the price for my sin? And what a terrible price to pay! The only way I know to show my appreciation is to serve You to the best of my ability. As a forgiven saint, I bow to You, I vow to serve You, and somehow I'll learn to walk in the total freedom of forgiveness —because of You and You alone. Thank You, Jesus!

Week 26 ❖ Day 2   Theme: Forgive/Pardon   Jun 25

LIVE FREE IN HIM

HIS WORD: "Do not judge, and you will not be judged. Do not condemn, and you will not be condemned. Forgive, and you will be forgiven."
Luke 6:37

"Forgive us our sins, for we also forgive everyone who sins against us."
Luke 11:4ab

MY CHALLENGE: *To forgive as He forgave me. Completely. Totally. Mercifully. Since He has forgiven me, I have no right to hold <u>anything</u> against anyone else. To live a life of true freedom, I must forgive everyone, everything, all the time.*

We have no right to hold a grudge,
Or take some hate into our soul.
Resentment and raw jealousy
Bring us a lack of self-control.

To not forgive brings bondage too;
It brings a knot you feel within.
Therefore break all bondage today.
Forgive, as He forgave your sin.

There are the things we must cast out,
In order we would be set free,
To live the life He has for us,
A life of living victory.

The greatest thing God wants for us,
To live our lives completely free,
And Holy Peace to satisfy,
With His great love and company.

LM

PRAYER AND PRAISE: My LORD and God, You have made it possible for me to live without aught against anyone, that is, completely free to love without limit. I confess, I'm not there yet, but am moving ahead, growing in You and making progress each day. Thank You, LORD, for making the way possible, for showing me the way and giving me the desire to do it.

Week 26 ❖ Day 3   Theme: Forgive/Pardon   **Jun 26**

HIS FORGIVENESS FOREVER

HIS WORD: "In him we have redemption through his blood, the forgiveness of sins, in accordance with the riches of God's grace that he lavished on us with all wisdom and understanding."
Ephesians 1:7-8

MY CHALLENGE: To know that I <u>have</u> received His forgiveness. As this scripture says, "We <u>have</u> redemption through His blood," that shed blood on the cross.

He shed His blood on the cross of Calvary,
Dealt with our sins forever.
Jesus is the One who took away our sin.
For all, He is the answer.

The sacrifice He paid was once and for all,
For all time a guarantee.
That Perfect Lamb gave His life in exchange
For our sins, to set us free.

Because we have received Him as our Savior,
We're clean as clean as can be.
We will not be judged for sins of the past.
They're buried deep in the sea.

Born-again Christian, whenever you sin,
Quickly confess it now.
He has paid the price for you for all time.
Make His praise and thanks your vow.

10 7.10 7

PRAYER AND PRAISE: *My LORD, that is my vow, to continually praise You for Your forgiveness wrought on the cross. Praise You, Jesus!*

Week 26 ❖ Day 4   Theme: Forgive/Pardon   Jun 27

HE HAS SET ME FREE

HIS WORD: "So if the Son sets you free, you will be free indeed."
John 8:36

"But now that you have been set free from sin and have become slaves to God, the benefit you reap leads to holiness, and the result is eternal life."
Romans 6:22

MY CHALLENGE: *To know that I am set free.*
Free from the necessity to sin. Free from worldly bondage.
Free to worship the LORD, *my God!*

Our God sees everything at all times
And is completely in control.
He knows everything to the very end.
There is nothing He does not know.

Why do you worry and fret so,
When things are not going your way?
Just put it all into His hands.
Give all to Him without delay.

Give up your foolish fretting now.
From the worldly cares you must flee.
Without the bondage others bring,
Enjoy a life of Godly glee.

Jesus paid the total price for us.
On that Calvary cross He suffered.
Then He rose again to show the way,
To follow Him, our Good Shepherd.

He alone is the bondage breaker,
The One who wrought the victory.
So you can shout it from the rooftops,
"Thanks to God, He has set me free!"

LM

PRAYER AND PRAISE: *I do thank You, my God, that You have set me free. And Your promise is that I am free indeed. No if's, and's or but's about it, I am free!* LORD, *what I ask is that I get this truth down deeper into my soul, and that I live my life in light of this truth. Thank You, Jesus!*

Week 26 ❖ Day 5   Theme: Forgive/Pardon   **Jun 28**

FORGIVENESS TO PERFECTION

HIS WORD: "Be perfect therefore, as your heavenly Father is perfect."
Matthew 5:48

"We proclaim him, admonishing and teaching everyone with all wisdom, so that we may present everyone perfect in Christ."
Colossians 1:28

MY CHALLENGE: *To live in such a way that reflects the perfectness of Christ in my life.*

Once you're a born-again Christian,
There is never a debate.
Your sins are washed away forever.
You're in a forgiven state.

This was done for once and for all.
Christ Jesus has paid it all.
You need not ask the LORD again,
To forgive you for your fall.

Just confess and repent of it,
Any sin there may have been.
Give thanks and praise to His Holy Name,
Over and over again.

Do not keep on asking forgiveness.
Accept the price He has paid;
For He forgave you once for all.
Your sins to Him were conveyed.

He is our precious LORD and God,
Master of our destiny.
He'll guide and lead us through this life,
To be free as free can be.

As we walk hand in hand with Him,
Forgiveness is not our plight.
We need not fret about past sins.
We are perfect in His sight.

87.87

PRAYER AND PRAISE: LORD, I confess, that when I think of being made perfect in Christ, I so often think in the worldly sense instead of the Biblical meaning. I thank You for continually reminding me of Christ's sacrifice and how that shed blood has covered my sins and has made me perfect in the Father's sight. I'm so grateful for the price You paid to bring me to this point.
Amen!

Week 26 ❖ Day 6　　Theme: Forgive/Pardon　　Jun 29

FORGIVE

HIS WORD: "Bear with each other and forgive whatever grievances you may have against one another. Forgive as the Lord forgave you."
Colossians 3:13

MY CHALLENGE: *To forgive! Jesus commands me to forgive. It is not just a suggestion. My forgiveness brings His freedom. When I release, He brings restoration. As I surrender, He brings success.*

To My Forgiven Child:

It matters not you have done wrong.
I love you as you are.
Pick up the pieces and move on.
Let not it leave a scar.

Others may hurt you without cause,
And you feel all alone.
Remember, my child, I'm with you.
I'm your Cornerstone.

As you have come to Me and prayed,
Forgiven others all,
Receive my joy and happiness,
You hear a bright new call.

My child, that call is to carry on,
Knowing I'm in control.
I've put you on a grand new path.
My light shines in your soul.

Let not the enemy steal your joy,
Making you feel aghast.
You've come to Me and repented.
You're free of that at last.

Know I have forgiven you, child.
You're free for evermore.
Just cling to my side every day.
Go with Me, I implore.

Your loving Dad

CM

PRAYER AND PRAISE: *Thank You, Father, for Your forgiveness of my sins. I confess my many shortcomings. I also confess You as my Lord and Savior, and I receive Your forgiveness, to live my life free in the Spirit. My joy is in Jesus. And, oh, what a joy it is!*

Week 26 ❖ Day 7   Theme: Forgive/Pardon   Jun 30

27

HIS CLEAR VOICE

His call to me is always clear.

In listening to His voice;

He lifts and guides me through each day.

He is my only choice.

I SEEK YOUR VOICE

HIS WORD: "While he was still speaking, a bright cloud enveloped them, and a voice from the cloud said, 'This is my Son, whom I love; with him I am well pleased. Listen to him!'"
Matthew 17:5

MY CHALLENGE: *To seek His voice, then listen!*

My Dear LORD:

I seek Your voice, speaking to me,
At all times of the day,
To know You have a word for me,
To follow in Your way.

To learn to be obedient to You
Is not an easy task.
For other voices are so loud,
I hear not what You ask.

But I am determined to hear
Your voice speaking to me.
I'll do whatever it takes, my LORD,
To be what You'd have me be.

I ask but one thing of You, LORD:
Help me be sensitive,
To hear the words You speak to me,
Teaching me how to live.

I know I need to trust in You
And not in my own strength.
I promise, LORD, to follow You.
I'll go to any length.

The one thing I know I must do,
In making the right choice:
To come to You with open heart.
My LORD, I seek Your voice.

Your Loving Child

CM

PRAYER AND PRAISE: *LORD, I confess that sometimes it's overwhelming to think about hearing Your voice! Just the same, that's what I want. I want to hear You, loud and clear. Thank You for helping me, as I seek Your voice.*

Week 27 ❖ Day 1   Theme: His Clear Voice   **Jul 1**

HIS GENTLE VOICE

HIS WORD: "The watchman opens the gate for him, and the sheep listen to his voice. He calls his own sheep by name and leads them out. When he has brought out all his own, he goes on ahead of them, and his sheep follow him because they know his voice."
John 10:3-4

MY CHALLENGE: *To listen to His voice, that I may follow Him.*

We learn to hear His gentle voice,
In stillness of the soul;
For He is with us all the time,
His words to us console.

He's with us till the end of time.
He'll never leave our side.
He brings to us His gentle nudge,
To listen and abide.

Fear not that He would leave you, child,
For that He cannot do.
His residence is in our hearts
And fills us through and through.

We still our lives and quietly,
Each moment make the choice;
To strive to hear His word to us.
We hear His gentle voice.

CM

PRAYER AND PRAISE: *My* LORD, *I have a confession to make. I struggle to hear Your voice. In fact, many times I don't think I hear it at all. I admit there are many worldly things swirling around in my head. But,* LORD, *I really do want to be able to hear Your voice clearly, follow You closely and adhere to Your Word confidently. So I ask You, in earnest prayer, please help me to listen and hear Your voice! Thank You, my* LORD *Jesus!*

Week 27 ❖ Day 2   Theme: His Clear Voice   Jul 2

GARDEN OF MY HEART

HIS WORD: "They asked her, 'Woman, why are you crying?'
'They have taken my LORD away,' she said, 'and I don't know where they have put him.' At this, she turned around and saw Jesus standing there, but she did not realize that it was Jesus.
'Woman,' he said, 'why are you crying? Who is it you are looking for?'
Thinking he was the gardener, she said, 'Sir, if you have carried him away, tell me where you have put him, and I will get him.'
Jesus said to her, 'Mary.'
She turned toward him and cried out in Aramaic,
'Rabboni!' (Which means Teacher).''
John 20:13-16

MY CHALLENGE: *To recognize Him when He speaks to me.*

In the garden of my heart,
We commune as One to one,
As His gentle voice whispers,
"I love you, My dear one."

As day begins quietly,
Before the din begins,
He comforts my hungry heart,
Confirms I am His kin.

His nudges are so subtle,
His voice to me asserts,
Guiding me gently forward,
As I remain alert.

He confirms His love for me.
His assurance He imparts.
I pleasure His presence in
The garden of my heart.

76.76

PRAYER AND PRAISE: LORD, when You speak to me, I pray to know for absolutely certain that it is You, and then to be able to hear exactly what You say. I want to listen. I want to hear. I want to know it's You!
Amen!

Week 27 ❖ Day 3   Theme: His Clear Voice   Jul 3

FOUNDING FATHERS, USA

HIS WORD: "Blessed is the nation whose God is the Lord."
Psalm 33:12a

"Submit yourselves for the Lord's sake to every authority instituted among men: whether to the king, as the supreme authority, or to governors, who are sent by him to punish those who do wrong and to commend those who do right."
1 Peter 2:13-14

MY CHALLENGE: *To keep this country free and under God!*
Our founding fathers met a challenge: To form a free country by choice.
We are blessed with this land today, Because our fathers heard His voice.

His voice spoke to a group of men,
Over two hundred years ago,
As they wrote a declaration,
To free them from England's control.

They formed a nation under God,
By following His Holy call,
With freedom of speech guaranteed,
Liberty and justice for all.

These men were the Founding Fathers,
And it was Freedom they pursued.
They gave their lives and possessions.
They're owed a debt of gratitude.

God has blessed this mighty nation.
For that blessing we must comply
And give Him all the glory due,
As He gives us His great supply.

No other nation in history,
Except for Israel alone,
Was founded under the banner,
With the Lord as our Cornerstone.

This country prospered mightily,
Under His care, showing the way.
We pray that God will continue
His blessing on the U.S.A.

LM

PRAYER AND PRAISE: *Our Fathers' God, to Thee, Author of liberty, to Thee we sing;*
Long may our land be bright, With freedoms Holy Light,
Protect us by Thy Might, great God our King.
(Verse 4, "America," words by Samuel F. Smith, 1832)
Amen!

Week 27 ❖ Day 4   Theme: His Clear Voice   **Jul 4**

HEAR THE VOICE OF GOD

HIS WORD: "After forty years had passed, an angel appeared to Moses in the flames of a burning bush in the desert near Mount Sinai. When he saw this, he was amazed at the sight. As he went over to look more closely, he heard the LORD's voice: 'I am the God of your fathers, the God of Abraham, Isaac and Jacob.' Moses trembled with fear and did not dare to look."
Acts 7:30-32

MY CHALLENGE: *To hear His voice without the need of a burning bush. That's the great advantage I have today. Because the Holy Spirit lives within me, I am able to hear directly from my LORD.*

If you want to hear your LORD God
Speak gently to your soul,
Then every moment of the day,
To Him give your control.

Put Him first in all your thinking,
In choices that you make.
Pay attention to His nudges.
He directs for your sake.

He will bring order to your thoughts,
Give His peace to your mind.
Let the LORD be in the forefront,
The rest all slip behind.

Know that to hear the voice of God
Takes practice on your part.
With patience and a listening ear,
Becomes a work of art.

Don't try to do it all at once.
Depend on the Divine
To guide you in your walk of life.
Take one step at a time.

If you will put your mind to it,
To clearly hear His voice,
You'll find that He will speak to you.
In Him, you'll then rejoice.

CM

PRAYER AND PRAISE: *LORD, I thank You that Your Holy Spirit lives within me, and I don't need a burning bush to hear Your voice. I just need to listen. I just need to live close to You on a daily basis. As I hear Your voice, I rejoice for the words You give me to lead me in Your way. Thank You, my Jesus!*

Week 27 ❖ Day 5   Theme: His Clear Voice   Jul 5

CHECK IN YOUR SPIRIT

HIS WORD: "Since we live by the Spirit,
let us keep in step with the Spirit."
Galatians 5:25

MY CHALLENGE: *To be certain that when I'm listening for His voice,
I will pay attention to any checks in my spirit,
to be certain I'm on the right track.*

Do you feel a check in your spirit?
Something may not be right.
You should stop what you're doing,
Ask God to give you light.

That's the time to pay heed to it,
A warning is in store.
Don't move ahead in that direction,
Till you hear from the LORD.

This is the way God cautions you,
As you travel along,
That you will go His chosen way,
And keep you from a wrong.

When you sense that tug on your heart,
That makes you stop and check,
Just turn to Him and quickly pray
And ask Him to direct.

Then, when you hear His word come through,
You're able to discern,
To heed His word and follow it,
And know which way to turn.

We thank You, LORD, for helping us,
To always make right choice,
To sense that check in our spirit,
And listen to Your voice.

CM

PRAYER AND PRAISE: *LORD, I need to remember to pay attention to the checks
in my spirit, as You guide me in this way. I know that when I sense a "check,"
I need to stop and allow You to show me the right thing to do
and the right thing to say, in order to go the right way—Your way.
I pray to continually grow and learn how to walk closer to Your Spirit.
Thank You and Amen!*

Week 27 ❖ Day 6   Theme: His Clear Voice   Jul 6

ON THE ROAD TO DAMASCUS

HIS WORD: "My companions saw the light, but they did not understand the voice of him who was speaking to me.
Then he said: 'The God of our fathers has chosen you to know his will and to see the Righteous One and to hear words from his mouth.'"
Acts 22:9,14 (6-16)

MY CHALLENGE: *To hear the words of the Righteous One from His mouth!*

To My Chosen Child:

It was on the road to Damascus.
I struck Paul with My Light.
I had his complete attention.
He had lost his eyesight.

I spoke to him and then questioned,
Why he persecuted me,
As I was Jesus of Nazareth,
And this was not to be.

I gave Him an order right there,
And told him what to do,
That he might be restored again,
And know that which is true.

With the help of his companions,
He did as he was told;
And I restored him to serve me,
And be a servant bold.

He became a great disciple,
And humble as can be.
He followed all my direction,
Serving passionately.

You need not fret I'll blind you, child,
In order you might see.
The role I have for you to play
In My own company.

Right now, my child, I'm calling you,
To follow after Me,
To hear My voice and heed My Word,
Fulfill your destiny.

All I ask is your obedience
And ears to hear My voice,
That as I lead you through this life,
I'll always be your choice.

Your Loving Jesus
CM

PRAYER AND PRAISE: Yes, my LORD Jesus, You will always be my choice. There is none other I care to lead me through this life. Therefore I come to You in humbleness, confessing my need for You, my desire to hear Your voice and committed to obedience. I thank You, my LORD, for everything! Amen!

28

OUR JESUS

Our Jesus is the only One

Who saves and sets you free.

He wants to help you through this day

And from your worries flee.

OUR SHEPHERD-KING

HIS WORD: "May the God of peace, who through the blood of the eternal covenant brought back from the dead our LORD Jesus, that great Shepherd of the sheep, equip you with everything good for doing his will, and may he work in us what is pleasing to him, through Jesus Christ, to whom be glory for ever and ever. Amen."
Hebrews 13:20-21

MY CHALLENGE: *To live my life looking constantly to Jesus as my Shepherd and King.*
A shepherd cares deeply for his sheep and does whatever is necessary to meet their every need. Jesus is my Shepherd! I will live like it!

My Loving King:

I deeply care for You, my LORD,
My Shepherd and my King.
I worship on Your Holy Ground,
Give praise for everything.

It matters not what lies ahead,
For You I know are there.
You have it all in Your control.
I trust You for Your care.

I need not worry, need not fret,
For You're my everything.
I trust in Your provision, LORD,
My Shepherd and my King.

Confessing You as Shepherd-King,
Each day I walk with You.
It leads me on to higher ground,
My life each day renews.

I'll worship You as King of Kings,
Throughout eternity,
Protector, Ruler o'er all things,
King Shepherd over me.

How can I give to You my thanks,
Your praises fully sing?
You're Jesus, LORD o'er everything,
My Shepherd and my King.

Your Loving Child
CM

PRAYER AND PRAISE: LORD Jesus, help me to live in such a way that I allow You to be my Shepherd and I follow You as one of Your sheep. I confess that in my humanness, I fall short so much of the time.
Jesus, You're my Shepherd; You're my King;
I trust You now for everything.
Amen!

Week 28 ❖ Day 1 Theme: Our Jesus Jul 8

NO ONE CAN TAKE HIS PLACE

HIS WORD: "A man of many companions may come to ruin, but there is a friend who sticks closer than a brother." *Proverbs 18:24*

"When Jesus saw their faith, he said,
'Friend, your sins are forgiven.'" *Luke 5:20*

MY CHALLENGE: To know and enjoy the fact that Jesus IS the friend that sticks closer than a brother. Because of this, no one can take His place.

Jesus, the Name above all names,
Brings victory over all.
When fate has dealt a cruel blow,
You're headed for a fall.

You know not where or how to go.
Your heart is filled with fear.
The road ahead is dark, unknown.
Your eyes are filled with tears.

You cannot comprehend the fact.
Your mind is filled with woe.
You must reach out to change your course,
Another way to go.

And so your heart cries out to Him.
He's waiting for you there.
He hears your call, a fearful plea.
You need His loving care.

"Lord Jesus, it is You I need.
There is no other friend,
Who helps me in my time of pain,
On whom I can depend."

And so it is, as we look up
And see His loving face;
For Jesus is this Friend of ours.
No one can take His place.

CM

PRAYER AND PRAISE: Lord Jesus, a Friend closer than a brother!
A Friend like no other.
A Friend that is always with me. A Friend that is always true.
My Jesus, I confess, there is no friend quite like You!
I pray to be the most faithful friend possible to You.
Amen!

Week 28 ❖ Day 2   Theme: Our Jesus   Jul 9

OUR HOLY ANTHEM

HIS WORD: "The Lord your God is with you, he is mighty to save.
He will take great delight in you,
he will quiet you with his love,
he will rejoice over you with singing."
Zephaniah 3:17

MY CHALLENGE: *To hear that Holy anthem of love that runs like a thread throughout the entire Bible. I must listen for it. That's my Jesus I hear! For He IS my Holy Anthem!*

He is our Most Holy Anthem,
Who takes great delight in us.
He quiets our hearts with His peace.
That's our precious Lord Jesus.

He is our Mighty Lord and God.
He gives us our song of life;
For He is our pure melody,
That carries us through our strife.

He is our melody of grace,
That penetrates deep within,
Comforts those aching hearts of ours,
Far above the worldly din.

He'll always be Lord and God,
Who comforts us with His Love.
He's our peace and our contentment,
Our Holy Anthem above.

87.87

PRAYER AND PRAISE: *My Lord Jesus, I pray to immerse myself in Your Holy Anthem today, so that my heart would be at peace, my soul be filled with Your joy and my lips praising You forevermore.*

OUR BLESSED HOPE

HIS WORD: "For the grace of God that brings salvation has appeared to all men. It teaches us to say 'No' to ungodliness and worldly passions, and to live self-controlled, upright and godly lives in this present age, while we wait for the blessed hope—the glorious appearing of our great God and Savior, Jesus Christ, who gave himself for us to redeem us from all wickedness and to purify for himself a people that are his very own, eager to do what is good."
Titus 2:11-14

MY CHALLENGE: *To live a Godly life while waiting for the blessed hope—Jesus Himself, to come in all His glory. I am to be ready. I am to be waiting. I am to be serving. I am to remain faithful. Even so, come, Lord Jesus, come.*

Our blessed hope, our blessed hope,
Jesus, our blessed hope,
Oh, how we long for Your appearing.
Will be of glorious scope.

Blessed are we who read Your Word,
Your coming anticipate.
The time is near, as Your Word says.
We look up as we wait.

For You will break that eastern sky.
Will be a glorious sight;
For You have come to rule on earth,
With all Your power and might.

We thank You, Lord, for hope we have,
Assurance as we wait.
We can joy in the knowledge that
We will participate.

We know that we'll have duties then,
No longer to discuss;
For we'll complete the work for You,
That You assign to us.

Lord Jesus, You're our blessed hope.
We wait for trumpet blast.
Then we can shout it with great joy,
"Praise God! He's here at last!"

CM

PRAYER AND PRAISE: *My Lord Jesus, all I can do at this time is to praise You and praise You again. My hope is in You, and in no other. I confess You and receive You again today—My Blessed Hope!*

A JESUS IMPRESSION

HIS WORD: "The man from whom the demons had gone out begged
to go with him, but Jesus sent him away, saying,
'Return home and tell how much God has done for you.'
So the man went away and told all over town
how much Jesus had done for him."
Luke 8:38-39

MY CHALLENGE: *To tell how much God has done for me! It's called
"giving your testimony," and when I do, I am to give God all the glory.
Also "being a testimony" for Jesus can be done in many ways.*

To leave a Jesus impression
In someone's life today,
Give a smile and a few kind words,
To help them on their way.

It may be a simple "Thank You,"
"And may the LORD bless you,"
Or words of His reassurance,
"Please know that God loves you."

It could be a good witness tool,
To demonstrate God's love,
To instill a desire in them,
To know Him Who's above.

It will take but little effort
To share that which we ought;
For He has given us power within,
To do as He has taught.

It is so easy to refrain
From doing what is right,
To share the love of Jesus, friend,
To help them see the Light.

So as you go throughout your day,
To all the ones you meet,
Just leave a Jesus impression.
They'll walk on lighter feet.

CM

PRAYER AND PRAISE: *My LORD Jesus, I want to do what You'd have me do,
that I would be a living, walking testimony for You.
This is what You call us to do. This is what You commission us to do.
I pray You give me the guidance and prodding to carry it out. Amen!*

Week 28 ❖ Day 5   Theme: Our Jesus   **Jul 12**

HIS NAME IS JESUS

HIS WORD: "That at the name of Jesus every knee should bow,
in heaven and on earth and under the earth,
and every tongue confess that Jesus Christ is LORD,
to the glory of God the Father."
Philippians 2:10-11

MY CHALLENGE: *To know His Name, but more importantly,
to <u>KNOW</u> Him as Savior and LORD,
all to the glory of God, the Father.*

Confess His Name.	Praise to His Name.
Pray to His Name for peace and contentment.	Speak forth His Name on every occasion.
Declare His Name.	Shout out His Name.
Proclaim His Name from the rooftops.	Reveal His Name to the lost.
Glorify His Name.	Spread forth His Name.
Sing out His Name with joy and thanksgiving.	Whisper His Name at every opportunity.
Mention His Name.	His Name is Jesus!
Offer His Name and Saving Grace to the afflicted.	IRR.

PRAYER AND PRAISE: *My LORD Jesus, it is in Your Name I have my life and my being. You fill me with Your Spirit, to lead and guide me along the path You have chosen for me. I praise You today as I remember the significance of Your Name.*
Amen!

Week 28 ❖ Day 6 Theme: Our Jesus **Jul 13**

THE LORD IS IN THIS PLACE

HIS WORD: "When Jacob awoke from his sleep, he thought, 'Surely the LORD is in this place, and I was not aware of it.' He was afraid and said, 'How awesome is this place! This is none other than the house of God; this is the gate of heaven.'"
Genesis 28:16-17

MY CHALLENGE: *To sense the Presence of the LORD in the place I am at this very moment, and every place at every moment during the day. Can I, at every moment, say, "Surely the LORD is in this place?"*

To My Child:

"Surely the LORD is in this place"
Are words I love to hear;
For they acknowledge My Presence,
And cast away all fear.

I live within your heart, My child.
I surround you with My love.
My Presence permeates your life,
Empowers you from above.

I'm sure I'll hear your voice cry out,
Awakened by My call,
"Surely the LORD is in this place;
I knew it not at all."

For just like Jacob long ago,
When sleeping on a stone,
Heard My voice to him in a dream,
In desert place alone.

Therefore, My child, if that is you,
Running away in fear,
Look up to Me in your valley.
Give Me a listening ear.

I want to give you assurance,
As we come face to face:
You will not doubt, but you will say,
"The LORD is in this place!"

Your Loving LORD

CM

PRAYER AND PRAISE: *I fall on my knees and praise You, LORD, for being in this place, at this time. You are always with me, and I need to sense Your Presence at all times. Yes, my LORD Jesus, I'm privileged to say, "Surely the LORD is in this place!"*
Amen!

Week 28 ❖ Day 7   Theme: Our Jesus   **Jul 14**

HIS WILL

He has a will for each of us,

To fellowship with Him,

To be together One on one;

For He's our closest kin.

SURRENDER TO SERVE

HIS WORD: "For I have come down from heaven not to do my will but to do the will of him who sent me. And this is the will of him who sent me, that I shall lose none of all that he has given me, but raise them up at the last day."
John 6:38-39

MY CHALLENGE: *To have the same determination Jesus had, that is, to do the Father's will.*

To My Lord:

I surrender my all to Your will.
I leave nothing behind.
I ask You to take all of me,
My body, will and mind.

That You will give me all Your will,
To mold to Your design,
As I conform to Your image,
And at Your table dine.

There is no other god who cares
For every bit of life,
To save and heal and deliver,
And raise above the strife.

As I step out to serve You, Lord,
Fulfilling Your command,
To take Your Name and saving grace
Proclaim throughout the land.

Your Loving Child

CM

PRAYER AND PRAISE: *My Lord God Almighty, I desire to do Your will. That is my intention, that is my prayer, and that is my determination. But, I confess, that so many times I fall short and find myself obeying my own selfish will and desires. Forgive me now, Lord. I give myself to You again and ask You to give me the strength, and even greater desire to do Your will. Thank You, Lord! Amen!*

Week 29 ❖ Day 1   Theme: His Will   Jul 15

HIS OPEN DOOR

HIS WORD: "I know your deeds. See, I have placed before you an open door that no one can shut. I know that you have little strength, yet you have kept my word and have not denied my name."

Revelation 3:8

MY CHALLENGE: *To see the open doors God has for me. I can be assured that His open doors cannot be shut by anyone. I am simply to remain faithful by keeping His Word and proclaiming His Name!*

Look for the open doors of the LORD,
That you can easily walk through.
They stand open, ready to enter,
Open doors prepared for you.

Do not force open closed doors you find.
They may bring troubles untold.
When you want to open a closed door,
Let His Spirit take a hold.

Is selfish desire being put ahead
Of listening to God to guide?
Or stubbornness forcing the issue,
Because of your headstrong pride?

It's like catching a snake by the tail.
It will turn and strike at you.
The results could be very painful,
With more trouble to ensue.

Sit back, relax and be determined,
That you'll not go in before
The LORD has it ready and open.
Then you can walk through the door.

You will find the wait has been worth it.
He has ready so much more.
Don't force open closed doors before you.
Just look for His open door.

87.87

PRAYER AND PRAISE: *My LORD and God, I pray to see Your open doors, to walk through them and, thereby, be obedient to Your will for me. I pray to give me all I need to do just that. Amen!*

Week 29 ❖ Day 2   Theme: His Will   Jul 16

HIS WILL FOR YOU

HIS WORD: "So do not worry, saying, 'What shall we eat?' or 'What shall we drink?' or 'What shall we wear?' For the pagans run after all these things, and your heavenly Father knows that you need them.
But seek first his kingdom and his righteousness, and all these things will be given to you as well. Therefore do not worry about tomorrow, for tomorrow will worry about itself. Each day has enough trouble of its own."
Matthew 6:31-34

MY CHALLENGE: To not worry as I follow His will for me, for He will supply my every need. Where God leads, He precedes. Where God guides, He provides. Where God directs, He protects.
It is my move, just to step out in faith.

What is the LORD asking of you?
Is it more than you're doing now?
You hear His voice speaking to you?
Or are you too busy somehow?

Too busy to spend time with Him?
Seeking after His will for you?
Wanting to know what is in store?
And just what may be coming due?

It's not as though life's a mystery,
By hiding things out of your way.
His Word reveals His truth to you,
As you learn what He has to say.

Latch on to our Savior and LORD.
Learn what He has in store for you.
As you walk with Him hand in hand,
His will for you comes breaking through.

LM

PRAYER AND PRAISE: My LORD Jesus, I confess that I need you every moment of every day, to walk in Your will. I know this is to be my way of life. I promise to do the very best I can, so that at the end of every day I can say, "Today, I have followed Your will!"
Amen!

HIS SOVEREIGNTY

HIS WORD: "The Lord is my light and my salvation—
whom shall I fear?
The Lord is the stronghold of my life—
of whom shall I be afraid?"
Psalm 27:1

MY CHALLENGE: *To recognize His Sovereignty, to rely on His strength, knowing He is the stronghold of my life.*

Your Sovereignty is our Stronghold
And our security.
You go far above and beyond,
To be our Guarantee.

Therefore we give You thanksgiving
In all things all the time.
We praise You in all circumstances,
Throughout our whole lifetime.

It matters not our situation;
For You are on the throne.
You guide, protect and help us,
To use us as Your own.

We thank You, Lord, as we comply
With Your commands to us.
We know You know what's best for us.
In You, we put our trust.

As Sovereign, God, absolute,
Reigns o'er the Universe,
Yet small enough to live within
Our hearts and to converse.

You, Lord, the Stronghold of our lives
And our security,
Reign in our hearts and guide our lives;
For You're our Sovereignty.

CM

PRAYER AND PRAISE: *Lord, I pray to have a deeper comprehension,
a fuller understanding and a greater knowledge of Your Sovereignty.
I know that, with our finite minds,
we cannot completely grasp the total significance of this.
However, I just want more of You.
Grant it, Lord, is my prayer. So be it!*

Week 29 ❖ Day 4   Theme: His Will   **Jul 18**

BE OPEN TO GOD

HIS WORD: "Therefore, when Christ came into the world, he said:
'Sacrifice and offering you did not desire,
but a body you prepared for me';
with burnt offerings and sin offerings you were not pleased.
Then I said, "Here I am—it is written about me in the scroll—
I have come to do your will, O God."'"
Hebrews 10:5-7

MY CHALLENGE: *To do just as Jesus did; that is, to look to God and say to Him, "Here I am. I have come to do Your will, O God."*

Keep your spirit and life open to God,
By putting everything aside.
Let His Spirit fill you completely now,
That in His Will you shall abide.

Do not let your heart be troubled and torn,
When people say wrong things of you.
You're not responsible for their actions,
For what they say or what they do.

When the world sets our morality,
To follow in their standard fare,
We've allowed their troubles into our lives,
To travel their road of despair.

It can't be a question to you at all,
Whether God has forgiven you;
For that is what He did upon the cross.
Let's believe what He did is true.

By His sacrifice He has made perfect
Forever those being made holy.
He remembers our sins and wrongs no more.
He paid it all for you and me.

Your spiritual life should be out in front,
To hear what the LORD has to say,
By communicating constantly,
To know the LORD's will for your way.

98.98

PRAYER AND PRAISE: *Yes, My LORD and God, this is my prayer: "Here I am, I have come to do Your will, O God." I submit my life to Your Will. Thank You, Jesus!*

Week 29 ❖ Day 5   Theme: His Will   **Jul 19**

DIALOGUE WITH HIM

HIS WORD: "For this reason, since the day we heard about you, we have not stopped praying for you and asking God to fill you with the knowledge of his will through all spiritual wisdom and understanding. And we pray this in order that you may live a life worthy of the LORD and may please him in every way: bearing fruit in every good work, growing in the knowledge of God, being strengthened with all power according to his glorious might so that you may have great endurance and patience, and joyfully giving thanks to the Father, who has qualified you to share in the inheritance of the saints in the kingdom of light."
Colossians 1:9-12

MY CHALLENGE: *To know His will, to grow in His Word, to fulfill His work by going His way. And to do this, I must dialogue with Him continually.*

A good and proper theology
May help you in endurance;
But experiential knowledge of God
Brings you blessed assurance.

The written Word of our Savior, God,
Is foundation for life's trip.
Daily having dialogue with Him
Builds personal relationship.

Dialogue is a two-way street
We humans tend to forget,
Because we do all the talking,
Without a single regret.

The LORD wills us to converse with Him,
That to you He may be real,
What e'er you do in your walk with Him,
Be sure to follow His will.

97.97

PRAYER AND PRAISE: *LORD Jesus, I admit that I am weak in this area—dialoguing with You on a continual basis. So much of the time I am very good at talking, but very poor at listening for Your voice.*
This is where I need to grow.
I pray for Your help in doing just that. Help me to listen, O LORD!
Amen!

Week 29 ❖ Day 6   Theme: His Will   Jul 20

BASK IN MY BEAUTY

HIS WORD: "Yet you have a few people in Sardis who have not soiled their clothes. They will walk with me, dressed in white, for they are worthy. He who overcomes will, like them, be dressed in white. I will never blot out his name from the book of life, but will acknowledge his name before my Father and his angels."
Revelation 3:4-5

MY CHALLENGE: To look forward to that time when I will truly bask in His beauty, dressed in white for the occasion and celebrating as an overcomer.

To My Beloved Child:

Now bask in the beauty of My pure love.
Let not sin keep you from Me, child.
Your sins are the reason I died for you.
I saw all had become defiled.

You're radiant in My righteousness, you see.
You are cleansed by the blood I shed.
My Spirit within you is teaching you
To recall all the words I've said.

I know you are seeking My will for you,
And you won't be dissatisfied.
I will empower you for all you need,
As you walk closely by My side.

My life within you is now changing you.
Let's rejoice in My love as such.
For when you reach out as My hands, you are
Reaching others who need My touch.

We'll walk hand in hand as we walk as one.
So give thanks unto Me today;
For this is the friendship I want with you,
As we're talking along the way.

Now march to My drumbeat in life for you,
Doing all that My will allows.
You'll cherish these days we have walked as one,
As you bask in My beauty now.

From your Loving LORD

10 8.10 8

PRAYER AND PRAISE: My LORD God, it is a wonderful reality to realize that I can bask in Your beauty right now, by walking close to You, talking with You and witnessing for You.
It's in Your Light and Beauty I desire to abide. Thank You, Jesus!

Week 29 ❖ Day 7   Theme: His Will   Jul 21

30

RELEASE

Release to Him your anxious ties,

That bring you times of fear,

That you may gain the victory,

And to your faith adhere.

RELEASE IT ALL TODAY

HIS WORD: "Do not judge, and you will not be judged.
Do not condemn, and you will not be condemned.
Forgive, and you will be forgiven.
(Release, and you will be released.)"

Luke 6:37

MY CHALLENGE: *To release everything in my life that is not of God: things like unforgiveness, hate, fear, indecisions, procrastination, etc., etc. The list can go on and on. The key is: If it isn't right, give it up.*

My Forgiving God:

Under Your mighty hand, my God,
I humble myself and pray.
I cast all anxiety onto You.
I release it all today.

I give all my trials unto You.
For me, the burden's great.
I give it all to You right now.
You've given this mandate.

There's no other freedom on earth
Like You impart to me,
To cleanse my conscience of my guilt,
And set completely free.

I lay my burdens at Your feet,
For You're the One Who cares.
I'm under Your mighty hand, my God,
With humbleness and prayer.

For You have wrought the victory,
That I'd be free indeed,
To forgive as You forgave me,
And from my sins be freed.

If ever there was a secret,
To find a freedom way,
It's simply to give all to You
And release it all today.

Your Loving Child

CM

PRAYER AND PRAISE: L ORD, as You know, we humans certainly have a difficult time in letting go of those things that hurt us, especially in our spiritual life. We know what's best for us—that is to give up all those negative things— but still we hang on to them. I make this promise, L ORD: I'm letting go now. I hang on no longer. It's all Yours. I'm set free. Thank You, my L ORD!

Week 30 ❖ Day 1   Theme: Release   Jul 22

RELEASING ANXIETY

HIS WORD: "Cast all your anxiety on him because he cares for you."
1 Peter 5:7

MY CHALLENGE: To cast all anxiety on Him, just as the scripture says. This is a huge challenge, as anyone who has ever tried to do it finds out. We humans tend to worry about most everything. This short scripture is telling me I don't have to do that. Just cast it all on Him!

When problems overshadow your thinking,
Things not as clear as they seem,
Anxiety is a problem for you,
Confusion will reign supreme.

At that time, bring your thinking to a halt,
To seek light of His Presence.
He will make the perfect analysis,
For He is your Providence.

He'll not let you down, if you look to Him.
Wait for the answer to come;
For He will send it in His perfect time
And give you to overcome.

His grace is far greater than all our need,
We humans tend to forget.
His promise was made many years ago.
We need not worry or fret.

As we have given everything to Him,
Trust is a must we have found;
For we're set free from the bondage of past,
And now we are heaven bound.

As we have released our problems to Him,
We know it's a certainty.
We put our trust in His provision for us,
Releasing anxiety.

10 7.10 7

PRAYER AND PRAISE: My LORD, I know and You know that I have difficulty in releasing to You all of my anxiety. But I also know that the more I do it, the greater blessing I receive, in the way of Your Peace and joy in my life. Thank You, my LORD.

Week 30 ❖ Day 2   Theme: Release   **Jul 23**

THE TWO-SIDED COIN

HIS WORD: "'In that day,' declares the Lord Almighty,
'I will break the yoke off their necks and will tear off their bonds;
no longer will foreigners enslave them.
Instead, they will serve the Lord their God and David their king,
whom I will raise up for them.'"
Jeremiah 30:8-9

MY CHALLENGE: To look to Him and serve Him, knowing that the Lord
has promised to break the yokes and bonds I may have.
In fact, He did that very thing when He gave His life for me.

Your trials are always part of life.
Accept this fact Today.
You can't escape problems to come.
They'll always have their way.

Yours is not to spend time fretting,
To be tied up in knots,
Or feel the pangs of anxious fear,
That puts you in a spot.

Our life is like two-sided coins.
We have a choice to make:
Just flip that coin to other side.
Forget your past mistakes.

On this side of your coin of life,
With God you take your stand.
You submit to His Sovereignty,
Walk with Him hand-in-hand.

To overcome your trials all,
He'll guide in every way;
For He has given you His power,
To follow every day.

So if the coin that you've been dealt
Is causing you divide,
Just take that coin and flip it, child.
He's on the other side.

CM

PRAYER AND PRAISE: Lord, I pray to be on Your side because You have wrought the victory for me. You have paid the price for my sins and have forgiven me. Therefore I "flip" the coin of my life to Your side. Thank You, Jesus!

Week 30 ❖ Day 3 Theme: Release **Jul 24**

TO HIM ALL THINGS RELEASE

HIS WORD: "The Spirit of the Sovereign LORD is on me,
because the LORD has anointed me to preach good news to the poor.
He has sent me to bind up the brokenhearted,
to proclaim freedom for the captives and release from darkness for the
prisoners, to proclaim the year of the LORD's favor
and the day of vengeance of our God,
to comfort all who mourn."
Isaiah 61:1-2

MY CHALLENGE: To be released from the darkness of this world into the freedom Christ wrought for me, starting with releasing all of my bondage unto Him.

Why is it all human kind
Will first look to their own,
To find direction for their lives
And trust in the unknown?

It all began in a garden.
The couple was misled;
For man did not listen to God,
But followed wrong instead.

And now we have this bondage here,
To keep us bound up tight.
The devil wants to bring defeat,
In order we can't fight.

We have good news to live this day,
In God's own freedom way;
For Jesus paid the price for us,
To live with Him each day.

We have the freedom He had wrought,
To live above the strife.
It's by His Name we have the power
To overcome in life.

Our secret to our freedom here,
And have His inner peace
Is break the bonds we have obtained.
To Him all things release.

CM

PRAYER AND PRAISE: Yes, my LORD, I release all to You, that I would glory in the freedom You wrought for me on the cross. I have trouble expressing the true and total joy I am blessed to live in because of You. Amen!

Week 30 ❖ Day 4   Theme: Release   Jul 25

LEARNING TO RELEASE

HIS WORD: *(Words of Jesus, quoting Isaiah 61:1-2)*
"The Spirit of the Lord is on me,
because he has anointed me to preach good news to the poor.
He has sent me to proclaim freedom for the prisoners
and recovery of sight for the blind,
to release the oppressed, to proclaim the year of the Lord's favor."
Luke 4:18-19

MY CHALLENGE: *To know that the Spirit of the Lord is on me, as I release all of my bondage unto Him. His Word says He has released the oppressed, therefore my challenge is to live in accordance with His Word.*

In walking with our Lord each day,
We look for perfect peace.
The secret in our walk of faith
Is learning to release.

We must give up our earthly wants,
Depend upon His care;
For then we will receive from Him
All things He has to share.

If we have the audacity
To beg Him to receive
And have not given all to Him,
Ourselves we have deceived.

Soul comfort is not based on things,
On which we can't rely,
But rather on our trust in Him.
All needs He will supply.

When we hang on to earthly goods,
To give security,
We find our life filled up with junk
And need to be set free.

But as we walk His way each day,
We find His perfect peace.
We learn to give up all our things,
To Him all things release.

CM

PRAYER AND PRAISE: *Jesus, I confess that I need to pay close attention to this scripture that You quoted from Isaiah. You are my Sovereign Lord, and I release to You all bondage and oppression that I am experiencing. You are the only One who can bring freedom. And the only way this comes about is by my total release to You, and I do it now. Thank You, Lord!*

Week 30 ❖ Day 5   Theme: Release   Jul 26

RELEASE FROM FEAR

HIS WORD: "So do not fear, for I am with you;
do not be dismayed, for I am your God.
I will strengthen you and help you;
I will uphold you with my righteous right hand."
Isaiah 41:10

MY CHALLENGE: *To not fear—anything at anytime—because God is with me, will help, strengthen and uphold me. I am to trust in Him.*

Let not your fear be your master,
To guide you in your life.
When you call upon our Savior Friend,
He'll help you through the strife.

Now give it all to Him, dear child.
Troubles you cannot bear.
To conquer all the fear you have,
Look to His loving care.

Rest in that love that never fails,
The kind our Savior gives,
A love paid for by sacrifice
He gave that all may live.

Let's thank the Lord, for He is good.
Lift up His Name on high,
That all the fears you've had in life
Have all said their good-bye.

He needs you free of all your bonds,
To be His guiding light,
That others see His love through you,
And put their fear to flight.

Be not afraid, reach out your hand,
With His endearing grace,
To touch a life that's hurting so,
Who needs a fond embrace.

To share His love with all you meet
Is what He asks of you,
That you will be His own right hand,
To touch and then renew.

It's in that love that conquers all
That all can find their peace
And know that He is King o'er all,
The One who brings release.

CM

PRAYER AND PRAISE: *Lord, I look to You, as I give You my fears and receive Your release from those fears. I thank You for my freedom from fear by being filled with Your faith. I will not fear, for You are with me. Amen!*

Week 30 ❖ Day 6   Theme: Release   **Jul 27**

RELEASE YOUR PAST

HIS WORD: "My eyes are ever on the LORD, for only he will release my feet from the snare."
Psalm 25:15

MY CHALLENGE: *To release my past and live in the present, with hope for my future, as the LORD releases me.*

To My Beloved Child:

You've been fretting about the past,
Spending time without cause.
I have everything in control.
There is no need to pause.

Just keep on trusting in Me, my child,
With things on earth you cope.
It is by My strength and My will,
For I'm Your only hope.

It matters not what others think,
As you follow My will;
For I will be with you always,
Until My time stands still.

Release your past to Me, my child,
As you live in the now,
Putting Your hope in My future
And in My written vows.

Your Loving Father

CM

PRAYER AND PRAISE: *Yes, my LORD, I give it ALL to You. My past. My present. My future. It all belongs to You. Just help me, LORD, to live it like I believe it! Let me say it one last time: LORD, I give it ALL to You! Amen!*

Week 30 ❖ Day 7   Theme: Release   Jul 28

31

WITNESS

To be a witness for our Lord,

To go as He has said,

Is to obey as He has asked,

Be fully in His stead.

AS YOUR EXTENDED HANDS

HIS WORD: "Then he (Ananias) said: 'The God of our fathers has chosen you (Paul) to know his will and to see the Righteous One
and to hear words from his mouth.
You will be his witness to all men of what you have seen and heard.
And now what are you waiting for?
Get up, be baptized and wash your sins away, calling on his name.'"
Acts 22:14-16

MY CHALLENGE: *To do as Paul did. He heard the word, got filled with the Spirit, saw the light, and became a witness for Jesus wherever he was sent. Now my challenge is the same as that of Paul—to be a witness.*

To My Loving Lord:

I pray to be Your extended hands,
Sharing Your enormous heart,
To all who would open the door,
Your salvation to impart.

It matters not our feelings in this,
For faith is the answer here,
To bring about God's eternal hope,
Eliminating their fear.

Lord, I ask You now to use me much,
In witnessing to Your plea.
You want all to be saved from their sin,
Setting all the captives free.

Lord, I give myself to You today,
To be Your extended voice,
To share the Gospel's eternal truth,
That the lost make You their choice.

Your Loving Child

87.87

PRAYER AND PRAISE: *My Lord Jesus, I confess I have not been witnessing as I should be. You've called me, You've charged me, You've challenged me, and You've commissioned me to do it. Now I've got to get out and do it. I thank You, Lord, for filling me with Your Holy Spirit, empowering me and lighting my way to follow You. I hereby promise to take a bold step of faith—and just do it! Amen!*

Week 31 ❖ Day 1   Theme: Witness   Jul 29

BE A WITNESS

HIS WORD: *(Words of Jesus)* "But you will receive power when the Holy Spirit comes on you; and you will be my witnesses in Jerusalem, and in all Judea and Samaria, and to the ends of the earth."
Acts 1:8

MY CHALLENGE: *To be a witness. A witness for Jesus Christ. A witness to the world, wherever my world may be.*

Have you ever told your story
How Jesus came to be
Your loving and living Savior,
In heaven's harmony?

Have you ever shared with anyone
His loving sacrifice?
He took our sins upon that cross
And paid the total price.

Isn't it right that we should take
A stand in His defense,
And share with others His great love,
By getting off the fence?

We need to share His love with all,
To bring His saving grace,
That they would find new life in Him,
And find His love embrace.

Show Him your appreciation.
Let your heart be aflame.
Bring others to His saving grace,
And Glorify His Name.

Therefore we ask Him for His power
To witness to the lost,
As we step out and then speak up,
No matter what the cost.

As a soldier in God's army,
Let's gather all as one,
Giving thanks to our God above,
And souls who've overcome.

His Great Commission is before us.
We make our solemn vow.
As His Holy Spirit empowers us,
We will fulfill it now.

CM

PRAYER AND PRAISE: Lord, Yesterday I promised to take a bold step of faith. I pray that You would lead me to the ones that need Your Good News! And then fill me so full of Your Holy Spirit that I will be utterly compelled to go! Thank You, Jesus. Amen!

Week 31 ❖ Day 2   Theme: Witness   Jul 30

AS AMBASSADORS

HIS WORD: "We are therefore Christ's ambassadors, as though God were making his appeal through us." *2 Corinthians 5:20a*

"Pray also for me, that whenever I open my mouth, words may be given me so that I will fearlessly make known the mystery of the gospel, for which I am an ambassador in chains." *Ephesians 6:19-20a*

MY CHALLENGE: To be an ambassador for Christ. And that means to be a witness to others wherever God leads—even if in chains.

He calls us as ambassadors,
To take His message clear,
Into a world that's lost in sin,
A world waiting to hear.

Let His light continually shine,
Within that life of yours,
To bring His loving, saving grace.
Lost souls be made secure.

The LORD will open all the doors
For you to walk on through.
He makes the opportunity.
Now it is up to you.

Therefore speak up and share the Word,
And save them from the grave.
Go and make disciples of all.
The grace of Jesus saves!

His call to us has been made plain,
From heaven's Counselor.
We're to take His Word to the world,
As His ambassador.

CM

PRAYER AND PRAISE: My God, as Your ambassador, may I be found worthy of the title. I represent You to the world I'm in each day. There is no greater honor, no greater responsibility and no greater privilege than to go forth each day to witness in Your Name. Thank You, my LORD. —Your ambassador.

Theme: Witness

TELL THE WHOLE WORLD

HIS WORD: "So do not be afraid of them. There is nothing concealed that will not be disclosed, or hidden that will not be made known. What I tell you in the dark, speak in the daylight; what is whispered in your ear, proclaim from the roofs."
Matthew 10:26-27

MY CHALLENGE: *To be an effective witness, by knowing His Word, revealing His truths, and sharing His saving grace.*

The One who shed tears at Bethany,
The One who shed blood on Mount Calv'ry;
Jesus is His Name,
Bearing all my shame,
Taking my sins, nailed them to the tree.

He walked the shore of Lake Galilee.
This Jesus walks life's pathway with me.
He is still the same,
And I bear His name,
His banner lift, for the world to see.

Then to the cross, filled His destiny.
No dignity, dying cruelly.
It's because of Him,
Taking all my sin.
He set me free for eternity.

We lift our praise, to His glory sing,
Shout out His praise. He gives everything.
Follow him and then,
Until He comes again,
Let's tell the world He's the saving King!

99.559

PRAYER AND PRAISE: *Yes, My LORD, I do want the whole world to know, but my world seems to be quite small. I know I need to start right where I'm at. So I thank You, LORD, for giving me the impetus (kick in the pants) that I need to get going. Relieve me of the fears that are holding me back. Relieve me of the doubts about failing. Relieve me of the leaded feet, enabling me to go and witness to the lost, just as You have asked. Thank You, LORD!*

Week 31 ❖ Day 4   Theme: Witness   Aug 1

OUR CIRCLE OF LIFE

HIS WORD: "Then Jesus came to them and said, 'All authority in heaven and on earth has been given to me. Therefore go and make disciples of all nations, baptizing them in the name of the Father and of the Son and of the Holy Spirit."
Matthew 28:18-19

MY CHALLENGE: *To witness to the lost, to fulfill the Great Commission. Jesus has given this commission. It's an order. Am I fulfilling His order to do it?*

Our Jesus calls not most of us
To travel very far;
But simply to take His message
At the place where we are.

That place is our circle of life,
Family, friends and neighbors.
With them to share the glorious news,
As Christ's ambassadors.

It's great to share our friendship
With family and with friends;
But comes a time when we must share
His Truth about the end.

We need not fear the end of life.
There is alternative.
If we would give our life to Him,
Forever we will live.

Now that's good news that must be shared.
Then there is no excuse
When Judgement Day confronts them all;
For they have heard the truth.

When you share the LORD's salvation,
To overcome their strife,
You have fulfilled the Great Commission,
With your circle of life.

CM

PRAYER AND PRAISE: *My LORD and my God, I need Your help in fully comprehending that You have given us all the power and authority we need to go and make disciples, bringing them into Your Kingdom, and getting them started on the road of faith. Fill me and fire me with Your Holy Spirit, that I will not hesitate to go as You have commanded. Thank You, Jesus!*

Week 31 ❖ Day 5   Theme: Witness   Aug 2

A MESSAGE FOR THE WORLD

HIS WORD: "Therefore go and make disciples of all nations, baptizing them in the name of the father and the Son and of the Holy Spirit, and teaching them to obey everything I have commanded you. And surely I am with you always, to the very end of the age."
Matthew 28:19-20

MY CHALLENGE: *To go and make disciples <u>and</u> teaching them to grow in the* LORD. *The most effective church fellowship doing the* LORD's *work is one in which the members are actively winning new converts to Christ <u>and</u> helping them to grow in the faith through teaching and example. I have that challenge.*

A message for the world we take,
By power of Heavenly Dove,
The message that He wrought for us,
Of faith and hope and love.

Simple is the command to love,
Just as Jesus has shown,
To follow in His leading path,
And make His Name be known.

There is no greater work to do
Than that He has for us,
To take His Word into the world,
To be His impetus.

It's the greatest story ever told,
This message we're to take.
'Twill change their lives for evermore,
For them, for heaven's sake.

"Go and make disciples," He said,
"And teach them to obey,"
Then made the promise eternal:
"I'll be with you always."

Therefore we joy in this delight,
To share this mighty pearl.
He gave His life that we might live,
A message for the world.

CM

PRAYER AND PRAISE: LORD, *as I continue in my service to You, it seems a never-ending process in learning, learning to witness to the lost, winning them to Christ, working in the Kingdom and worshiping You continually. But I thank You that it is a never-ending process because I can't imagine what it would be like if it were not. Thank You for empowering, teaching and leading me to be Your witness, wherever You lead. Amen!*

Week 31 ❖ Day 6 Theme: Witness Aug 3

MY BANNER UNFURLED

HIS WORD: "The apostles left the Sanhedrin, rejoicing because they had been counted worthy of suffering disgrace for the Name. Day after day, in the temple courts and from house to house, they never stopped teaching and proclaiming the good news that Jesus is the Christ."
Acts 5:41-42

MY CHALLENGE: *To never stop witnessing, teaching and proclaiming the Good News, even in the face of persecution.*

To My Witnessing Child:

It is recorded in My Word,
"Go into all the World.
Preach My Good News to everyone."
Be My banner unfurled.

I use you as extended hands,
To reach out to the lost,
That they would come to know My love,
With fire of Pentecost.

You are a disciple of My Love.
I also call you friend.
I have filled and empowered you,
To share where e'er I send.

You can trust in My provision,
For I'll provide your needs,
To gather in the harvest ripe,
From all My planted seeds.

Step out now with boldness and love.
Speak words I give to you.
Then you will see many miracles,
Through what I've called you to.

Now go, fulfill My call for you,
Into this fallen world.
All will know you're a servant of Mine,
For you're My banner unfurled.

Your Appreciative Lord

CM

PRAYER AND PRAISE: *I humble myself in prayer before You, my God, for Your power in my life to continually be a witness for You. My desire is to fulfill my call and follow You to the very end. To You I give my all. In Jesus' Name.*

Week 31 ❖ Day 7   Theme: Witness   Aug 4

32

HIS CALL

He calls us to His Kingdom.

He calls us to serve.

He calls us to follow Him.

Have we got the nerve?

MARCHING TO HIS CALL

HIS WORD: "He said to them,
'Go into all the world and preach the good news to all creation.
Whoever believes and is baptized will be saved,
but whoever does not believe will be condemned.'"
Mark 16:15-16

MY CHALLENGE: *To honor His call. To hear His Call. To heed His call.*

To Our Calling Lord:
We've received our marching orders,
To go into all the world,
Preach Good News to all creation,
Give them His gems and pearls.

For Your words are precious to hear.
Your words will save and heal.
When we take them into our heart,
They are a Holy meal.

Jesus, You satisfy the soul,
And bring deep peace within,
As we look to Your saving grace,
To follow as Your kin.

You said to go and do as You did,
To reach out to the lost,
To be a marching disciple,
No matter what the cost.

We march to the drumbeat of Him,
Following every word,
As we go into all the world,
To those who have not heard.

Your Word satisfies hungry souls,
Looking for Your embrace,
Having their lives make a U turn.
Praise God it's by Your Grace!

Your Listening Child

CM

PRAYER AND PRAISE: *My Lord, You call Your children to honor, hear and heed Your call to go into the world with Your Good News. That call of Yours is to be our commitment. Help me keep my ears and eyes open to everything You would have me say and do. I give myself to You and to Your service now. Amen!*

Week 32 ❖ Day 1   Theme: His Call   Aug 5

HIS CLARION CALL

HIS WORD: "For it is commendable if a man bears up under the pain of unjust suffering, because he is conscious of God. But how is it to your credit if you receive a beating for doing wrong and endure it? But if you suffer for doing good and you endure it, this is commendable before God. To this you were called, because Christ suffered for you, leaving you an example, that you should follow in his steps."
1 Peter 2:19-21

MY CHALLENGE: *To hear His call and then to answer it, by living as He would have me live.*

Daily listen and live
The clarion call of Jesus.
Rely on Him continually.
Living in dependence
On Him is adventure,
To the very highest degree.

Never scurry around,
With your nose to the ground,
Thinking you'll go to any length,
Attempting to receive
The world's wealth for yourself,
To gain it all by your own strength.

Rather look to the One,
Who has given His all,
Dependent for all things on Him.
Accept your weaknesses
As a gift from the Lord,
Living as one His paradigm.

Just relax in His care,
Knowing you're in His hands,
Watching to see what He will do.
Look for the miracles
Taking place all around,
Rejoicing for His life in you.

His vict'ry is assured,
Living your life in Him,
Filling you with His mighty power,
To carry out His will,
Accomplishing His work,
Leading by His strength every hour.

Intentionally live and
Have your being in Him.
His plans are superior o'er all.
Rejoice and be glad for
The adventures He gives,
As you follow His clarion call.

12 8.12 8

PRAYER AND PRAISE: *My Lord, I ask You to help me in hearing Your call on my life, and then answering that call by living in obedience to You. Thank You, Lord!*

Week 32 ❖ Day 2   Theme: His Call   Aug 6

HE CALLS ON US

HIS WORD: "Therefore, my brothers, be all the more eager to make your calling and election sure. For if you do these things, you will never fall, and you will receive a rich welcome into the eternal kingdom of our Lord."
2 Peter 1:10-11

MY CHALLENGE: *To receive His call with joy and be ready to fulfill that call, whatever it may be.*

He calls on us to take His Word,
To use for His increase,
And fill the empty hearts of those,
Who have not found their peace.

That peace we need is Him alone.
No other can compare.
That's why He calls us to serve Him,
And with His love to share.

We know His love and sacrifice
Provide salvation free;
Therefore we hear His call to us,
To "Come and follow Me."

We know we need to know His Word,
And be at one with Him,
To follow what He'd have us do,
And spread that joy within.

No other to whom we can turn,
Who forgives and forgets.
With our sins washed away for good,
He's fully paid our debts.

Therefore, as we walk in His way,
Though our pace be a crawl,
We know one thing is always true,
A joy to hear His call.

CM

PRAYER AND PRAISE: *My Lord, how awesome it is to hear Your call on my life, to know that You have not only forgiven me, but You have a plan I am to fulfill. You know, and I know, that I need all the help I can get. So I thank You now for that needed help, that I can fulfill Your plan for my life, thus, having heard and heeded Your call. Amen!*

Week 32 ❖ Day 3 Theme: His Call **Aug 7**

HIS CALL

HIS WORD: "As Jesus walked beside the Sea of Galilee, he saw Simon
and his brother Andrew casting a net into the lake, for they were fishermen.
'Come, follow me,' Jesus said,
'And I will make you fishers of men.'
At once they left their nets and followed him."
Mark 1:16-18

MY CHALLENGE: *To hear His call and answer it!
In these verses, He calls me to follow Him and be a fisher of men.
Do I hear His call? Will I answer it?*

The world matters not at all,	Fear not what future may bring.
When we have heard His clear call.	Worry not about anything.
Starting today,	Trusting in Him,
Follow His way.	He is our hymn.
He gives us the wherewithal.	Therefore we praise Him and sing.
We must always remember,	His promises, we recall,
Be in complete surrender,	Will sustain us over all.
Trusting His call,	We seek His face.
Giving our all,	We're under grace,
Focusing on His splendor.	As we follow His great call.

77.447

PRAYER AND PRAISE: LORD Jesus, I hear Your call, and I am answering it. Even though sometimes I have doubts in my ability to do what You have called me to do, I must remember that You provide all my needs to fulfill Your call. You are all I need. Thank You, Jesus!

Week 32 ❖ Day 4   Theme: His Call   Aug 8

LOVE OUR MATES

HIS WORD: "Husbands, love your wives, just as Christ loved the church and gave himself up for her to make her holy, cleansing her by the washing with water through the word." *Ephesians 5:25-26*

"However, each one of you also must love his wife as he loves himself, and the wife must respect her husband." *Ephesians 5:33*
(See also verses 27 through 32)

MY CHALLENGE: *To follow His call to love my mate as Christ loves me; remembering that Christ loves me so much He gave His life for me.*

God calls on us to love our mates,
As much as He loves us,
And gave His life that we may live,
In His own righteousness.

"Love each other as I've loved you,"
He spoke as a command.
Therefore we need to honor Him,
By doing what He planned.

To love my mate as He loved me,
As He has made so clear;
For if I do as He has said,
A challenge we have here.

But that's what He has planned for us.
Our life be hid in Him,
To do for Him what He has said.
He fills us to the brim.

We honor the one He's giv'n us,
To help perpetuate,
By bringing forth some progeny.
That's why He gives us mates.

We confess that we love Him so,
And with our mates our call,
To honor His life lived through us,
We give our lives, our all.

CM

PRAYER AND PRAISE: *Yes, my LORD, I need to love my mate as You love me. That's a tall order for me, but I confess I feel great when I do it and terrible when I do not. My promise to You is to do it more intently and purposefully, in keeping with Your Word. I thank You for Your Holy Spirit help in this.*
Amen!

THE FINAL CALL

HIS WORD: "And the God of all grace, who called you to his eternal glory in Christ, after you have suffered a little while, will himself restore you and make you strong, firm and steadfast. To him be the power for ever and ever. Amen."
1 Peter 5:10-11

MY CHALLENGE: To give my life to Him each day, until the final call.

The final call will sound for us,
Someday on down the road,
When life on earth has run its course.
We leave behind its load.

We cannot see His glory now,
Can only dream of it,
As we spend our time here on earth,
To Him our lives commit.

Our hearts are beating with His love,
Fulfilling life for Him,
To reach out in His Name each day,
E'en as the lights grow dim.

We honor His commission great,
No matter what befall.
We give ourselves to Him each day,
Until the final call.

CD

PRAYER AND PRAISE: My God, I give my life to You this day, to use me as You will. You have called me to Yourself, and to You I have come.
You have called me to love, and love I will.
You have called me to serve, and serve I will.
I pray to serve You until I hear Your final call.

ANSWER MY CALL

HIS WORD: "You did not choose me, but I chose you and appointed you to go and bear fruit—fruit that will last. Then the Father will give you whatever you ask in my name."
John 15:16

MY CHALLENGE: To go in answer to His call. I am to do that which He has called me to do without question. He calls me to save the lost, heal the sick and deliver the oppressed in His Name.

To My Beloved Disciple:

Be willing, child, to answer Me,
As quickly as can be.
Do not delay and hesitate.
My call to you is key.

There are so many hungry souls,
Hurting, lost and needy,
Wanting to be relieved of all,
Their pain and agony.

I hear their cries and plead their case.
Hungry they are for Me.
I'll use you, child, as My right hand,
To heal them and set free.

Their bondage has been great indeed.
The devil kept them bound.
But as they turned their eyes to Me,
Salvation they have found.

It's in My Name they're healed of all,
In spirit, flesh and soul.
We bring them into My Kingdom,
For now they are made whole.

And now, My child, as you reach out,
No matter what befall,
Reach out as My extended hands,
In answer to My call.

Your Loving Jesus

CM

PRAYER AND PRAISE: To answer Your call! That's my prayer. Jesus, my LORD! I pray to know what that call is, to hear it clearly, to honor it dearly and to heed it quickly. Thank You, Jesus!

THANKSGIVING

Give thanks in all circumstances,

For all things at all times;

This is what His Word asks of us,

Throughout our whole lifetime.

BEAUTIFUL DAY OF THANKS

HIS WORD: "Come, let us sing for joy to the LORD;
let us shout aloud to the Rock of our salvation.
Let us come before him with thanksgiving and extol him with music and song.
For the LORD is the great God, the great King above all gods."
Psalm 95:1-3

MY CHALLENGE: *To give Him thanks with joy!
I do this with singing, shouting, music and song.*

My LORD and my God:

What a beautiful day to say,
"We give You thanks for all.
You are the Giver of good gifts,
Of all things big and small."

We thank You for the greatest Gift.
As sacrificial Lamb,
You took our sins upon Yourself.
You, the great I AM!

You showed the way to Your great power:
Receive the Heavenly Dove;
Be touched by You and You alone.
You fill our hearts with love.

Your joy that fills our lives today
With others we will share.
Oh, Glory! Hallelujah! LORD,
Your joy beyond compare!

There is no greater God than You,
Comforter and our Guide.
Created all there ever was,
Yet lives down deep inside.

Our thanks to You, our LORD and God.
With words we can't express.
You've made the beauty of this day.
We give You thanks with YES!

Your Loving Child

CM

PRAYER AND PRAISE: LORD, I come to You with thanksgiving in my heart for all You have done, for all You will do, and for Who You are! You are my LORD and God, and I praise You now for all things. May my praise continually be lifted to You. May my grateful thanksgiving bring glory to Your Name!

Week 33 ❖ Day 1   Theme: Thanksgiving   Aug 12

GIVE THANKS, THE WAY TO GO

HIS WORD: "And whatever you do, whether in word or deed, do it all in the name of the LORD Jesus, giving thanks to God the Father through him."
Colossians 3:17

MY CHALLENGE: To give thanks to God the Father through our LORD Jesus, in everything I do and everything I say.

When you give thanks, it opens doors,
And blessings come to you.
When you lose hope, hope comes to you.
His light comes shining through.

For thankfulness is key for growth,
While on your journey walk.
It matters not what reasons are.
Make "thanks" a gift of talk.

It shows appreciation for
All others' efforts too.
Then hearts are blessed as they, in turn,
Give Him thanks, just like you.

It's a multiplying factor
In motion has been set,
As freely you give thanks for all.
It's simple etiquette.

There is a factor that is divine.
It stores up in your bank.
Then dividends will be poured out,
When giving out your thanks.

It never ceases, never ends,
When it is set in flow.
So pour it out in abundance.
Give thanks, the way to go!

CM

PRAYER AND PRAISE: My LORD, I know that giving thanks is the way to go. I know that I have not been doing this as I should. Therefore I repent of it. Thank You for Your forgiveness. Please, LORD, help me by instilling in me a great desire and pleasure to consistently thank You and others!

Week 33 ❖ Day 2   Theme: Thanksgiving   Aug 13

GIVE THANKS FOR EVERYTHING

HIS WORD: "Speak to one another with psalms, hymns and spiritual songs. Sing and make music in your heart to the Lord, always giving thanks to God the Father for everything, in the name of our Lord Jesus Christ."
Ephesians 5:19-20

MY CHALLENGE: *To always give thanks for everything!*

Would you like to have a sample
Of heaven in your life?
Try giving thanks for everything,
Regardless of the strife.

For that is what God asks of us.
Make it a top concern.
As daily we will practice it,
It helps us then to learn.

For God is true in all His Word,
If we but will obey.
Let's give Him thanks for everything,
All things throughout the day.

From standpoint of our human way,
Most difficult to bring.
But as we grow, we learn the truth:
Give thanks for everything.

CM

PRAYER AND PRAISE: Lord, I pray to grow in Your truth, the truth of Your Word, as I know it says that we are to give You thanks for everything. I know it's true, and I promise to do my best to do just that. Amen!

FAUCET OF THANKSGIVING

HIS WORD: "With praise and thanksgiving they sang to the Lord: 'He is good; his love to Israel endures forever.' And all the people gave a great shout of praise to the Lord, because the foundation of the house of the Lord was laid."
Ezra 3:11

MY CHALLENGE: *To recognize the accomplishments of the Lord and then to give Him the praise for them.*

Turn on the faucet of thanksgiving.
Pour out your gratitude.
Let it run out, a mighty stream,
A gracious attitude.

His grace pours out abundantly.
It never will run dry.
He has promised us provision.
God has endless supply.

We give Him thanks for everything,
For all things great and small.
We praise His Name for all that comes,
Regardless what befalls.

We find that victory is ours,
As we live out each day,
Open faucet of thanksgiving.
He'll guide in every way.

CM

PRAYER AND PRAISE: *As I bow to You in prayer, I recognize the many things You have built into my life to bring victories. In fact, I would ask You to help me recall all of them, so that I may give You more praise!*
Amen!

THANKSGIVING, THE LANGUAGE OF LOVE

HIS WORD: "You are my God, and I will give you thanks;
you are my God, and I will exalt you.
Give thanks to the LORD, for he is good;
his love endures forever."
Psalm 118:28-29

MY CHALLENGE: *To daily make my thanksgiving for His love
a language of love to others.*

Your thankfulness is a language.
It speaks of His pure love,
That Christ gave you to share with all,
From endless stores above.

It matters not why you give thanks;
It matters most you do;
For as you give abundantly,
It will come back to you.

The more you give, the more you get.
Please try to comprehend.
Unless you stop the flow of it
The cycle will not end.

In fact, it will do more than that,
As habit it becomes.
You'll find you're filled with His great love,
And to His love succumb.

The gratitude that you receive
Is greater than you give;
For you will receive the measure.
The Good News you will live.

Make thanks, your language of giving,
Your love for Him above;
For these two things are as one:
Thanksgiving and your love.

CM

PRAYER AND PRAISE: *My LORD, I do give You thanks for Your enduring love.
And may Your love so fill me that it will be a "language" to others
that they know and understand.
Therefore I give You thanks for Your overflowing love today.
Thank You, Jesus. Amen!*

Week 33 ❖ Day 5   Theme: Thanksgiving   Aug 16

GIVE HIM THANKS FOR ALL

HIS WORD: "Give thanks in all circumstances, for this is God's will for you in Christ Jesus."
1 Thessalonians 5:18

MY CHALLENGE: *To know and understand that giving God thanks in all circumstances for all things brings me victory beyond understanding.*

*(Therefore, read the rhyme **slowly**, because the repetitive lines will cause an urge to speed through it. Go slow. Let it sink in.)*

The foundation for our prayers:
Give Him thanks for all,
And in every circumstance,
Give Him thanks for all.

It matters not the trial, child.
Give Him thanks for all.
Nor how long the journey's been.
Give Him thanks for all.

Are you hurting and in need?
Give Him thanks for all.
In all struggles of your life
Give Him thanks for all.

Is end of the rope in sight?
Give Him thanks for all.
Your energy but a dream?
Give Him thanks for all.

We have in Him victory.
Give Him thanks for all.
There is no other like Him.
Give Him thanks for all.

There's no other name on earth,
Give Him thanks for all,
That will give us new birth.
Give Him thanks for all.

We shout it from the housetops:
Give Him thanks for all.
Praise His Name throughout the earth;
Give Him thanks for all.

We proclaim it evermore:
Give Him thanks for all.
One last time we shout it out:
Give Him thanks for all!

75.75

PRAYER AND PRAISE: *I accept the challenge. My God, I will give You thanks in all circumstances, all the time, for all things. I trust in You, for You hold my present and my future, as I give it all to You. Thank You, my LORD!*

Week 33 ❖ Day 6   Theme: Thanksgiving   Aug 17

THANKSGIVING PRAISE

HIS WORD: "For everything God created is good,
and nothing is to be rejected if it is received with thanksgiving,
because it is consecrated by the word of God and prayer."
1 Timothy 4:4-5

MY CHALLENGE: *To receive everything with thanksgiving and
continually give Him praise for all things.*

To My Beloved Child:
> I receive your thanksgiving praise.
> I take it to My heart.
> With rejoicing here in heaven,
> My love to you impart.
>
> As I have stated in My Word,
> "Give thanks for everything,"
> I love to shower My love and care,
> With a soul that's yearning.
>
> I love to fill your every need
> And help in every task.
> Just come to Me in humbleness.
> Then in My love you'll bask.
>
> How I desire that all would know
> The joy that fills me so,
> When My children praise Me for all.
> That sets My heart aglow.
>
> So now, My child, keep up the thanks,
> For everything you own
> And everything that comes your way.
> Give Me the praise alone.
>
> In every circumstance you have,
> Give thanks to Me always;
> And I will bless you greater still,
> Through your thanksgiving praise.

Your Ever-Loving Lord

CM

PRAYER AND PRAISE: *My Lord, I am humbled by Your words. I more clearly
understand the desire to have a thousand tongues to sing Your praise.
I pray that I would grow into a deeper relationship with You,
in learning by experience to give You thanksgiving praise continually.*

34

GATHERING

He gathers His children together

At the end of our time,

To be with Him forever and ever,

With a royal suppertime.

I WILL GATHER YOU

HIS WORD: "Since you are precious and honored in my sight, and because I love you, I will give men in exchange for you, and people in exchange for life. Do not be afraid, for I am with you; I will bring your children from the east and gather you from the west. I will say to the north, 'Give them up!' And to the south, 'Do not hold them back.' Bring my sons from afar and my daughters from the ends of the earth—every one who is called by my name, whom I created for my glory, whom I formed and made."
Isaiah 43:4-7

MY CHALLENGE: To know with absolute certainty that I am called by His Name. I have been created for His glory, and it is He Who has formed and made me. When I can fully grasp that,
it will humble me and honor Him!

To My Precious Lord:

Lord, as You shout to "give them up,"
You gather from all around,
To bring your children from far and near,
As they are homeward bound.

For our true home is with you, Lord,
Wherever that may be.
Ascending high or staying here,
It matters not to me.

I know that wherever You are,
From there I want to serve,
That I may bring You the Glory,
That only You deserve.

Gather us to Your bosom, Lord.
We're ready to gather in,
To feel the warmth of Your embrace,
And serve You to the end.

Your Loving Child
CM

PRAYER AND PRAISE: Lord, I humble myself before You and pray in the Holy Spirit. I thank You that I'm in Your Family. I also pray for those who are not, and I pray that You would use me to bring them in.
I give myself to You to be Your extended hands, sharing Your enormous heart that I would see many join the Family of God.
Thank You, Lord!

Week 34 ❖ Day 1   Theme: Gathering   **Aug 19**

GATHER AT HIS ELECT

HIS WORD: "At that time the sign of the Son of Man will appear in the sky, and all the nations of the earth will mourn. They will see the Son of Man coming on the clouds of the sky, with power and great glory. And he will send his angels with a loud trumpet call, and they will gather his elect from one the four winds, from one end of the heavens to the other."
Matthew 24:30-31

MY CHALLENGE: To keep my head in the present, as I look forward to that great Day of the LORD and the glory of it all. There is a lot of work to do for Him while I'm abiding on this earth. I can't allow myself to become so heavenly bent I'm no earthly good.

What a glorious Day that will be,
At just the right moment,
When the sign of the Son appears:
Glorious Second Advent.

The Son of Man, coming on clouds,
With great Glory and pow'r.
The nations of the earth will mourn,
For this, their final hour.

The angels sound the trumpet call.
The elect are gathered in;
And all the faithful will rejoice,
A new life to begin.

Oh thank You, LORD, as we look up.
We know there's no delay,
When You shall gather Your elect,
And gather them that Day.

CM

PRAYER AND PRAISE: LORD, I want to shout and sing Hallelujah! The vision of your coming helps keep the present tolerable. I pray to be used of You so that when that gathering time comes, I'll feel good about what's been done. I want to be a faithful child and serve You, not a task-shirker. Thank You, LORD, as I step out in faith right now.

Week 34 ❖ Day 2   Theme: Gathering   **Aug 20**

THE GATHERING DAY WARNING

HIS WORD: "Concerning the coming of our Lord Jesus Christ and our being gathered to him, we ask you brothers, not to become easily unsettled or alarmed by some prophecy, report or letter supposed to have come from us, saying that the day of the Lord has already come."
2 Thessalonians 2:1-2

MY CHALLENGE: To be extremely cautious about listening to the voices of the world over the written Word and My Lord's assurance spoken to my heart. There are those who would lead me astray, some intentionally and others in ignorance. Either way, I know the Lord will NEVER lead me astray.

We thank You, Lord, for Your caution to us.
We can so easily go astray.
We hear so many voices in this world;
They all claim they know the true way.

Some bring us reports of tremendous fear,
And some bring prophecy of doom.
There are those who claim they have word from You,
That cover us with clouds of gloom.

You bring to us the greatest hope of all.
It's Your voice we need listen to,
As we rely on Your Holy written Word,
Our trust to be only in You.

Therefore we rejoice, no matter the talk,
And set all gloom and doom aside.
Oh, Lord, how great it is to look to You,
And know we're on the winning side!

10 8.10 8

PRAYER AND PRAISE: I pray to keep my focus on You and You alone, measuring the words of others by Your written Word.
Help me to listen more intently to that
which You are speaking to my heart.
Thank You, Lord!

Week 34 ❖ Day 3   Theme: Gathering   Aug 21

GATHER THE WHEAT

HIS WORD: "Let both grow together until the harvest. At that time I will tell the harvesters: First collect the weeds and tie them in bundles to be burned; then gather the wheat and bring it into my barn."
Matthew 13:30

"As the weeds are pulled up and burned in the fire, so it will be at the end of the age. The Son of Man will send out his angels, and they will weed out of His Kingdom everything that causes sin and all who do evil. They will throw them into the fiery furnace, where there will be weeping and gnashing of teeth. Then the righteous will shine like the sun in the kingdom of their Father. He who has ears, let him hear."
Matthew 13:40-43

MY CHALLENGE: To know that I am a wheat and not a weed.
Then I'm to be assured of being gathered to Him.
I am to hear with my spiritual ears.

We see the evidence today,
Together weeds and wheat,
Both will grow to maturity,
With each other compete.

Harvest angels collect the weeds
And burn them in the fire.
So it will be at end of the age,
When evil does expire.

The wheat is then all gathered in
And brought into His barn.
The LORD does the separating
In just the way He warned.

There's weeping and gnashing of teeth,
For all the weeds need fear,
While righteous will shine in the sun.
He who has ears, let him hear.

CM

PRAYER AND PRAISE: Dear LORD, I want to be certain to hear loud and clear. I want my antenna pointed directly to You. I pray my receptors are receptive. Yes, I have ears and I want to hear. I will hear. I am determined. I thank You, LORD, for these ears You've given me, to listen to you, learn from You and to live in Your Presence. Thank You, LORD!

Week 34 ❖ Day 4   Theme: Gathering   Aug 22

FOCUSING ON THE FUTURE

HIS WORD: "At that time men will see the Son of Man
coming in clouds with great power and glory.
And he will send his angels and gather his elect from the four winds,
from the ends of the earth to the ends of the heavens."
Mark 13:26-27

MY CHALLENGE: To be anticipating the great gathering, to be ready for it and to look forward to the sight of His great glory!

Fast Forward to the future:

I bring to you an announcement,
The most amazing thing:
Jesus has returned to the earth,
To rule as King of kings.

We have been waiting for this time,
To hear His trumpet call;
And now that it is here, dear one,
Will you stand or will you fall?

From Jerusalem comes the news
That we've been waiting for,
A time to cheer and clap our hands,
A time our spirits soar.

He has entered the Golden Gate,
As promised long ago.
We see it all so vividly.
We see it blow-by-blow.

He put His enemies under feet,
Has won the victory,
Overcoming all opposing Him.
Oh, see His Majesty!

We all shall take our place with Him,
In peace and harmony.
His rule will last a thousand years,
To rule with Holy duty.

Focusing Forward
CM

PRAYER AND PRAISE: I pray, Lord, to be watching and ready with great anticipation. Your coming again in all Your glory will be a one-time event, never seen before and never to be seen again. How grateful we are!

Week 34 ❖ Day 5   Theme: Gathering   Aug 23

ARE YOU READY?

HIS WORD: "Therefore keep watch because you do not know on what day your Lord will come. But understand this: If the owner of the house had known at what time of night the thief was coming, he would have kept watch and would not have let his house be broken into. So you also must be ready, because the Son of Man will come at an hour when you do not expect him."
Matthew 24:42-44

MY CHALLENGE: *To be ready! Am I keeping watch for the signs and times? Am I ready for His return to earth? I know not the hour, but I DO know He is coming. Therefore, I must challenge myself with the question: Am I ready?*

We're looking with anticipation
Toward the eastern sky,
Awaiting His glorious appearing,
His earth to occupy.

The signs have all been recognized.
It's but a breath away.
It won't be long until we're changed,
As promised for that Day.

The world is vastly unaware
Of the approaching scene.
They carry on with all their sin,
In living lives obscene.

But that's all coming to an end,
As Christ prepares to come,
To set His Kingdom up on earth,
His enemies overcome.

The Great Tribulation soon past,
With months and months of hell;
But all the saints have been guarded
In God's protective shell.

And so, we saints are all ready.
It is the Harvest Moon.
We ask you, child, are you ready
For His appearing soon?

CM

PRAYER AND PRAISE: *Lord, I think I'm ready, but my prayer to You is this: if there is any area in my life that is not ready for Your return, I ask that You do whatever is necessary so that area gets ready. Don't hold back on anything. I'll keep watching for the signs and times. You're coming soon. I am ready! Even so come, Lord Jesus!*

Week 34 ❖ Day 6   Theme: Gathering   Aug 24

I HAVE LONGED TO GATHER

HIS WORD: "O Jerusalem, Jerusalem, you who kill the prophets and stone those sent to you, how often I have longed to gather your children together, as a hen gathers her chicks under her wings, but you were not willing! Look, your house is left to you desolate. I tell you, you will not see me again until you say, 'Blessed is he who comes in the name of the LORD.'"
Luke 13:34-35

MY CHALLENGE: *To keep my eye on the future, my head on earth and my body in readiness until He comes again.*

To My Waiting Child:

The key to a "successful" life,
In the world you're living:
Keep your focus where it should be,
On Me, your living King.

So-called "success" in the workplace
Is far different from Mine;
For I measure not by bank accounts,
Nor by where they dine.

I measure not by cars they drive,
So they'll look impressive,
Nor about clothes in latest style,
Or homes in which they live.

What matters most to Me, my child,
Is found within the heart.
Is it beating with love for Me
Or focused far apart?

Is it the desire of the soul
To serve in every way,
Your LORD and Master and your Friend,
To please Me every day?

My child, I've longed to gather
My entire family,
To give all my blessing and joy,
For all eternity.

Your Soon-Coming Lord

CM

PRAYER AND PRAISE: *LORD, I so look forward to that Day, that will settle things once and for all; and to see You reign as King of kings and LORD of Lords, rejoicing in your victory. I simply pray for Your help in walking the narrow path while I trod the steps to the glory goal ahead.*

Week 34 ❖ Day 7   Theme: Gathering   **Aug 25**

35

HIS REST

He has a rest awaiting you,

When life on earth is done;

But as you serve Him be at rest,

And be His holy beacon.

JESUS, JESUS, JESUS

HIS WORD: *(Words of Jesus)* "Come to Me, all you who are weary and burdened, and I will give you rest. Take my yoke upon you and learn from me, for I am gentle and humble in heart, and you will find rest for your souls."
Matthew 11:28-29

MY CHALLENGE: *To come to Him to find His rest for my soul.*

To My Loving LORD:

Jesus, Jesus, Jesus,
I thank You for Your Word,
For all the things You have told me,
For all things I have heard.

Thank You, thank You, thank You,
For this one thing I know:
I'm thankful for the peace I have.
It's my internal glow.

Jesus, Jesus, Jesus,
You are the only One
Who gave His life that I would live,
And my salvation won.

Praise You, praise You, praise You.
Some day I will ascend;
But in the meantime, here on earth,
You'll always be my Friend.

Jesus, Jesus, Jesus,
For my life You have blessed.
Your Name is always on my lips.
I'm ever in Your rest.

Your Loving Child
SM

PRAYER AND PRAISE: LORD Jesus, it's such a great comfort to think of the rest I have in You, a rest beyond description, and a rest not only for today, but for eternity. So I humbly thank You for that rest, as I place myself into Your hands again today, LORD. I ask You to help me to do this every day because I'm so inclined to depend upon myself instead of You.
I need to strive more for Your rest and less for what I think is best. Amen!

Week 35 ❖ Day 1   Theme: His Rest   **Aug 26**

DESIRE TO REST IN HIM

HIS WORD: "This is what the Lord says:
'Stand at the crossroads and look; ask for the ancient paths,
ask where the good way is, and walk in it,
and you will find rest for your souls.'"
Jeremiah 6:16

MY CHALLENGE: *To find that rest He has promised me.*

The world has taught us to elevate
The role of self-sufficiency,
That we could walk with heads held high,
The master of our destiny.

We all can be so very proud,
In achieving our self-made goals,
And show the world how great we are,
With everything under control.

This is not what the Lord designed,
To live an independent flair,
Without acknowledgment of Him,
For us to live outside His care.

For He has created in us all
A hunger and a longing need,
To seek His way and trust in Him,
Desire to follow in His lead.

What joy it is to lean on Him
And know He holds onto the reins,
To guide us in our daily life,
Until eternal life we gain.

He calls for us to rest in Him,
Assured He has for us the best,
That we not fret on what we see,
But simply to receive His rest.

LM

PRAYER AND PRAISE: *Lord, I thank You for Your Rest! I confess I desperately need Your rest, both now and forever. I also confess I have been so busy with my own interests and everyday living that I haven't stopped to receive and enjoy the rest You have for me. Therefore, as I bow my head now, I give it all to You and thank You for the rest and peace You give me at this time. In Jesus' precious Name.*

Week 35 ❖ Day 2   Theme: His Rest   **Aug 27**

HIS QUIET REST

HIS WORD: "Therefore, since the promise of entering his rest still stands, let us be careful that none of you be found to have fallen short of it. For we also have had the gospel preached to us, just as they did; but the message they heard was of no value to them, because those who heard did not combine it with faith.
Now we who have believed enter that rest, just as God has said, 'So I declared on oath in my anger, "They shall never enter my rest."'
And yet his work has been finished since the creation of the world."
Hebrews 4:1-3

MY CHALLENGE: *To take the promise of entering His rest and combine it with faith.*

The world has been in great turmoil.
Evil has been displayed.
The devil has a dire control,
Since Adam disobeyed.

Since then the conflicts of this world
Have gained intensity,
Until all hope seemed far too gone,
Without a peace to see.

But then the LORD has promised us,
And gives to us His best:
Since we are in His Family,
We will enter His rest.

The kind of rest that comes to us,
The world has never known;
For it's given to God's children,
From our LORD Jesus alone.

The rest that permeates the heart
Brings comfort to the soul.
It brings a peace to the body,
The Spirit in control.

Know He cares for your hurts and needs.
He wants for you the best.
We look to Him, He gives to us
A peace of quiet rest.

CM

PRAYER AND PRAISE: *My LORD, My faith is in You, and I stand on Your promises. And, oh, what a beautiful promise it is, that I will enter the peace of Your quiet rest. Thank You for the blessed assurance, as it brings peace to my heart. There is none like You! Amen!*

Week 35 ❖ Day 3   Theme: His Rest   Aug 28

ENTER HIS REST

HIS WORD: "For somewhere he has spoken about the seventh day in these words: 'And on the seventh day God rested from all his work.' And again in the passage above he says, 'They shall never enter my rest.' It still remains that some will enter that rest, and those who formerly had the gospel preached to them did not go in, because of their disobedience."
Hebrews 4:4-6

MY CHALLENGE: To be certain I maintain obedience and retain that blessed assurance that I shall enter His rest, for it is that which gives me peace beyond understanding and joy unspeakable.

To enter His rest
Is a promise of His,
When into the family we came.
As kids of the King,
We are privileged to praise
That Name that is above all names.

We carry that Name,
Who paid our total debt,
And He cleansed our guilty conscience.
We follow His will,
As we obey His Word.
We have that blessed assurance.

We rest in His peace,
With joy unspeakable.
With His love we are truly blessed.
With faith in that Name
Our future guaranteed,
Forever we enter His rest.

11 8.11 8

PRAYER AND PRAISE: Lord, I give myself to You in worship of Your Holy Name, for I do carry Your Name, "Christian," and I pray to be obedient and honor that Name. I do this with joy in my life, love in my heart and peace in my mind, as I am privileged to live in Your rest today.
Amen!

Week 35 ❖ Day 4   Theme: His Rest   **Aug 29**

COMPLETENESS IN HIS REST

HIS WORD: "Therefore God again set a certain day, calling it Today, when a long time later he spoke through David, as was said before: 'Today, if you hear his voice, do not harden your hearts.' For if Joshua had given them rest, God would not have spoken later about another day."
Hebrews 4:7-8

MY CHALLENGE: To hear His Voice with a warm, pliable heart, relishing His present rest while, at the same time, looking forward to that eternal rest.

In His rest is our completeness,
Our wholeness in His hands;
For He has brought us peace to live
And follow His commands.

His peace is that deep, inner sense
That calms all worry and fear,
Knowing He has it in His hands.
Our trust in Him sincere.

There is no other one on earth,
Nor any thing we see
That can bring us peace like His alone,
For all eternity.

We look forward to that last day.
To earth we say goodbye,
And sail on home to be with Him,
To live in Paradise.

'Twill be our final place of rest,
Beyond that distant shore,
To praise His Name throughout the time,
And joy forevermore.

In meantime, we'll serve on earth
And do our very best.
We know that here on earth we have
Completeness in His rest.

CM

MY PRAYER: My Eternal God, how blessed I am to know You and Your rest for my soul, both now and forevermore.
Help me hear Your voice ever so clearly, that I'll not miss a single direction You have for me—until such time I enter my eternal rest. Thank You, LORD!

Week 35 ❖ Day 5   Theme: His Rest   Aug 30

UNTIL OUR SABBATH-REST

HIS WORD: "There remains, then, a Sabbath-rest for the people of God; for anyone who enters God's rest also rests from his own work, just as God did from his. Let us, therefore, make every effort to enter that rest, so that no one will fall by following their example of disobedience."
Hebrews 4:9-11

MY CHALLENGE: To be certain I am going to enter that Sabbath-rest. It may also be called a final rest, in which all believers will enter upon their departure from earth and arrival at their heavenly home.

In what God has called us to do,
We strive to do our best,
To give Him all the glory due,
Until our Sabbath-rest.

We trust in Him; it matters not
Whatever we may say.
We give to Him, surrender all,
To let Him have His way.

We know that we can trust in Him
All aspects of our life,
To lean on Him throughout our walk,
Regardless of the strife.

Therefore we give Him all our thanks.
We raise to Him our praise.
For He's the One who gave His all,
And set the world ablaze.

He sent the Holy Spirit fire,
To give us all we need,
That we would follow in His path,
And do His Godly deeds.

Therefore what God has called us to,
Let's strive to do our best,
To follow Him and His commands,
Until our Sabbath-rest.

CM

PRAYER AND PRAISE: My Lord God, I look forward to that day when You call me heavenward to Yourself, to a home You have prepared for me. I confess, I'm doing everything I can to live as long as I can here on earth. I give thanks to You as I look forward to that day You call me home.

Week 35 ❖ Day 6   Theme: His Rest   Aug 31

MY BLESSED REST

HIS WORD: "Then I heard a voice from heaven say,
'Write: Blessed are the dead who die in the LORD from now on.'
'Yes,' says the Spirit, 'they will rest from their labor,
for their deeds will follow them.'"
Revelation 14:13

MY CHALLENGE: *To be certain to receive His promise of His blessed rest.
I can be certain and will be assured when I know I am God's child.
As Jesus said: "You must be born again."* (See Feb 2)

To My Beloved Child:

From Genesis to Revelation,
My promises are given.
So grasp them and hold on tightly,
For they're your Holy Beacon.

In the first book of the Bible,
You are never to forget,
I rested on the seventh day,
An example I had set.

In the book of Revelation,
My promises continue.
Believers will rest from their labor,
My blessings poured out on you.

Just keep in mind, for you're my child,
As you trust Me for the best:
Just look to Me for all your needs,
As I give My blessed rest.

Your Loving Dad

87.87

PRAYER AND PRAISE: *Thank You, LORD, that I've had the opportunity to focus on Your rest these past few days. I confess I don't think about that enough. You have promised us rest, for now and for eternity. The present life and the life to come. What a blessing indeed! Thank You, Jesus!*

Week 35 ❖ Day 7   Theme: His Rest   Sep 1

36

COMFORT

The comfort You bring to us each day

We gratefully extol;

For as we hear Your words for us,

They're comfort for our soul.

YOU'RE MY COMFORT

HIS WORD: "Praise be to the God and Father of our LORD Jesus Christ, the Father of compassion and the God of all comfort, who comforts us in all our troubles, so that we can comfort those in any trouble with the comfort we ourselves have received from God."
2 Corinthians 1:3-4

MY CHALLENGE: To _know_ that He is the God of all comfort and that comfort is mine. All I need do is to acknowledge and accept it, for He's already given it to me!

To My Comforting Jesus:

You bring comfort to my soul, LORD Jesus,
Knowing You are my destiny.
It matters not the offers of the world,
For only You can comfort me.

The cry of the world is loud in my ears,
But I hear Your still, inner voice,
Bringing to me Your total peace and joy.
For Your comfort I make the choice.

It's You and You alone I seek, my LORD,
For You're my Counselor and Guide.
I bring my life and lay it at Your feet.
My promise in You I'll abide.

LORD, the more of myself I give to You
The more of Yourself I perceive.
Through it all, I can only shout and claim,
"LORD Jesus, You're a comfort to me!"

Your Loving Child

10 8.10 8

PRAYER AND PRAISE: My God of all comfort, I bow to You in humble prayer. I do acknowledge and accept Your comfort to me, the compassion You have for me and the care You give to me. What a blessed LORD You are! Amen!

Week 36 ❖ Day 1   Theme: Comfort   Sep 2

A COMMUNICATION OF COMFORT

HIS WORD: "For just as the sufferings of Christ flow over into our lives, so also through Christ our comfort overflows. If we are distressed, it is for your comfort and salvation; if we are comforted, it is for your comfort, which produces in you patient endurance of the same sufferings we suffer."
2 Corinthians 1:5-6

MY CHALLENGE: To bring comfort to others, just as the apostle Paul was doing in His second letter to the Corinthians.

A communication of comfort
Is who the LORD can use
To bring His words of solace to all,
The words of Jesus' Good News!

Not the world's words of negativity,
That drown a person in gloom.
But needed are His words of comfort,
A fresh fragrance in the room.

It is His work to build up the soul
And bring them help to assure
That they can gain their spiritual strength,
To help His children mature.

If we will but lean on Him today
And know that He will supply,
We can relax and fret not at all.
His comfort will satisfy.

97.97

PRAYER AND PRAISE: My LORD, You have comforted me so many times. May I so comfort others who are looking for a little solace in their lives. Use me as Your extended hands to do just that. Thank You, my LORD!

Week 36 ❖ Day 2   Theme: Comfort   **Sep 3**

MY COMFORTING WORDS

HIS WORD: "And our hope for you is firm,
because we know that just as you share in our sufferings,
so also you share in our comfort."
2 Corinthians 1:7

MY CHALLENGE: *To share with others the comfort
that Christ brought to me.*

Give encouragement to His children:
To touch another soul in your walk each day.
Give them an encouraging word.
Let the words of your mouth speak peace to their hearts,
That they would be greatly assured.

As their hearts are burdened by their trials in life
And bodies may be suffering pain,
Help them to be built up in the most Holy Faith,
Encouragement that will help them sustain.

Let your life be a life of encouragement.
Spreading oil on their troubled seas.
That will enable them to have ears to listen.
Then will open their ears to Me.

I'll confirm the words you have given to them.
They will know they were words from above.
Reach out in My Name, as you speak to their need,
To give them all My Comforting Love.

11 9.11 9

PRAYER AND PRAISE: *My loving and leading God, put me in touch today,
with someone who needs an encouraging word from You.
May I be Your conduit to bless their life today. Thank You, my LORD!*

Week 36 ❖ Day 3   Theme: Comfort   **Sep 4**

WORDS OF COMFORT AND HOPE

HIS WORD: "Comfort, comfort my people, says your God."
Isaiah 40:1

MY CHALLENGE: *To minister in the Name of our LORD, to bring His hope and comfort to others, just as God has asked me to do.*

Give Comfort and Hope to My Children:
**Each day you have the opportunity
To minister in My Name.
Everyone you meet along the way
Needs My words that you proclaim.**

**You only need give them words of Mine,
Kind words of comfort and hope,
Words that help their problems today,
In helping them to cope.**

**Each one is a precious soul to Me.
Each one needs help of some kind.
So be My mouthpiece, giving My Words.
New peace in their life they'll find.**

**Speak out the words I lay on your heart.
Fear not, as for words you grope.
I use you as a channel of Mine
To bring them comfort and hope.**

97.97

PRAYER AND PRAISE: *My LORD and God, forgive me. Far too often I focus on the comfort that I think I need, rather than on the needs of others. I know that when I take the time and effort to comfort others in their need, You, in some way, meet my own needs. Help me now to remember that and look to the needs around me, that I can bring someone Your comfort today.
Thank You, my LORD!*

Week 36 ❖ Day 4   Theme: Comfort   **Sep 5**

HIS PEACEFUL PRESENCE

HIS WORD: "The Lord is my shepherd, I shall not want.
He maketh me to lie down in green pastures;
He leadeth me beside the still waters.
He restoreth my soul:
He leadeth me in the paths of righteousness for his name's sake.
Yea, though I walk through the valley of the shadow of death,
I will fear no evil: for thou art with me;
Thy rod and thy staff they comfort me.
Thou preparest a table before me in the presence of mine enemies:
Thou anointest my head with oil; my cup runneth over.
Surely goodness and mercy shall follow me all the days of my life:
And I will dwell in the house of the Lord forever."
Psalm 23, KJV

MY CHALLENGE: *To take this most beloved of psalms and the comfort it gives and live it!*

We walk in His peaceful Presence,
Talk with Him one on One.
We keep our mind in constant prayer,
Until our day is done.

And then we give Him thanks for all.
To Him, our praise we sing.
Our hearts rejoice with Him in song,
For the comfort He brings.

We sit quietly in His Presence,
As He speaks to our hearts,
Of glorious things in His domain,
In perfect time imparts.

This brings us comfort to our souls,
As we wait in reverence,
And walk with Him in the interim,
With His peaceful Presence.

CM

PRAYER AND PRAISE: Lord, I am so comforted by the words of the psalm and knowing You are my Shepherd, and I truly do have everything I need. And, thanks to You, I will dwell in Your house forever.
Thank You, my Lord, for Your comfort to me.

Week 36 ❖ Day 5   Theme: Comfort   Sep 6

YOUR COMFORT IN SERVICE

HIS WORD: "But you, O Lord, are a compassionate and gracious God, slow to anger, abounding in love and faithfulness.
Turn to me and have mercy on me; grant your strength to your servant and save the son of your maidservant.
Give me a sign of your goodness, that my enemies may see it and be put to shame, for you, O Lord, have helped me and comforted me."
Psalm 86:15-17

MY CHALLENGE: *To keep focused on my service to Him, while at the same time, knowing I am being comforted by Him. Whomever and whenever He calls, He comforts.*

You, my Lord, are compassionate,
Full of mercy and grace.
You are abounding in faithfulness.
I sense You in this place.

Thank You for Your mercy to me
And strength You've given me,
That I can serve You faithfully,
All through eternity.

Continue to teach me Your truth,
That I'll walk in Your way.
Give me an undivided heart,
That I will never stray.

I'll serve You with a passion, Lord.
All effort I will make;
For You have always given me
Your comfort for my sake.

CM

PRAYER AND PRAISE: *My compassionate and comforting God, how great You are! As I cast my eyes on You, You cast Your comfort on me. As I seek Your Presence, You soak me with Your love. Help me to keep my eyes upon You, that I may continually sense Your comfort. Amen!*

Week 36 ❖ Day 6   Theme: Comfort   Sep 7

MY COMFORT IN PERFECT TIME

HIS WORD: "For the LORD will ransom Jacob and redeem them from the hand of those stronger than they. They will come and shout for joy on the heights of Zion; they will rejoice in the bounty of the LORD—the grain, the new wine and the oil, the young of the flocks and herds. They will be like a well-watered garden, and they will sorrow no more. Then maidens will dance and be glad, young men and old as well. I will turn their mourning into gladness; I will give them comfort and joy instead of sorrow."
Jeremiah 31:11-13

MY CHALLENGE: To know the promise of the LORD to give His comfort and joy in place of my sorrow. He said it. He promised it. He'll give it!

To My Sorrowful Child:

When you come to a valley in your life,
Mountains of worry surround,
You imagine things that haven't come,
As you're constantly looking down.

Lift up your eyes to the heavens, child.
See My glory put in place.
I created all you see and more.
I comfort you with My grace.

I can do that, if you'll look to Me,
With your Holy Spirit's eye;
For I have come to live within you.
You're the apple of My eye.

Therefore, My child, I will hold you close,
As your tears fall on My breast.
I bring to you My assuring words:
You'll receive My very best.

So now, lay back and relax, My child.
I will lead you by the hand,
As we face your problems together,
Though you may not understand.

Therefore I will mold you and shape you,
On your path of life we climb.
I'll bring you each step of the way,
My comfort in perfect time.

Your Comforting Father
97.97

PRAYER AND PRAISE: Thank You, my LORD, that in Your perfect timing, You bring Your comfort to me. Your comfort that is encouragement and joy. Amen!

Week 36 ❖ Day 7 Theme: Comfort Sep 8

37

FRIEND

We call you Friend and Friend you are,

For You have said the same,

As You have shared Your love with us

And given us Your Name.

YOUR EXTENDED HAND

HIS WORD: "My command is this: Love each other as I have loved you. Greater love has no one than this, that he lay down his life for his friends."
John 15:12-13

MY CHALLENGE: *To focus on Jesus as my greatest Friend, for He is! That's why I can go forth as His extended hand.*

My LORD and my Friend:

I keep my eyes focused on You,
For You're my greatest Friend.
No other One has loved me so,
Will carry me through to end.

Let me tingle with Your Glory,
To sense Your Presence near,
To feel my heart warmed with Your love,
With nothing left to fear.

For now I know You're with me, LORD.
I'll do what e'er You say.
You've filled me now with Your great power.
I'm ready for this day.

I want to sense Your Spirit deep,
To fill up every pore,
To walk together hand in hand,
New ventures to explore.

I sense the weights are lifted now.
My body's light as air.
It seems that I could soar through space,
And meet You over there.

So now, my LORD, I rise to serve,
Wherever You command,
As I go forth as friend with Friend,
As Your extended hand.

Your Loving Child and Friend
CM

PRAYER AND PRAISE: *My LORD Jesus and Friend, I bow before You now to give You thanks for my having discovered You as Savior, as LORD and as Friend. Since that time, I find myself drawing closer to You each day. This drawing closer never ends, my growing in faith will never cease and my love for You has no boundaries. I give You all the glory now and forever. Amen!*

Week 37 ❖ Day 1   Theme: Friend   Sep 9

JESUS, MY FRIEND, I CONFESS

HIS WORD: "You are my friends if you do what I command."
John 15:14

MY CHALLENGE: To demonstrate my friendship with Him by doing and being what He has asked of me.

Jesus, my friend, I confess I:
    Love You,
    Adore You,
    Bow down before You,
    Praise Your Name,
    Sense Your Presence,
    Rejoice in You,
    Lift Your Name,
    Live Your life,
    Love Your tenderness,
    Sense Your nearness,
    Glory in You,
    Worship You,
    Give You Thanks.

Jesus, I will continually do my best to:
    Submit to You,
    Trust in You,
    Obey Your Word,
    Please Your heart.

For I:
    Am Your Bride,
    Am Yours

You are my friend
For ever and ever.
Amen!

IRR.

PRAYER AND PRAISE: My LORD, what an awesome God You are!
I confess that I love You with my whole heart and soul.
I confess that I desire to follow in Your way, to do what You'd have me do and to be what You'd have me be.
That's my desire; that's my delight. Thank You, my LORD!

Week 37 ❖ Day 2   Theme: Friend   Sep 10

SERVING AS A FRIEND

HIS WORD: "I no longer call you servants, because a servant does not know his master's business. Instead, I have called you friends, for everything that I learned from my Father I have made known to you."
John 15:15

MY CHALLENGE: *To know, for an absolute certainty, that I am His friend and not called a servant. Even though I serve Him, I serve Him as a friend, not as a servant.*

My Jesus, what an awesome thought:
You give to us this day
To know we serve You as a friend,
Though You're the great Yahweh

Nor do You call us bond servants,
As though we were a slave;
For we are in Your family.
It's Your Presence we crave.

You call us not to be employed,
As though a hired hand;
But live our lives as Your best friend.
It's absolutely grand.

We give thanks to You, LORD Jesus,
Able to comprehend:
We live the greatest privilege,
To walk with You as Friend!

CM

PRAYER AND PRAISE: *My LORD Jesus, I confess that sometimes I have a struggle thinking of You as the Most High God (which You are) while, at the same time, knowing that You are a closer Friend than anyone on earth. I thank You, my LORD, for helping me to wrap my mind around this, so that I can capture it, hold it and enjoy it, as You would have me do.*
On You, my Master,
I can depend.
This will always be.
You are my Friend.

Week 37 ❖ Day 3   Theme: Friend   Sep 11

JESUS IS MY FRIEND

HIS WORD: "A man of many companions may come to ruin, but there is a friend who sticks closer than a brother."
Proverbs 18:24

"He who loves a pure heart and whose speech is gracious will have the king for his friend."
Proverbs 22:11

MY CHALLENGE: To know this King of kings as the best Friend of all! On Him I can always depend. He'll never leave me nor forsake me.

My Jesus is a friend of mine.
He's my Greatest Helper.
He sticks with me through thick and thin,
Closer than a brother.

That's why I lean on Him so much,
Depending on His strength.
As I do my best to follow,
He'll go to any length.

I strive to have a heart that's pure,
My lips always praising.
Therefore I have a King as Friend.
Yes, Jesus is my King!

I look to Jesus as my LORD.
On Him I do depend.
He meets my every need for all,
For Jesus is my Friend.

CM

PRAYER AND PRAISE: My LORD, my God, my Savior, my King and my Friend, without the help of Your Holy Spirit, I cannot begin to understand how "LORD," "God," "Savior" and "King," can all be wrapped up in "Friend!" But it is true, and I'm eternally grateful to You that it is true. It is real and available to all who will receive You as such. Thank You, Jesus!

Week 37 ❖ Day 4   Theme: Friend   Sep 12

I WANT TO LIVE

HIS WORD: "He called out to them, 'Friends, haven't you any fish?'
'No,' they answered.
He said, 'Throw your net on the right side of the boat and you will find some.'
When they did, they were unable to haul the net in
because of the large number of fish."
John 21:5-6

MY CHALLENGE: To listen to Him as Friend because He will always call me to the "right" side, without fail.

You are my Friend, I know is true,
For You have said as much.
I take You at Your Word, my LORD
And feel Your friendly touch.

I want to live in Your embrace
And know that You are near.
Give comfort to this aching heart
And take away the fear.

I want to serve with You, my LORD,
To win lost souls to You,
Bring life anew to hurting ones.
I know Your Way is true!

I want to love as You have loved,
To cause them faith release,
That those who want Your saving grace
Will find Your joy and peace.

I want to live for You alone,
With all my heart to give,
My service to My LORD and Friend.
For You I want to live.

CM

PRAYER AND PRAISE: My Friend, Jesus, I know You call me friend, just as You did those disciple fishermen in the boat. I ask that You help me get this concept deeper into my heart and soul, so that there's never a doubt of this fact. I listen now and hear You now, as You call me "friend." Thank You, LORD!

Week 37 ❖ Day 5   Theme: Friend   Sep 13

DELIGHT OURSELVES IN HIM

HIS WORD: "Trust in the L{sub}ORD{/sub} and do good;
dwell in the land and enjoy safe pasture.
Delight yourself in the LORD and he will give you the desires of your heart.
Commit your way to the LORD; trust in him and he will do this:
He will make your righteousness shine like the dawn,
the justice of your cause like the noonday sun."
Psalm 37:3-6

MY CHALLENGE: *To learn to delight myself in Him at all times, regardless of what is going on in the world around me.*

Seek to please the LORD above all.
He's your Friend in all ways.
Strive to please Him in the small things,
As you journey through the days.

Seek to please Him every moment,
As any friend would do,
So your relationship can grow
And in His love pursue.

What life may give to you each day
Is not your source of joy.
It's only through our LORD Jesus,
Our Holy Viceroy.

It gives us joy to be assured
His love will never end.
We will delight ourselves in Him,
For He's our greatest Friend.

CM

PRAYER AND PRAISE: *I cannot give You anything but praise at this time, my LORD, as I consider You my greatest Friend and, therefore, desire to please You above all others and all earthly things.*
It is my prayer, as Your friend, to bring You glory in all I do and say.
May it be so, my dear LORD!

Week 37 ❖ Day 6   Theme: Friend   Sep 14

MY BEST FRIEND

HIS WORD: "And this is love: that we walk in obedience to his commands. As you have heard from the beginning, his command is that you walk in love."
2 John 1:6

"And the scripture was fulfilled that says, 'Abraham believed God, and it was credited to him as righteousness,' and he was called God's friend."
James 2:23

MY CHALLENGE: *To live the truth of what He has said: that is, to live in obedience to Him because I am His friend, just as Abraham believed God and was considered His friend.*

To My Child, My Friend:

Your best friend has forsaken you,
Know not how to respond,
Having confided in that soul,
As in a holy bond.

You shared so many private things,
Personal in nature;
And now they're being bantered about.
You wonder your future.

Remember one thing, my dear child:
Your future's Mine to hold.
You look to Me in spite of all,
My Glory to behold.

See in Me your Answer to all.
I AM your Strong Tower.
Do not sweat your earthly problems.
Receive My Holy Shower.

For I AM filling you with Me,
My presence to employ,
That your soul will be satisfied,
Your life be filled with joy.

Worry not about earthly grief.
I'll love you to the end.
Just come along and walk with Me,
For I AM your best Friend!

Your Forever Friend
CM

PRAYER AND PRAISE: *I commit myself to You again today, to walk in obedience to Your commands, simply because I am Your friend, and You are mine.*

Week 37 ❖ Day 7   Theme: Friend   **Sep 15**

38

IN HIS LOVE

Love each other as I have loved you.

You must love one another.

All will know you're my disciples,

If you love one another.

LIFE A LOVE SONG

HIS WORD: "Be imitators of God, therefore, as dearly loved children and live a life of love, just as Christ loved us and gave himself up for us as a fragrant offering and sacrifice to God."
Ephesians 5:1-2

MY CHALLENGE: *To be an imitator of God, to give myself in service to others, just as He did for me.*

To My Loving Lord:
> Lord, let my life be a love song,
> And set my heart aflame,
> To raise Your banner to the heights,
> And glorify Your Name.
>
> My life is nothing without You;
> With You it's everything;
> For I can trust You completely.
> You're always King of kings.
>
> So take my life and make it be
> A lovely lullaby;
> For Your great love and gift to all,
> A life to glorify.
>
> Your Loving Child
> CM

PRAYER AND PRAISE: *Thank You, my Lord, that I am a loving child of Yours. As I serve others in Your Name, may it be a gift of Your love through me. In Jesus' Name.*

Week 38 ❖ Day 1   Theme: In His Love   Sep 16

A FIELD OF LOVE

HIS WORD: "I pray that out of his glorious riches he may strengthen you with power through his Spirit in your inner being, so that Christ may dwell in your hearts through faith. And I pray that you, being rooted and established in love, may have power, together with all the saints, to grasp how wide and long and high and deep is the love of Christ, and to know this love that surpasses knowledge—that you may be filled to the measure of all the fullness of God."
Ephesians 3:16-19

MY CHALLENGE: To grasp the greatness of Christ's love, that I may grow in Him, be filled with Him and know this fullness of God.

A field of love God cultivates
Is found right in our heart.
He sows the seeds of love down deep
And helps them get their start.

He waters and He nourishes,
As love begins to grow.
It breaks the surface with a sprout,
To capture Sonlight's glow.

This plant of love sends down its roots
And grows a mighty stem,
From which the fruit will then burst forth.
This is God's stratagem.

Then, as these plants of love mature,
Their roots deep in the sod,
Fulfill their Godly purpose then,
Bring forth the fruit of God.

Receive the seed He wants to plant
And let it penetrate;
For you and I are fields of love
For God to cultivate.

This is our role in life, dear one,
We simply can deduce:
To bear His fruit in perfect time.
His garden will produce.

CM

PRAYER AND PRAISE: Having received the blessings of Your love, Jesus, I pray that I will continuously produce fruit, the fruit of Your love. Thank You, Jesus!

I OWE MY LIFE TO YOU

HIS WORD: "Dear friends, let us love one another, for love comes from God. Everyone who loves has been born of God and knows God. Whoever does not love does not know God, because God is love. This is how God showed his love among us: He sent his one and only Son into the world that we might live through him. This is love: not that we loved God, but that he loved us and sent his Son as an atoning sacrifice for our sins. Dear friends, since God so loved us, we also ought to love one another."
1 John 4:7-11

MY CHALLENGE: To give my life as a gift to God, because of His love for me. His sacrifice for my sins was a debt I could not pay.

I owe my life to You, my LORD,
For You have cleansed my heart,
Given new life for me to live,
From this old world apart.

I cannot fathom a love so great,
Willing to pay the price,
To suffer and give all for me
And make the sacrifice.

I know no other such as You,
Who gave His life for me,
Willing to suffer a cruel cross
In order I'd be free.

My sin, a debt I could not pay.
A life gone wrong I knew.
Thank You, my LORD, this gift to me.
I owe my life to You.

CM

PRAYER AND PRAISE: On bended knee I come to You, to lift You up, to praise and glorify You. You are my Savior, my LORD, my Master and my Everything. You have saved me from my life of sin and from the pits of hell. You have brought me into Your Kingdom, to live forever in Your Presence. Glory! There is nothing greater than that! All praise to You, my LORD!

OVERFLOWING LOVE

HIS WORD: "The good man brings good things out of the good stored up in his heart, and the evil man brings evil things out of the evil stored up in his heart. For out of the overflow of his heart his mouth speaks."
Luke 6:45

"May the LORD make your love increase and overflow for each other and for everyone else, just as ours does for you. May he strengthen your hearts so that you will be blameless and holy in the presence of our God and Father when our LORD Jesus comes with all his holy ones."
1 Thessalonians 3:12-13

MY CHALLENGE: *That the overflow of my heart would be an overflow of Christ's love through me, touching the lives of others.*
Can I see myself as His hands extended in love to others? If so, will I?

Do you have love deep in your heart,
That brings cascading joy?
A love that focuses on Him
The world cannot destroy.

A love that overflows your heart
And floods to others 'round.
They sense that beating of a heart,
With love that knows no bound.

Our challenge, as His progeny,
Is follow in His way,
To reach out with His loving heart,
Give out His love each day.

The most amazing thing occurs,
As we do as He shows.
He keeps on filling us with Him,
A love that overflows.

CM

PRAYER AND PRAISE: *LORD, I open my heart to You, that You would overflow it with such quantity that I couldn't help but affect others and that they would receive Your love increasingly. Thank you, LORD, for all opportunities to share Your love with others.*

Week 38 ❖ Day 4   Theme: In His Love   Sep 19

IN LIGHT OF YOUR LOVE

HIS WORD: "No one has ever seen God; but if we love one another, God lives in us and his love is made complete in us. We know that we live in him and he in us, because he has given us of his Spirit. And we have seen and testify that the Father has sent his Son to be the Savior of the world. If anyone acknowledges that Jesus is the Son of God, God lives in him and he in God. And so we know and rely on the love God has for us. God is love. Whoever lives in love lives in God, and God in him."
1 John 4:12-16

MY CHALLENGE: To live in love, with God's love in me.

God's mercy will move your mountains
And fill your valleys with love.
He smooths out the way of your life,
If you'll look to Him above.

His Spirit lives within your heart.
He will guide you through the maze.
Because of His great love for you,
He is with you through all days.

He'll never leave nor forsake you.
His love wants only the best,
If we can but comprehend it
And trust till our final rest.

Thank You, Lord, for Your mighty love.
I will never doubt again.
I'll trust Your guidance for all times,
In light of Your Love, Amen!

87.87

PRAYER AND PRAISE: In light of Your love, my Lord, I have a mandate, and that is to love others as You have loved me. The more I ponder that, Lord, the greater understanding I receive of sacrificial love. That is contrary to what the flesh desires, so I ask You to help me follow in Your steps and demonstrate the kind of love You have given to me. Thank You, Lord!

Week 38 ❖ Day 5   Theme: In His Love   Sep 20

NO GREATER LOVE

HIS WORD: "And a voice from heaven said, 'This is my Son, whom I love; with him I am well pleased.'"
Matthew 3:17

"Greater love has no one than this, that he lay down his life for his friends. You are my friends if you do what I command."
John 15:13-14

MY CHALLENGE: *To love as He has loved, which He has commanded.*

There's no greater love ever known
That's greater than our LORD's;
For He has saved us from the pit,
By His almighty Sword.

He won the victory for all.
He paid the total cost.
There is no other love like His,
Example by the cross.

He gave us the Great Commandment,
To love as He has loved.
We follow Him obediently,
His orders from above.

We take His love to all the world.
We lift His Name on high,
Fulfilling what He asks of us,
His Name to magnify.

Therefore, as we confess His Name,
We can be rest assured:
There is no love as great as His.
We're in His love secured.

"This is My Son whom I do love,"
The words God spoke above.
"This is My One and only Son."
There is no greater love.

CM

PRAYER AND PRAISE: *My LORD Jesus, I confess that no matter how hard I try I still find it difficult to love some people. However, on the other hand, I know that You have commanded us to love as You have loved. That is to love without condition. Therefore, my LORD, I will try to do that, knowing that I will grow in You through this experience. Amen!*

Week 38 ❖ Day 6   Theme: In His Love   **Sep 21**

LET MY LOVE TAKE HOLD

HIS WORD: "I no longer call you servants, because a servant does not know his master's business. Instead, I have called you friends, for everything that I learned from my Father I have made known to you."
John 15;15

MY CHALLENGE: *To let His love take control of my life, as I serve Him as a Friend. I am to listen, learn and love, just as He did with His Father. I am to follow His example.*

My beloved child:

My little ones, I plead with you:
Let not your fears take hold.
Just lean on Me and trust My way,
That you will be consoled.

You are my love; I come to you,
For your companionship,
That you and I together, we
Will both enjoy this trip.

For that's what life is all about:
A trip to honor Me;
For I created you and all,
Everything you see.

Whenever you scurry around,
You find no place to land,
You'll probably end up empty.
You haven't heard My command.

Now stop and get your bearings, child,
And make the proper choice,
To quiet yourself before Me.
Be still and hear My voice.

My precious ones, I ask you now:
Do you want to be consoled?
Just lean on Me and trust My way.
Now let My love take hold.

Your Loving LORD

CM

PRAYER AND PRAISE: *Thank You, my LORD, and my God, that I have the honor and privilege of serving You as Your friend. Just to think that my God and I are friends! I give myself to You now and let Your love take hold of me. Praise the LORD!*

Week 38 ❖ Day 7   Theme: In His Love   Sep 22

39

SALVATION

It is by grace you have been saved,

Nothing you could afford.

Has nothing to do with yourself.

Only by grace of our L ORD.

I FOLLOW ONLY YOU

HIS WORD: "The man who loves his life will lose it, while the man who hates his life in this world will keep it for eternal life. Whoever serves me must follow me; and where I am, my servant also will be. My Father will honor the one who serves me."
John 12:25-26

MY CHALLENGE: *To follow the Lord in my service to Him, because of the salvation He has wrought for me.*

To My Saving Jesus:

I turn to You for my greatest need,
This empty heart to fill.
My Lord, I'm sorry for my sins.
Forgiveness is Your will.

I thank You for Your forgiveness.
You've cleansed my heart and soul.
You've set my feet upon Your rock,
Saved me and made me whole.

Today, again, I give my all,
My life and all I own,
To walk the road You'd have me go.
Praise God, I'm not alone.

Holy Spirit, come and fill me,
To live Your life and way.
It's my desire to faithful be,
To follow every day.

You have saved me and You've filled me,
To be Your servant true,
That I'd reach out to other souls,
To bring them Your Good News!

I thank You, Lord, for open doors,
That You would lead me through;
For now I have Your salvation.
I follow only You.

Your Grateful Child

CM

PRAYER AND PRAISE: *My Lord, in gratitude for my salvation and in response to it, I follow Your leading for whatever You'd have me do and wherever You'd have me go. I am Yours because of Your great salvation.*

Week 39 ❖ Day 1   Theme: Salvation   Sep 23

THANKS FOR MY SALVATION

HIS WORD: "Come, let us sing for joy to the LORD;
let us shout aloud to the Rock of our salvation.
Let us come before him with thanksgiving and extol him with music and song.
For the LORD is the great God, the great King above all gods."
Psalm 95:1-3

MY CHALLENGE: *To continually thank Him for my salvation.*

Open your heart and ask Him in.
Open it up today.
Welcome the gracious King of kings
And ask Him in to stay.

LORD Jesus, You are Savior mine.
You now reside in me,
To guide and direct along the path
To final victory.

I have repented of my sin;
I have confessed to Thee.
They are gone because of Your gift,
For You have set me free.

I rejoice in my salvation.
My life is turned around.
No longer do I seek the world.
No longer by it bound.

I know salvation isn't free.
It cost You everything.
You paid the price on Calvary,
For You are LORD and King.

There are not words I can express
My new-found relation.
I simply put it my own way:
"Thanks for my salvation!"

CM

PRAYER AND PRAISE: *My LORD, I confess that simply thanking You
for my salvation seems so little.
I thank You with my tongue. I thank You with my spirit.
I thank You with my whole being. Praise Your Name on high!*

Week 39 ❖ Day 2   Theme: Salvation   **Sep 24**

HIS UNFAILING LOVE

HIS WORD: "But I trust in you, O LORD; I say, 'You are my God.'
My times are in your hands; deliver me from my enemies and from
those who pursue me. Let your face shine on your servant;
save me in your unfailing love.
Praise be to the LORD, for he showed his wonderful love to me
when I was in a besieged city."
Psalm 31:14-16,21 (see verses 14-21)

MY CHALLENGE: Once He has given me His salvation, I am to give Him my trust. He gave me His unfailing love, therefore, I am to give Him my love.

I put my trust in You, my LORD.
I say, "You are my God."
My times I place into Your hands,
While on this earth I trod.

Deliver me from my enemies,
With power from above.
May Your face shine on your servant,
With Your unfailing love.

Let me not be ashamed, O LORD,
As I cry out to You.
Let wicked men be put to shame.
You only I pursue.

How great is Your goodness stored up,
For those who come in fear.
You give to them who trust in You
Your whole salvation here.

In the shelter of Your Presence,
You hide us from men's pride.
You keep us safe in Your Domain,
Put all their guile aside.

All praise and thanks to You, my LORD,
For You have magnified
The greatness of Your gift to me,
Your wondrous love inside.

CM

PRAYER AND PRAISE: *My LORD, I pray to have the necessary boldness to pursue You with all my strength, that I may demonstrate my love for You. Yes, as I put my complete trust in You, I want to shout from the housetops, "You are my God!"*

Week 39 ❖ Day 3   Theme: Salvation   **Sep 25**

SAVED BY GRACE

HIS WORD: "For it is by grace you have been saved, through faith—and this not from yourselves, it is the gift of God—not by works, so that no one can boast. For we are God's workmanship, created in Christ Jesus to do good works, which God prepared in advance for us to do."
Ephesians 2:8-10

MY CHALLENGE: *To keep in mind that His salvation for me is a gift and not because of any works I have ever done or ever will do.*

Because of His great love for us,
He paid the sacrifice.
God, who is so rich in mercy,
Made us alive with Christ.

Even in our transgressions dead,
He saved us by His grace.
He raised us up and seated us
In His most Holy Place.

Through faith it is a gift of God.
Salvation is by grace.
It is not by the works we do,
But simply is by faith.

We believe He is our Savior.
He's LORD o'er all the earth.
This Jesus comes to give to us
His Spirit and new birth.

There is no other Name we take
To be our very own;
For it's that Name of Christ we raise,
As Christians to make known.

We take His Name to all the world,
For we're His workmanship,
Created in Him to do good work,
As one in fellowship.

CM

PRAYER AND PRAISE: *Please forgive me, my LORD, for all too often I have done good works with the wrong attitude. I can't earn Your favor, for You've already given it. I can't earn Your love, for You've already shared it. I can't earn Your forgiveness, for You've already forgiven from the cross. Therefore, I simply bow down and praise You, my LORD!*

SOJOURNERS IN THE FAITH

HIS WORD: "He said to them, 'Go into all the world and preach the good news to all creation. Whoever believes and is baptized will be saved, but whoever does not believe will be condemned.'"
Mark 16:15-16

MY CHALLENGE: *To go into the world to share my faith with others, proclaiming His great salvation.*

My brothers and my sisters all,
Sojourners in the faith,
We work together hand in hand,
To share with all His grace.

Let's have a thankful attitude,
As we make Him be known.
Giving praise to Him for everything,
We bow before His Throne.

Together we'll be pliable,
As putty in His hands,
To go and do as He directs,
Wherever in the land.

We will act out our love for Him.
He blesses mightily,
As we share the Good News of God,
Raising Him for all to see.

We hear the words He gave to us,
"Go into all the world,"
"Making disciples of all men,"
Creating mighty pearls.

We'll fulfill the Great Commission.
As one, we'll keep the pace.
Together we will follow Him,
Sojourners in the faith.

CM

PRAYER AND PRAISE: *I ask You, L*ORD*, to fill me again today with the power of Your Holy Spirit, that I may be a witness to Your great salvation. I know it's only by Your power and through Your love I can do it. Thank You, Jesus!*

Week 39 ❖ Day 5　　　Theme: Salvation　　　**Sep 27**

FOUR "C's" TO CHRIST

HIS WORD: "As God's fellow workers we urge you not to receive
God's grace in vain. For he says,
'In the time of my favor I heard you, and in the day of salvation I helped you.'
I tell you, now is the time of God's favor, now is the day of salvation."
2 Corinthians 6:1-2

MY CHALLENGE: *To do as the rhyme below says.*

I Call on Your most Holy Name,
For You are God over the earth.
Our Creator and Master of life,
I come to You now for new birth.

I Confess my sins unto You,
All that I have ever done wrong.
I empty myself of all self,
To be filled with Your Spirit's song.

I Connect as I ask You in,
Into my heart to rule and reign.
I give my all to You right now,
My Jesus to obtain.

I Commit to You my praise, dear Lord.
Thanksgiving to You I employ.
Lord, take my life and make it be
A life filled with Your love and joy!

LM

PRAYER AND PRAISE: *My prayer, my Lord, is simply to follow this:
To call on You, to confess to You, to have connection with You,
by committing my life to You. Thank You, my Lord Jesus!*

Week 39 ❖ Day 6   Theme: Salvation   Sep 28

SALVATION TO MY CHILD

HIS WORD: "Surely God is my salvation; I will trust and not be afraid. The Lord, the Lord himself, is my strength and my song; he has become my salvation. With joy you will draw water from the wells of salvation."
Isaiah 12:2-3

"Salvation is found in no one else, for there is no other name under heaven given to men by which we must be saved."
Acts 4:12

MY CHALLENGE: *To joy in my salvation! For His Name is the only Name by which I am saved, therefore I rejoice and am glad in it.*

To My Beloved Child:

Oh how I yearn to hold you, child,
To feel your love embrace;
For I will grant to you the same,
When we meet face to face.

You have given your life to Me,
To walk in all My ways,
To listen to My guiding voice,
In all your waking days.

There will come a time at the end,
When I will call you home.
You'll be changed in the wink of an eye,
Never again alone.

That day is coming soon enough,
In just My perfect time,
To welcome you to heaven's home.
It will be suppertime.

Rejoice in My deliverance, child,
From bondage of the earth,
As I bring you unto Myself,
To show you what you're worth.

I've saved you from your sins of past
And set you wholly free.
When comes the time to leave the earth,
It's eternal life with Me.

Your Loving Lord
CM

PRAYER AND PRAISE: *My soul takes great comfort in knowing You and Your salvation, my Lord. It gives me peace of heart and assurance of eternity. My praise to You forevermore!*

Week 39 ❖ Day 7   Theme: Salvation   Sep 29

40

HEAVEN AHEAD

A glory and joy await us

In heaven's glory land,

As we look forward to the time

He takes us by the hand.

OUR BLESSED CORNERSTONE

HIS WORD: "Consequently, you are no longer foreigners and aliens, but fellow citizens with God's people and members of God's household, built on the foundation of the apostles and prophets, with Christ Jesus himself as the chief cornerstone. In him the whole building is joined together and rises to become a holy temple in the Lord. And in him you too are being built together to become a dwelling in which God lives by his Spirit."
Ephesians 2:19-22

MY CHALLENGE: *As a part of God's Temple, I am to look to Jesus as my chief, blessed Cornerstone. With all other believers, we are being built together to become a dwelling in which God lives by His Spirit.*

My Blessed Lord:

You've made the most majestic trip,
From heaven to earth and back,
To lower Yourself as one of us,
Knowing We had a lack.

We needed a Savior to come here,
Defeat the devil's plan,
And bring to us the victory:
A promise of Your land.

A place that is called Glory Land,
Awaiting for us there,
When we complete our life on earth,
Our final sail in air.

For there we will abide with You,
Forever and a day,
On golden streets of purity.
For You have made the way.

That will be a joy to behold.
We can't imagine how;
For it is far beyond the realm
Of thinking in the now.

We have the promise You have made,
When we became your own:
That we'd forever live with You,
Our blessed Cornerstone.

Your Loving Child
CM

PRAYER AND PRAISE: *Thank You, Lord, as I look forward to our life eternal with You. You have a work for us to do throughout eternity. Glory Land awaits! Thank You, Jesus, our Chief Cornerstone!*

Week 40 ❖ Day 1   Theme: Heaven Ahead   **Sep 30**

HOPE OF HEAVEN

HIS WORD: "I saw heaven standing open and there before me was a white horse, whose rider is called Faithful and True. With justice he judges and makes war. His eyes are like blazing fire, and on his head are many crowns. He has a name written on him that no one knows but he himself. He is dressed in a robe dipped in blood, and his name is the Word of God."
Revelation 19:11-13

MY CHALLENGE: *To know this beautiful Lord Jesus is my hope of heaven, my coming King, my Savior, who is also Faithful and True. He is my All in All.*

Lord Jesus is our love and joy.
He is our promised One.
We're looking to that final day,
When work on earth is done.

We'll continue to carry on
Our service to Him here,
While living on this earth below,
His Presence always near.

When that time comes to soar away
And feet have left the ground,
With earth behind and glory ahead,
To heaven's gates were bound.

Our trip from earth to Glory Land,
In the twinkling of an eye.
Our Lord is waiting for us there,
To welcome us on high.

We'll know Him in ecstatic joy,
When meeting face to face.
Our earthly words cannot describe
Our meeting in that place.

We'll always be refreshed while here,
In acting out His will.
The Hope of heaven is our Lord.
We wait for Him until.

CM

PRAYER AND PRAISE: *My Lord, as I look forward to being with You in Your perfect timing, I glory in the assurance that I will see You, and it will be perfect joy. Thank You for living in me and giving me this assurance, pure joy and Your love.*
Amen!

Week 40 ❖ Day 2 Theme: Heaven Ahead Oct 1

HALLELUJAH! I'M ALIVE!

HIS WORD: "After this I heard what sounded like the roar of
a great multitude in heaven shouting:
'Hallelujah! Salvation and glory and power belong to our God.'"
Revelation 19:1

"Then I heard what sounded like a great multitude, like the roar of
rushing waters and like loud peals of thunder, shouting:
'Hallelujah! For our Lord God Almighty reigns.'"
Revelation 19:6

MY CHALLENGE: *To look to my future time in heaven when I'll be
shouting "Hallelujah!" with great joy!*

I wonder what I'll say to Him,
When we meet face to face.
Will I express pure words of joy,
Or will we just embrace?

I will have left old earth behind.
New life in Him I gain.
Will receive my heavenly abode
With joy I can't explain?

There are not words in my own tongue,
To let my heart reveal,
And thank Him for the price He paid,
Expressing how I feel.

On that great day in Glory Land,
My having just arrived,
I'll shout it with new strength of voice:
"Hallelujah! I'm Alive!"

CM

PRAYER AND PRAISE: *My Lord, in thinking on this future time,
I can do nothing but give You all the praise!
To catch a glimpse of this glory is so gratifying as to cause me
to shout it once again:
"Hallelujah!"*

Week 40 ❖ Day 3   Theme: Heaven Ahead   Oct 2

THE LADDER OF THE LORD

HIS WORD: "Then he added, 'I tell you the truth, you shall see heaven open, and the angels of God ascending and descending on the Son of Man.'"
John 1:51 (Also see Genesis 28:10-22)

MY CHALLENGE: To look upward toward that Day. For that Day will come when each believer will ascend into heaven, to live with Him for eternity. Our lives will be better used here if we keep our eyes toward that Day.

When Jacob saw that Ladder of God,
With the LORD standing above,
Instructions, blessings and promises
Poured out with Almighty Love.

"I AM the LORD God of Abraham.
I now give you all this land.
The people on earth will be blessed
And o'er the whole earth expand."

"Surely the LORD God is in this place,"
Jacob cried out from his heart.
LORD Jesus spoke of this, Jacob's dream,
In His teaching at the start.

For truth you will see heaven open,
Angels of God ascending
And descending on the Son of Man.
You shall see these greater things.

Jesus is our Ladder to Heaven,
Angels treading up and down,
As we head to final upward climb,
To receive our golden crown.

We look forward to that final Day.
As on that Ladder we board,
We will ascend, with angels to guide,
Up the Ladder of the LORD.

97.97

PRAYER AND PRAISE: LORD, we know not when that day will be that You guide us up the Ladder of the LORD to Glory Land and eternity. I pray that until that day comes I will continue to keep my eyes on it, while, at the same time, being an effective follower of Yours.
Thank You, Jesus!

Week 40 ❖ Day 4   Theme: Heaven Ahead   Oct 3

GRADUATION INTO GLORY

HIS WORD: "All these people were still living by faith when they died. They did not receive the things promised; they only saw them and welcomed them from a distance. And they admitted that they were aliens and strangers on earth. People who say such things show that they are looking for a country of their own. If they had been thinking of the country they had left, they would have had opportunity to return. Instead, they were longing for a better country—a heavenly one. Therefore God is not ashamed to be called their God, for he has prepared a city for them."
Hebrews 11:13-16

MY CHALLENGE: *To be waiting in anticipation of my graduation into glory: that is, the day the LORD calls me home to Glory Land, a place He has prepared.*

When your graduation to Glory
Is coming 'round the bend,
You know not when the moment be.
You know earth's time will end.

You sense the quickening of your heart.
You're waiting for His voice
That says it's time to come on home:
"My child, you've made the choice."

It's okay, friends and family
To say goodbye and know
To release me from this body
And let my spirit go.

It's homeward bound to heaven land,
To see Him face to face,
To rest my head upon His breast
And thank Him for His grace.

'Twill be a mighty moment then,
To feel His fond embrace,
To know that I will ever be
A child in heaven's place.

That day will be a blessed time.
His love has covered all.
I'm looking up and watching, LORD.
I'm waiting for Your call.

CM

PRAYER AND PRAISE: *I know, my LORD, even now, You are preparing my heart and mind for that special day ahead, when I graduate to a new home, a new land and a new life. How blessed I'll be! Thank You, LORD!*

Week 40 ❖ Day 5   Theme: Heaven Ahead   Oct 4

A DANCE OF VICTORY

HIS WORD: "Then I saw a new heaven and a new earth, for the first heaven and the first earth had passed away, and there was no longer any sea. I saw the Holy City, the New Jerusalem, coming down out of heaven from God, prepared as a bride beautifully dressed for her husband. And I heard a loud voice from the throne saying, 'Now the dwelling of God is with men, and he will live with them. They will be his people, and God himself will be with them and be their God. He will wipe every tear from their eyes. There will be no more death or mourning or crying or pain, for the old order of things has passed away.'"
Revelation 21:1-4

MY CHALLENGE: *To look forward with great anticipation to that great Day, knowing the Day will surely come, and I will see it!*

There is a dance to dance today,
A dance of victory,
A time to sing and shout for joy,
To dance eternally.

The time to mourn has come and gone;
The time to dance has come;
For Jesus has returned to earth,
His rule on earth begun.

All His believers have been changed,
In twinkling of an eye.
New glorious bodies are received.
No more shall ever die.

His promise of old has been fulfilled,
The devil put in chains.
The wicked and unrighteous folk
Have gone where Satan reigns.

No more sorrow and no more tears.
All of it passed away.
We glory in this newfound life
Forever and a day.

Raise the banners; shout out with joy.
He's the One we adore.
Let's celebrate the world's sole King
And dance like ne'er before.

CM

PRAYER AND PRAISE: *Glory be! What a day that will be to behold! Thank You, LORD, that we have the promise and assurance that we see that day in our future. I ask, my LORD, that You help me keep this in my sights.*

Week 40 ❖ Day 6   Theme: Heaven Ahead   Oct 5

I'LL CALL YOU HOME

HIS WORD: "Now we know that if the earthly tent we live in is destroyed, we have a building from God, an eternal house in heaven, not built by human hands. Meanwhile we groan, longing to be clothed with our heavenly dwelling, because when we are clothed, we will not be found naked. For while we are in this tent, we groan and are burdened, because we do not wish to be unclothed but to be clothed with our heavenly dwelling, so that what is mortal may be swallowed up by life. Now it is God who has made us for this very purpose and has given us the Spirit as a deposit, guaranteeing what is to come."
2 Corinthians 5:1-5

MY CHALLENGE: To always know—blessed assurance—that when the time comes, I'll discard this old body and be clothed with my heavenly dwelling.

To My Beloved One:

I want to see your face light up,
In heaven your first day.
I want to hear your joy pour out,
Hear what you have to say.

You'll cast your eyes upon the home
Designed by your Divine;
For I have made it just for you.
It's all by My guideline.

The beauty I designed on earth
Is but a small foretaste
Of Glory in My heavenly realm,
You'll forever embrace.

To you, My child, I wait for you.
Your time is in My hands.
Please joy in your journey on earth,
And follow My commands.

For there is much I have for you,
As you reach out for Me,
To take My love and bring them in,
Into our family.

When work I've planned for you is done,
There's no place else to roam,
Look forward to your rest in peace,
For then I'll call you home.

Your Loving Jesus
CM

PRAYER AND PRAISE: My LORD, I want to serve in Your work as long as I live, and I desire to live as long as I can be fruitful for You.

Week 40 ❖ Day 7   Theme: Heaven Ahead   Oct 6

41

RENEWAL

His Word says we will be transformed

By renewing of our mind.

For this we are ever grateful.

That is what God designed.

I HUMBLE MYSELF

HIS WORD: "Humble yourselves, therefore, under God's mighty hand,
That he may lift you up in due time.
Cast all your anxiety on him because He cares for you."
1 Peter 5:6-7

"For whoever exalts himself will be humbled,
and whoever humbles himself will be exalted."
Matthew 23:12

MY CHALLENGE: *To remain humble, dispensing all pride.
In my humanity, this is difficult because pride raises itself above all else.
It takes a conscious effort on my part to be humble at all times.*

My Precious Lord:
I humble myself under Your mighty hand,
   That You may lift me up in time due.
I give myself to You, a living sacrifice,
   Holy and acceptable to You.

The lower I get in submitting myself
   The more I give to trusting in Thee.
Therefore I give my all to Your loving care,
   All that I have and ever will be.

If ever I exalt self, I'll be humbled,
   Because our pride goes before a fall;
But whoever humbles himself will be exalted.
   Therefore I submit to You my all.

I humble myself in my worship of You,
   As I rise to You on bended knee;
For You are the great Lord of lords over all.
   Therefore I humble myself to Thee.

Your Loving Child
11 9.11 9

PRAYER AND PRAISE: *My Lord, I submit to Your Lordship, as I humble myself before You.
Thank You for doing whatever is necessary in me to remain humble before
You in all I say and do. Amen!*

Week 41 ❖ Day 1   Theme: Renewal   Oct 7

THE TIME TO RECONNECT

HIS WORD: "Very early in the morning, while it was still dark, Jesus got up, left the house and went off to a solitary place, where he prayed."
Mark 1:35

MY CHALLENGE: To get up early, go into a solitary place and spend time alone with Him in prayer and praise.

Every morning is a reconnect.
After your hours of sleep,
Look to your Shepherd and His way,
To follow as His sheep.

For He was with you during the night;
He ne'er leaves you alone.
You left to visit your dreamland,
Where time is not your own.

It all belongs to our Father.
With Him we must stay close,
By going to Him first thing in morn
And getting Spirit's dose.

We must connect with Him, our LORD,
To hear His gentle voice.
We give our lives for Him to lead,
To always make right choice.

Don't start in with your daily work
'Til after you have prayed,
In order you connect with Him,
With plans that He has made.

We go to Him with prayer and praise.
We pay Him our respect.
Every morning's a new beginning,
The time to reconnect.

CM

PRAYER AND PRAISE: My Jesus, my LORD, You have said in Your Word that we will do what You have been doing. Okay, that means I need to get up early, go into a special private place and spend time with You.
Hear me now, Jesus: tomorrow morning, I'll be there calling on You.
In the meantime, LORD, help me to get out of that bed in the morn.
Amen!

Week 41 ❖ Day 2   Theme: Renewal   Oct 8

OUR DRIVING FORCE

HIS WORD: "When the day of Pentecost came, they were all together in one place. Suddenly a sound like the blowing of a violent wind came from heaven and filled the whole house where they were sitting. They saw what seemed to be tongues of fire that separated and came to rest on each of them. All of them were filled with the Holy Spirit and began to speak in other tongues as the Spirit enabled them."

Acts 2:1-4

MY CHALLENGE: *To be filled with the Holy Spirit, and allow Him to be the driving force in my life.*

Don't lean on promises of the world.
They're based on wrong resource.
But look to God for everything.
He is the driving force!

To take a step, an act of faith,
Into the wild unknown
Demands our trust completely in
Our LORD and God alone.

For if we could see far ahead,
Know what the future brings,
We'd no longer trust in our God.
All would be our own doings.

It is so difficult in life
To let go of the reins
And give our all to Him alone,
To His power that sustains.

As we trust in Him for everything
And worry not our care,
It's then His blessings will pour out.
Our load then He will bear.

Therefore we give it all to Him,
To follow in His course,
Be filled with the Holy Spirit.
He is our Driving Force.

CM

PRAYER AND PRAISE: LORD, as I give all to You, please hold nothing back. I want everything You have for me, so that I may be effective in Your service. I ask You now to fill me with the power of Your Holy Spirit. I thank You, my Jesus, for filling me with Your Holy Spirit, giving me Your gifts and setting me on fire for You and the Gospel. Amen!

Week 41 ❖ Day 3   Theme: Renewal   Oct 9

IN MY CLOSET OF PRAYER

HIS WORD: "And when you pray, do not be like the hypocrites, for they love to pray standing in the synagogues and on the street corners to be seen by men. I tell you the truth, they have received their reward in full. But when you pray, go into your room, close the door and pray to your Father, who is unseen. Then your Father, who sees what is done in secret, will reward you."
Matthew 6:5-6

MY CHALLENGE: To get before You, my LORD, in prayer and to humbly bow before You privately every day, for time alone with You. Jesus, You set the example for prayer, as You got off by yourself and spent time with Your Father. You call us to do the same. We know we must. I know Satan will do anything to keep me from my time with You. Therefore, Satan, I rebuke you now and command you to get behind me, as I go before my LORD Jesus in prayer.

Before rise of sun,
My day has begun,
Time spent in my closet of prayer.
To this I admit.
To Him I submit.
Everything with You I will share.

It's still dark of night.
By dim candlelight
I hear Your voice come breaking through.
Quietly and soft
I hear it so oft,
Each time as though it were anew.

When quiet prevails,
To You my heart sails.
I'm so glad as my spirit sings.
Your heavenly Dove
Pours out Your pure love.
I rejoice the pleasure it brings.

I can take my stand.
With my list in hand,
I submit all my needs to Your care.
As I bend my knee,
Make my needed plea,
With time in my closet of prayer.

5 5 8.5 5 8

PRAYER AND PRAISE: I thank You, my LORD, for the joy I sense, as I spend time with You in my closet of prayer. For it is there You speak to me with words of assurance, encouragement and instruction.

Week 41 ❖ Day 4   Theme: Renewal   Oct 10

KEEP JESUS ON YOUR THRONE

HIS WORD: "If you do what is right, will you not be accepted? But if you do not do what is right, sin is crouching at your door; it desires to have you, but you must master it."
Genesis 4:7

"My dear children, I write this to you so that you will not sin. But if anybody does sin, we have one who speaks to the Father in our defense—Jesus Christ, the Righteous One. He is the atoning sacrifice for our sins, and not only for ours but also for the sins of the whole world."
1 John 2:1-2

MY CHALLENGE: To accept and live the responsibility to do that which is right and not sin. But I know if I do sin, I can go to Jesus Who forgave me on the cross.

*There is a power in our lives
That wants to rule and win.
It tries to overtake our will,
That power o'er us is sin.*

*We know it's crouching at the door.
It wants to enter in,
That it may gain a full access,
To every part within.*

*There is a battle to be fought,
A price that must be paid.
If we are to win the victory,
Decisions must be made.*

*We cannot use the law to win.
That would be absurd.
It's by the Holy Spirit's power
And God's own Holy Word.*

*When sin is knocking at your door,
Then exercise your right.
Rebuke it with His powerful Name.
Then you will win the fight.*

*We're aliens living in this world,
For heaven is our home.
So keep your life free of all sin.
Keep Jesus on your throne.*

CM

PRAYER AND PRAISE: LORD, I stop now and confess the following sins in my life _____.
I deeply regret them, therefore I confess and repent of them.
I now accept and receive Your forgiveness provided on the cross of Calvary.

Week 41 ❖ Day 5   Theme: Renewal   Oct 11

PRIVATE DEVOTIONAL TIME

HIS WORD: "Humble yourselves, therefore, under God's mighty hand, that he may lift you up in due time."
1 Peter 5:6

MY CHALLENGE: *To humble myself before my God in private devotional time each and every day.*

Humble yourself under the mighty Hand of God.
Submit to His Lordship anew,
Giving to Him every aspect of your life,
Holding on to that which is true.

Speak out your praises to the LORD with great joy.
Sing out your thanksgiving with cheer.
Shout aloud the praises that are due His Name.
Then sense His Holy Presence near.

In your private devotion time with the LORD,
Cast aside all thoughts of the world,
To focus on His Presence and give Him ear.
Let your praise to Him be unfurled.

As you pray out to Him, "I surrender all,"
And ask His Presence to invade,
Then open your life to receive His glory
And relish the joy He has made.

The daily time you spend worshiping the LORD
Will make your spirit rise and shine.
So humble yourself under God's mighty hand
In private devotional time.

11 8.11 8

PRAYER AND PRAISE: *As I humbly bow before You, my LORD. I thank You for this time alone, just You and me. Thank You, Jesus!*

Week 41 ❖ Day 6   Theme: Renewal   Oct 12

REFILL YOUR TANK

HIS WORD: "Therefore do not be foolish, but understand what the Lord's will is. Do not get drunk on wine, which leads to debauchery. Instead, be filled with the Spirit."
Ephesians 5:17-18

MY CHALLENGE: To be filled with the Holy Spirit, to help me understand the Lord's will and to follow His leading.

To My Beloved Child:

"You need to have your tank refilled.
You feel it running low?
It keeps you from your very best.
You feel you've lost control?"

"The world is rushing past you now.
Your wheels stuck in the mud.
The energy you're expending,
You feel like you're a dud?"

"Cheer up, dear one, for there is hope,
In which you will be thrilled:
There is a way that upward leads
To get your tank refilled."

"For I desire to cuddle you
And hug you in My arms,
To have you feel My Presence now,
To be above all harms."

"I give to you My precious kiss,
The kiss of My pure love.
When you receive this love, My child,
You'll know it's from above."

"When you receive this refill mode,
It's Me you have to thank.
My peace I give to you with joy,
As I have filled your tank."

Your Loving Dad

CM

PRAYER AND PRAISE: Thank You, Lord, for filling my tank and then refilling it many times. Because of the filling of Your Holy Spirit, I'm able to follow Your leading and listen to and learn from the Word You give me. To that, I give a great AMEN!

Week 41 ❖ Day 7   Theme: Renewal   Oct 13

HIS WORD

In the beginning was the Word,

And the Word was with God.

His Word is our very life itself.

His Word, our Lord, our God.

YOUR WORD TO ME

HIS WORD: "Let the peace of Christ rule in your hearts, since as members of one body you were called to peace. And be thankful. Let the word of Christ dwell in you richly as you teach and admonish one another with all wisdom, and as you sing psalms, hymns and spiritual songs with gratitude in your hearts to God. And whatever you do, whether in word or deed, do it all in the name of the Lord Jesus, giving thanks to God the Father through him."
Colossians 3:15-17

MY CHALLENGE: *To let His words so richly dwell in me that I would do everything in the Name of my Lord Jesus, and that it would all be done in accordance with His written Word.*

To My Lord:

My mind is open to receive.
My heart is ready too,
That I would hear Your Word to me,
A Word that's fresh and new.

For as I read Your printed Word,
Words that have no sin,
To know I can rely on it,
Gives me true joy within.

It's on Your Word I can depend,
As nothing else on earth;
For I have learned to walk with You,
Since You gave me new birth.

Then as I am in pray'r with You,
I sense Your victory.
I know that all aligns today,
With words You give to me.

Your Waiting Child

CM

PRAYER AND PRAISE: *Thank You, my Lord, for Your words to me, words on which I can depend and words in which I can put my trust. It is Your Word that creates and sustains life. Help me, Lord, to remember that, as I live my life each day. Because of Your Word, I have victory. And now, my Lord, I am still and listening—waiting for more word from You. Speak to me now. Your child is waiting and listening. Amen!*

Week 42 ❖ Day 1 — Theme: His Word — Oct 14

PSALM 119:33-40

HIS WORD: *Psalm 119:33-40 as given below in poetic form*

MY CHALLENGE: *To follow His Word and walk His way, filled with His goodness.*

33 My Lord, **teach me to follow Your Word,**
  And to Your Spirit divine,
 That I'd obey to the very end,
  To stay on Your Holy line.

34 Give Your understanding unto me,
  That I would fully comply
 With all the words You've given to me,
  In my heart, to keep them nigh.

35 Make me to walk the path of Your Word,
  The path You've outlined for me;
 For there I would find a great delight,
  As I follow after Thee.

36 Please turn my heart to Your Presence, Lord.
  In my life, Your Word shall reign,
 As You turn my heart to Your Spirit,
  And not toward my selfish gain.

37 Turn my eyes away from worthless things,
  In Your good and precious way,
 In accordance with Your Holy Word,
  To preserve my life this day.

38 Fulfill to me Your promise, O Lord,
  So that You may be revered.
 Establish Your Word to Your servant,
  In order You may be feared.

39 Help me abandon my shameful ways.
 Your judgements are always good;

40 I long to follow Your Spirit, Lord,
  Your goodness in me renewed.

97.97

PRAYER AND PRAISE: *Yes, my Lord, I ask for Your help and power in each one of these verses above. Each verse is a prayer I need to pray to You. Collectively they are my prayerful desire for today. And so, my Lord, I read them again as my prayer to You. Thank You for Your mercy!*

Week 42 ❖ Day 2   Theme: His Word   Oct 15

DON'T BELIEVE THE DEVIL

HIS WORD: "Submit yourselves, then, to God. Resist the devil, and he will flee from you."
James 4:7

"And I saw an angel coming down out of heaven, having the key to the abyss and holding in his hand a great chain. He seized the dragon, that ancient serpent, who is the devil, or Satan, and bound him for a thousand years. He threw him into the Abyss, and locked and sealed it over him, to keep him from deceiving the nations anymore until the thousand years were ended. After that, he must be set free for a short time."
Revelation 20:1-3

MY CHALLENGE: *To resist the devil, knowing that Christ is in control.*

Don't ever believe the Devil,
Nor any of his schemes.
He will try to throw you off-track
And make some ugly scenes.

He knows his time is limited,
Until Christ comes again.
So he will do all he can do
To destroy the Great Amen.

We know the answer to his plight.
God has it in His Word:
Christ will come and rule over all
And make him look absurd.

He will be a defeated foe,
Bound for a thousand years.
Jesus will be our King of kings,
With nothing left to fear.

Therefore we celebrate today,
With Christ, God's only Son.
As we rejoice in victory,
The battles have been won.

Reject the Devil and his work.
Let not him rule your way;
For on the cross Christ won the fight,
Gained victory for today.

CM

PRAYER AND PRAISE: *Thanks be to You, LORD, I have the victory over sin and Satan, because of Your sacrifice and resurrection. And what a joy it is to know that this will ever be so. You are the Victor, we the benefactors.*

Week 42 ❖ Day 3   Theme: His Word   **Oct 16**

WHEN GOD IS SILENT

HIS WORD: "I waited patiently for the LORD;
he turned to me and heard my cry. He lifted me out of the slimy pit,
out of the mud and mire;
he set my feet on a rock and gave me a firm place to stand.
He put a new song in my mouth, a hymn of praise to our God.
Many will see and fear and put their trust in the LORD.
Blessed is the man who makes the LORD his trust."
Psalm 40:1-4a

MY CHALLENGE: *To wait patiently for the LORD, knowing His timing is perfect. My timing is extremely imperfect. That's why the call to trust in Him.*

When God is silent and there's no word,
You wonder why this is so.
Just keep on praying and praising Him,
Regardless of how it goes.

It's never because of displeasure,
But rather of discipline,
To bring teaching and maturity,
A time of growing in Him.

Wait for God's timing in all of this.
Don't rush ahead on your own.
Relax and be more focused on Him.
Allow self to be dethroned.

During a time of waiting on Him,
Don't let confidence be lost;
But make it a time to build it up,
Determined no matter the cost.

When your faith is based on God alone,
Matters not the length of wait.
Matters not what others say and do,
Nor what they may contemplate.

For the LORD is the One you look to,
Having put all else aside,
Determined to trust, the silent time,
Only in Him to abide.

97.97

PRAYER AND PRAISE: *LORD, help me to learn to have more patience and to trust You much more than I do. I realize that's a dangerous thing to pray for because I know we develop patience through tribulation. But, so be it. I need more patience. Thank You, my LORD, as I trust You to take me through whatever is necessary to gain maturity in You.*

Week 42 ❖ Day 4   Theme: His Word   Oct 17

HAIL, YOUR MAJESTY!

HIS WORD: "In the beginning was the Word, and the Word was with God,
and the Word was God. He was with God in the beginning.
Through him all things were made;
without him nothing was made that has been made.
In him was life, and that life was the light of men.
The light shines in the darkness, but the darkness has not understood it."
John 1:1-5

MY CHALLENGE: *To know, honor and understand the Light, the Word,
our God, our Savior—the Light of men.*

Hail, Your Majesty, LORD Jesus,
Our eternal King!
Your Glory reigns far above all
And over everything.

There is none other can compare
To your glory supreme,
And to Your Glory here on earth.
You set the Holy Theme.

You are God, and You are the Word.
The Bible tells us so.
Therefore we pick up Your banner,
For the whole world to know.

In light of Your reign here on earth,
We will wait patiently,
Until that last day we can shout:
All hail, Your Majesty!

CM

PRAYER AND PRAISE: *Yes, my LORD! All hail, Your Majesty!
You are King of kings and LORD of lords!
We look forward to that Day, when the whole world will finally
see the truth—their Creator has returned!
You, the Word, will endure forever.
Amen!*

Week 42 ❖ Day 5   Theme: His Word   Oct 18

JESUS, THE WORD OF GOD

HIS WORD: "He is dressed in a robe dipped in blood, and his name is the Word of God. The armies of heaven were following him, riding on white horses and dressed in fine linen, white and clean. Out of his mouth comes a sharp sword with which to strike down the nations. 'He will rule them with an iron scepter.' He treads the winepress of the fury of the wrath of God Almighty. On his robe and on his thigh he has this name written: KING OF KINGS AND LORD OF LORDS."
Revelation 19:13-16

MY CHALLENGE: *To know the names, titles, identities and characteristics of Jesus, so that I may more fully know Him, understand Him and appreciate Him.*
I desire to grasp and appreciate all the great things He has done for me.

Jesus, You Are the:

Alpha and Omega,	Lord of Lords,
Author of Life,	Messiah,
Baptizer,	Mediator,
Bread of Life,	Mighty God,
Comforter,	Name Above All names,
Counselor,	Prince of Peace,
Creator of All,	Redeemer of Mankind,
Deliverer from Evil,	Great Provider,
Good Shepherd,	Savior of the World,
Healer of All,	Son of the Living God,
King of Kings,	Son of Man,
Lamb of God,	Victor,
Light of the World,	Word of God.

IRR.

PRAYER AND PRAISE: *I give You thanks, my Lord and God, for giving me a greater depth of knowledge and appreciation of all that You Are! It causes me to fall on my knees and worship You, and You alone!*

Week 42 ❖ Day 6   Theme: His Word   Oct 19

MY WORD FOR YOU

HIS WORD: "Then Peter, filled with the Holy Spirit, said to them: 'Rulers and elders of the people! If we are being called to account today for an act of kindness shown to a cripple and are asked how he was healed, then know this, you and all the people of Israel: It is by the name of Jesus Christ of Nazareth, whom you crucified but whom God raised from the dead, that this man stands before you healed.'"
Acts 4:8-10

MY CHALLENGE: *To <u>know</u> that it is by the Name of Christ Jesus that I am saved, healed and delivered! There is no other Name in heaven or on earth by which this can be said.*

To a Child of My Word:

I have a word for you today.
Please listen what I say.
Slow down your pace and look to me.
I AM your only Way.

You know not what's ahead of you,
Nor what the world may bring;
But as you trust My loving care,
My praises you will sing.

Child, let Me save you from yourself,
Your struggle to release;
But when you do, you'll always find,
There comes My inner peace!

I will deliver you, My child,
From pain and heartaches too.
If you'll release it all to Me,
It's then I can renew.

My healing is for you today.
Just look to Me, your Source,
That I may do a work in you,
To keep on healthy course.

Just trust in Me, I ask of you.
I know what's best for you.
My Word has promised you My love.
My Word is always true!

Your Tender Loving LORD
CM

PRAYER AND PRAISE: *My* LORD*, there are struggles and strife in life that I needlessly hang on to. I give up and release them all to You now. I trust You. I love You. I receive all You have for me. Thank You, my Jesus!*

Week 42 ❖ Day 7   Theme: His Word   Oct 20

43

CONTENTMENT

"But godliness with contentment

Is great gain," Paul has said.

Let's be content with what we have,

In all that is ahead.

RHYTHM OF LIFE

HIS WORD: "Come, let us bow down in worship,
let us kneel before the Lord our Maker;
for he is our God and we are the people of his pasture,
the flock under his care."
Psalm 95:6-7

MY CHALLENGE: *To know the contentment that is mine,
as part of the flock under His care.*

My Lord Jesus:

*I joy in my rhythm of life,
Living close to You each day,
Trusting You for Your Providence,
Knowing You will lead the way.*

*I thank You, Lord, for this lifestyle,
Far above all worldly ways.
Depending completely on You,
I can rest in You each day.*

*It matters not what comes my way,
For You have me in Your hands.
I merely need to trust in You,
Though I may not understand.*

*Oh, what a blessedness it is,
With You all trials to share,
And know beyond shadow of doubt,
I'll always be in Your care!*

*It's up to me to follow You
And let You have full control.
No matter what may come my way,
You're the Guardian of my soul.*

*I thank You, my Lord and my God,
For guiding me through the strife,
As I live close to You each day
And joy in rhythm of life.*

Your Humble Child

87.87

PRAYER AND PRAISE: *My Lord, You have given life to me, and how blessed I am! I pray to learn more of Your contentment in me and practice it in my everyday life. Thank You, my Lord!*

Week 43 ❖ Day 1   Theme: Contentment   Oct 21

REST CONTENT

HIS WORD: "The fear of the LORD leads to life:
Then one rests content, untouched by trouble."
Proverbs 19:23

*MY CHALLENGE: To rest content in Him.
It sounds so small and simple, however it is a big challenge.*

*The fear of the LORD leads to life.
Then one will rest content,
Untouched by the troubles one has,
Knowing they're heaven bent.*

*We cannot trust in our own way,
For we will go awry.
When left to our own life to live,
We trust in our supply.*

*Then, as we fear the LORD our God,
Abiding in His will,
He'll guide and lead as He knows best.
His work we will fulfill.*

*So through our LORD we learn this truth:
To fear Him is to live.
To trust in Him and rest content,
In this one life we give.*

CM

PRAYER AND PRAISE: *And now, my LORD, as I remember this, I commit my life again to You. I rest in You and am content. Thank You, Jesus!*

Week 43 ❖ Day 2   Theme: Contentment   Oct 22

HIS PEACE IS CONTENTMENT

HIS WORD: "I am not saying this because I am in need, for I have learned to be content whatever the circumstances. I know what it is to be in need, and I know what it is to have plenty. I have learned the secret of being content in any and every situation, whether well fed or hungry, whether living in plenty or in want."
Philippians 4:11-12

MY CHALLENGE: To be content, <u>no matter the circumstances.</u> This is not possible in the flesh, only through the power of the Holy Spirit.

Never be in such a hurry
You lose your inner peace;
For it is not God's will for you,
That all your calm should cease.

He wants to fill you, as He said,
"I give to you My Peace.
I do not give as the world gives.
My peace will never cease."

When His peace resides in your heart,
Which brings His best to you,
Then you can live without a fret
And have contentment too.

Contentment is a way of life
We all need to ensue.
Because we're in God's family,
He wants the best for you.

"But godliness with contentment
Is great gain," His Word states.
Our spoken words of peace to all
Contentment will create.

We must "seek peace and pursue it"
And make it our intent.
Following the path that He has made
We'll always be content.

CM

PRAYER AND PRAISE: I bow on bended knee, as I make my prayer request.
I pray for this kind of contentment,
the contentment that only You—my Jesus—can bring.
For I know that as I live my life in this kind of peace and contentment,
nothing can move me from the path You have made for me.
Thank You, my LORD!

Week 43 ❖ Day 3   Theme: Contentment   Oct 23

HAVING ALL THAT YOU NEED

HIS WORD: "And God is able to make all grace abound to you, so that in all things at all times, having all that you need, you will abound in every good work."
2 Corinthians 9:8

MY CHALLENGE: *To know that because of His grace I have all I need to abound in every good work He gives me.*

Our God will make all grace abound,
As He gives out His blessings.
You will have everything you need,
At all times and in all things.

You'll abound in every good work,
The promise He's made to you,
As you meet the call on your life
And all He'd have you pursue.

As you move ahead in His will,
Follow Him very closely.
Keep looking to His leading way,
To fulfill your destiny.

His reward is given to you,
That in Him you will succeed.
Recall His grace is abundant,
In having all that you need.

87.87

PRAYER AND PRAISE: *My God, it is my desire to follow Your leading so closely that there will be no doubt as to my fulfilling the destiny You have for me. I praise You now for giving me all I need to abound in every good work You give me.*
Amen!

Week 43 ❖ Day 4 Theme: Contentment **Oct 24**

GIFT OF CONTENTMENT

HIS WORD: "But godliness with contentment is great gain. For we brought nothing into the world, and we can take nothing out of it. But if we have food and clothing, we will be content with that. People who want to get rich fall into temptation and a trap and into many foolish and harmful desires that plunge men into ruin and destruction. For the love of money is a root of all kinds of evil. Some people, eager for money, have wandered from the faith and pierced themselves with many griefs."
1 Timothy 6:6-10

MY CHALLENGE: *To joy in His contentment, to hold on to and treasure it as a precious gift.*

Saints of God, forever forgiven,
Why carry a load of remorse,
When Jesus forgave you from the cross,
For you a life-changing course?

Why worry and fret and carry on
And anxious about your day,
When all you need do is to look to Him,
And let Jesus have His way?

He has given you a special gift,
To bring you joy and His peace,
The gift of His loving contentment,
To give your worries release.

Ask for His gift and receive it now.
It is free and limitless.
Take His contentment into your life,
For with this gift you are blessed.

97.97

PRAYER AND PRAISE: *I confess, my LORD, that I haven't taken advantage of Your contentment as I should have because I've been fretting about many things in my life. I know this need not be. Therefore, I give You all my troubles, pains and strife right now and bask in the delight of Your contentment. Thank You, my LORD!*

Week 43 ❖ Day 5   Theme: Contentment   **Oct 25**

BE CONTENT WITH WHAT YOU HAVE

HIS WORD: "Keep your lives free from the love of money and
be content with what you have, because God has said,
'Never will I leave you;
never will I forsake you.'"
Hebrews 13:5

MY CHALLENGE: *To take my eyes off the things of the world
and put them on the things of God's Kingdom.*

"Never will I leave you,
Nor will I forsake you"
Are words our LORD God has promised.
You're to accept as true.

Do not love your money.
You're to keep your lives free,
To be content with what you have,
Giving God the glory.

As we go on in life,
With all its roil and rife,
We're to lean on Him for all things,
Regardless of the strife.

Our LORD God has said it.
Let us not forget it,
"I'll never leave nor forsake you,"
To Him our lives commit.

SM

PRAYER AND PRAISE: *LORD, I would ask that You help me be content with
what I have and to know that I know You'll never leave me nor forsake me.
That is great assurance, comfort and, yes, even contentment.*

Week 43 ❖ Day 6   Theme: Contentment   Oct 26

BE CONTENT IN LIFE

HIS WORD: "Therefore, since we are surrounded by such a great cloud of witnesses, let us throw off everything that hinders and the sin that so easily entangles, and let us run with perseverance the race marked out for us.

Let us fix our eyes on Jesus, the author and perfecter of our faith, who for the joy set before him endured the cross, scorning its shame, and sat down at the right hand of the throne of God. Consider him who endured such opposition from sinful men, so that you will not grow weary and lose heart."
Hebrews 12:1-3

MY CHALLENGE: *To fix my eyes on Jesus and relish His great contentment, by drawing close to Him and living His words.*

To My Contented Child:

*Now be content in daily life
And joy in perfect peace.
Shut out the worldly sounds you hear
And fix your eyes on Me.*

*Throw off the things that hinder you,
With all the chains of sin,
To break the worldly bonds of greed.
And then My Peace you'll win.*

*I want the very best for you,
Which doesn't always mean
It's measured by the world's standard,
But trust in Me, not seen.*

*I AM the Author of your faith,
Protector of your soul.
So fix your eyes upon Me, child,
And let Me have control.*

*To keep your mind focused on Me,
Shut out the world you hear,
Then listen for My gentle voice.
You'll hear it soft and clear.*

*There you have it, My dear child.
To live above the strife,
Draw close to Me and live My words.
You'll be content in life.*

Your Comforting Jesus
CM

PRAYER AND PRAISE: *I pray to draw closer to You, my Jesus, to experience more of Your contentment in my life. I seek more of You. I seek more of Your will and way. Thank You, my precious LORD!*

Week 43 ❖ Day 7   Theme: Contentment   Oct 27

44

PRAISE

Praise His Holy and wonderful Name,

That Name above all Names.

No other name on earth saves us.

It's Jesus we proclaim.

PRAISE OF PSALM 150

HIS WORD: "Let everything that has breath praise the LORD.
Praise the LORD."
Psalm 150:6

MY CHALLENGE: *To praise Him. With my every breath to praise Him!*

To My Holy LORD:

I praise You in Your sanctuary.
I praise You in Your heavens.
I praise You for Your acts of power.
I praise because You've risen.

I praise You with the trumpet sound.
I praise You with the harp.
I praise You with the tambourines.
I praise You with my heart.

Let everything that has a breath
All praise in one accord
That Name that is above all names.
I praise my Holy LORD.

How good it is His praises sing,
Thanksgiving to my God!
How pleasant to give Him my praise,
As o'er the earth I trod!

I praise Him with the cymbal's clash,
With harp and with the lyre.
I praise Him with the strings and flute
And for His Godly fire.

I praise Him in the day and night.
He'll always be the same.
And as I end this time of praise,
I Lift His Holy Name.

Your Praising Child

CM

PRAYER AND PRAISE: *How can I do anything but praise You, my LORD, for Your Word compels me to do such and to lift Your Name continually in praise. Help me to remember that even during difficult days and times, when I may not feel like doing it. I am to do it anyway. So, I will praise You at all times for all things. Amen!*

Week 44 ❖ Day 1   Theme: Praise   Oct 28

OUR PRAISE TO YOU ALONE

HIS WORD: "'I am the Lord; that is my name!
I will not give my glory to another or my praise to idols.
See, the former things have taken place, and new things I declare;
before they spring into being I announce them to you.'
Sing to the Lord a new song, his praise from the ends of the earth,
you who go down to the sea, and all that is in it,
you islands, and all who live in them.
Let the desert and its towns raise their voices;
let the settlements where Kedar lives rejoice.
Let the people of Sela sing for joy; let them shout from the mountaintops.
Let them give glory to the Lord and proclaim his praise in the islands."
Isaiah 42:8-12

MY CHALLENGE: *To praise Him alone,
for He is my God and the only true God.*

O Lord, our God, we worship You.
Our praise to You alone;
For You are Master of this world.
Your glory has been shown.

For we have seen Your Majesty,
In Your creation here.
Your mighty hand has worked it all.
It should be loud and clear.

That You alone are mighty God.
No other can there be.
Therefore we give our all to You
Throughout eternity.

We'll always shout it from the heights:
Your Name would be made known;
For You're our Lord, and You're our God,
Our praise to You alone.

CM

PRAYER AND PRAISE: Your Word expresses praise so well. I can only repeat what it says, as I look to You and praise Your Name! I worship You and praise You alone! I praise you throughout eternity. Amen!

Week 44 ❖ Day 2   Theme: Praise   Oct 29

PRAISE, THE PATHWAY TO PEACE

HIS WORD: "In a loud voice they sang:
'Worthy is the Lamb, who was slain, to receive power and wealth and wisdom and strength and honor and glory and praise!'
Then I heard every creature in heaven and on earth and under the earth and on the sea, and all that is in them, singing:
'To him who sits on the throne and to the Lamb be praise and honor and glory and power, for ever and ever!'"
Revelation 5:12-13

MY CHALLENGE: To constantly give Jesus a flow of praise that will give Him the glory due, as I see in this example from Revelation above.

Our praise is the pathway to peace.
So give Him thanks today.
As we rejoice, He then redeems,
Sets us free from the fray.

The blessings God gave to Abraham
Are also ours today.
Jesus secured them on the cross,
A bloody price to pay.

He gave His life as an exchange
For sins that were so vast.
It was for us He paid the price,
That we'd be free at last.

His love for us was so profound
He did not hesitate
To pay a price He did not owe.
That's why we celebrate.

Therefore our thanks should always be
A constant flow of praise,
To give Him all the glory due,
For now and all our days.

Today we give Him thanks and praise.
Each day may it increase,
As all as one we sing it out,
On pathway of our peace.

CM

PRAYER AND PRAISE: My LORD, it shouldn't be necessary that I be reminded to praise You. However I sometimes need this prodding, even though I discovered long ago that the more I praise You the better things go in my life.
Thank You and praise You, my LORD Jesus!

Week 44 ♦ Day 3   Theme: Praise   Oct 30

HE INHABITS OUR PRAISE

HIS WORD: *"But thou art holy, O thou that inhabitest the praises of Israel."*
Psalm 22:3, KJV

"Shout for joy to the LORD, all the earth. Worship the LORD with gladness;
come before him with joyful songs.
Know that the LORD is God. It is he who has made us, and we are his;
we are his people, the sheep of his pasture.
Enter his gates with thanksgiving and his courts with praise;
give thanks to him and praise his name.
For the LORD is good and his love endures forever;
his faithfulness continues through all generations."
Psalm 100

MY CHALLENGE: *To shout with joy His Name as I praise Him, knowing that He inhabits my praise!*

If we desire a greater sense
Of His Presence in us,
We need only to look at His Word.
On it we're to focus.

For His Word says He inhabits
The praises of His own.
Therefore, if we want more of Him,
Give Him more praise alone.

Praise Him in all circumstances.
At all times give Him praise.
Praise Him for all things in your life.
You'll find your spirit raised.

His Presence will be real to you.
You'll sense like ne'er before,
Because you've done as He has asked,
To praise Him more and more.

This all adds up to realize,
To sense His Presence in
The need to praise Him evermore,
From this moment we'll begin.

Yes, our LORD, we'll focus on You
And give You all the praise,
To give you all the glory due,
From now through all our days.

CM

PRAYER AND PRAISE: *Thank You, my LORD, as I praise You and sense You inhabiting my praise. What joy that is! My prayer is to take the initiative to praise You much more than I have been doing. Praise Your Name!*

Week 44 ❖ Day 4 Theme: Praise **Oct 31**

A TIME OF PRAISE

HIS WORD: "Come, let us sing for joy to the Lord;
let us shout aloud to the Rock of our salvation.
Let us come before him with thanksgiving
And extol him with music and song."
Psalm 95:1-2

MY CHALLENGE: To come and sing for joy!
I will shout aloud and bring thanksgiving,
extolling Him with music and song.
In doing that, I discover that my eyes are off "self" and are
focused on the Lord, right where they should be.

We thank You with the trumpet sound
And with our voices raise,
To glory in Your Holy Name,
And lift Your Name in praise.

We give thanksgiving for all things
And lift Your Name on high.
We give You all the glory, God,
To praise and glorify.

You give us Your provision, Lord,
Supplying all our need.
We thank You for Your gift of grace,
As to Your Word we heed.

We sing to You, our Lord, a song
And praise with other saints,
To make You known throughout the world.
Let not our hearts be faint.

It is Your Name we raise on high.
In You we take delight.
We children joy in Your true Word.
Together we unite.

We saints rejoice in this, our gift.
To You, our joy we raise.
We take the cross and follow You.
A trail of thanks we blaze.

CM

PRAYER AND PRAISE: Lord, I confess I haven't lifted Your Name in praise to the
extent that I could or should. I give You my thanksgiving for all
Your provision, and I am determined to give You the glory for all things.
May my thanks to You be on my lips now and continually. Thank You, my Lord!

Week 44 ❖ Day 5   Theme: Praise   Nov 1

PRAISE YOU, PRAISE YOU

HIS WORD: "With praise and thanksgiving they sang to the LORD;
'He is good; his love to Israel endures forever.'
And all the people gave a great shout of praise to the LORD,
because the foundation of the house of the LORD was laid."
Ezra 3:11

MY CHALLENGE: *To praise, sing and shout thanks to Him.
The people of Ezra's time expressed great joy on the
completion of the temple restoration.
They praised, they sang and they shouted.
I, too, can praise Him because of His goodness and great love for me.*

Praise You! Praise You! Praise You, LORD!
Praise Your Holy Name.
Holy! Holy! Holy, LORD!
Light in me Your flame.

Honor! Honor! Honor, LORD!
Lift Your Name on high.
Glory! Glory! Glory, LORD!
For Your Name I die.

Keep me! Keep me! Keep me, LORD!
Keep me right in line.
Mold me! Mold me! Mold me, LORD
To Your will divine.

Serve You! Serve You! Serve You, LORD!
Serve by Your design.
Love You! Love You! Love You, LORD
With this heart of mine.

75.75

PRAYER AND PRAISE: *LORD, I simply come to you now, fall on my knees,
give thanks to You in praise and shout Your Name for joy!
I am the temple of Your Holy Spirit, and You are building me to perfection
in every way. Fill me again today with Your Holy Spirit desire,
to give You praise and thanksgiving continually!*

Week 44 ❖ Day 6 Theme: Praise Nov 2

A PEACE OF PRAISE

HIS WORD: "I extol the LORD at all times;
his praise will always be on my lips.
My soul will boast in the LORD; let the afflicted hear and rejoice.
Glorify the LORD with me; let us exalt his name together."
Psalm 34:1-3

MY CHALLENGE: *To lift His Name and give the LORD praise
and glory at all times.*

To My Beloved Child:

Now live in the light of My Peace,
My words of grace for you,
That you will know the peace I give,
The path you're to pursue.

I do not give as the world gives.
They know not what is true.
My peace beyond understanding
Is, nonetheless, for you.

I give it out in full measure
To overflow your heart,
That you will be assured of this:
We'll never be apart.

Then, as your peace brings praise to Me,
Together we will grow.
Our fellowship as one on one
'Twill set our hearts aglow.

May praise be always on your lips,
In gratitude to Me,
For all that I have done for you
And all that is to be.

I live within that praise of yours
And joy in your delight.
The more you sing My praises, child,
The more you'll see My Light!

Your Inhabiting LORD

CM

PRAYER AND PRAISE: *Thank You, my loving Father, for giving to me a life of
gratitude to praise Your Name for all You are and have done.
My LORD, I praise You for all things, even though I may not understand it all.
I want to be obedient to You and give You all the glory.
I thank You for the sacrifice of Jesus and the power of the Holy Spirit.
Glory to Your Holy Name!*

Week 44 ❖ Day 7   Theme: Praise   Nov 3

45

JESUS

Our Jesus is the Son of God,

Our God, our Deity.

We worship Him and love Him so,

For all eternity.

JESUS

HIS WORD: "She will give birth to a son,
and you are to give him the name Jesus,
because he will save his people from their sins."
Matthew 1:21

"But these are written that you may believe that Jesus is the Christ,
the Son of God, and that by believing you may have life in his name."
John 20:31

MY CHALLENGE: *To acknowledge that Jesus is my God, my Creator
and my All in All. I accept it and adhere to it,
and I worship Him as each Name listed below.*

To My Lord Jesus:
JESUS, You are:

My Comforter,	My Maker,
My Counselor,	My Master,
My Deliverer,	My Power,
My Friend,	My Protector,
My Glory,	My Provider,
My God,	My Redeemer,
My Healer,	My Righteousness,
My Husband,	My Savior,
My King,	My Teacher,
My Lord,	My All in All,
My King of Kings,	My Jesus!
My Lord of Lords,	

Your Loving Child

IRR.

PRAYER AND PRAISE: *My Lord Jesus, as I pray to You and call You by each of these names, I am humbled by the immensity of it all. Help me to comprehend Your greatness. Help me to understand that You are these and so much more! I submit to Your Lordship my whole being.*

Week 45 ❖ Day 1   Theme: Jesus   **Nov 4**

YOU ALONE

HIS WORD: "Who will not fear You, O Lord,
and bring glory to Your Name?
For You alone are holy.
All nations will come and worship before You,
for Your righteous acts have been revealed."
Revelation 15:4

MY CHALLENGE: To put Jesus first above all, before anything else,
and put Him first in every step of my life. I am to seek Him and Him alone
for my salvation, my deliverance and my spiritual maturity.

Lord Jesus, it is You alone
Who saves me from my load of sin,
Setting me on the Solid Rock
With You, a new life to begin.

I love to walk with You as Friend,
Learning to trust You for all things.
My Desire is to please Your heart.
To You forever I will cling.

As I trod on this path of faith,
Going and growing in Your grace,
And look forward to Your Great Day,
To see each other face to face.

Your praises I will ever sing,
And to this lost world make You known.
No one will ever take Your place.
Lord Jesus, it is You alone.

LM

PRAYER AND PRAISE: Lord, My prayer is to look to You alone
to forgive my sins, heal my body and meet my needs, as I walk this path
of life, looking forward to the day I hear You call me home.

Week 45 ❖ Day 2   Theme: Jesus   Nov 5

SOMEONE WONDERFUL

HIS WORD: "For to us a child is born, to us a son is given,
and the government will be on his shoulders.
And he will be called Wonderful Counselor,
Mighty God, Everlasting Father, Prince of Peace."
Isaiah 9:6

MY CHALLENGE: *To grasp how wonderful He is!
I am filled with wonder as I ponder the
life of my Lord Jesus and all that He did for me.
Even the word "wonderful" doesn't do Him full justice,
for He is far greater even than that! Can I comprehend it?*

Isn't our Jesus wonderful?
His victory we proclaim.
He's Master o'er our destiny.
We praise His Holy Name!

I know not why He loves me so,
Shedding His blood for me.
I can't repay the debt I owe.
His act has set me free.

I give You thanks, my Lord Jesus.
Your commands I obey,
Telling all of Your saving grace,
Following in Your way.

Your steps will lead me to heaven.
You are all-powerful.
Let me ask the question again:
Isn't He wonderful?

CM

PRAYER AND PRAISE: Yes, Lord, You are more than wonderful, and I confess my love for You. I ask You to give me greater vision of Your Majesty, Your Holiness and Your Righteousness, that I might grasp a greater sense of Your wonder, my "Wonderful!"

Week 45 ❖ Day 3   Theme: Jesus   **Nov 6**

SONG OF LIFE

HIS WORD: "The LORD is my strength and my song;
he has become my salvation."
Psalm 118:14

"Surely God is my salvation; I will trust and not be afraid.
The LORD, the LORD is my strength and my song;
he has become my salvation."
Isaiah 12:2

MY CHALLENGE: To live my life as a life of love, just as Jesus did.
Since Jesus is my Song of Life, He is also my Song of Love.
You cannot separate the two, for His life was given as a love gift.

Jesus is my Song of Life.
He is my Melody.
Together we walk the road,
In total harmony.

I feel the beat of His heart
And His loving embrace.
As I keep in stride with Him,
He fills me with His grace.

In eternal covenant,
This path will never end,
As we walk along His road,
Much closer than a friend.

I acknowledge His Presence,
As we walk side by side.
He's my Savior and Lover
And I'm His lovely bride.

That's why I'm so elated,
Overcoming the world's strife.
No matter what's ahead,
He is my Song of Life!

76.76

PRAYER AND PRAISE: My loving God, You have given me the greatest song in life: that is, Your love causing a new melody in my heart. I praise You for that, and I pray to keep my heart open and warm to continue singing Your Song to those who have never heard it. Thank You, LORD!

Week 45 ❖ Day 4   Theme: Jesus   Nov 7

JESUS IS HIS NAME

HIS WORD: "I will show you what he is like who comes to me
and hears my words and puts them into practice.
He is like a man building a house,
who dug down deep and laid the foundation on rock.
When the flood came, the torrent struck that house but
could not shake it, because it was well built."
Luke 6:47-48

MY CHALLENGE: *To put into practice His Presence, by putting His Word
into practice. The words of Jesus above state that I am to put
His words into practice. Jesus is the Word of God.
That is my challenge every day.*

The practice of His Presence
Is no mystery.
Commune with Him at all times,
You will be set free.

To worship at His altar,
Glory to receive.
Then you will find the answers,
Answers to your pleas.

The problem with us humans
Is ourselves within.
Our throne of life is filled up.
Pride has entered in.

But now we have the answer.
Practice is our aim.
His Presence is to fill us.
Jesus is His Name!

75.75

PRAYER AND PRAISE: L̪ᴏʀᴅ, *putting Your Word into practice and following after
You seems like such a daunting task. And yet, I wish to obey and do as
Jesus did, to walk as Jesus walked and to talk as Jesus talked.
Now I give myself to You, to be trained to do just that.
I step out in faith believing today.*

Week 45 ❖ Day 5   Theme: Jesus   Nov 8

OUR PRECIOUS CORNERSTONE

HIS WORD: "As you come to him, the living Stone—rejected by men but chosen by God and precious to him—you also, like living stones, are being built into a spiritual house to be a holy priesthood, offering spiritual sacrifices acceptable to God through Jesus Christ. For in Scripture it says:
'See, I lay a stone in Zion,
a chosen and precious cornerstone,
and the one who trusts in him
will never be put to shame.'"
1 Peter 2:4-6

MY CHALLENGE: *To come to the full realization that Jesus IS my precious, living Cornerstone, and I am like a living stone, being built into His spiritual house. What a responsibility! What a privilege! What an honor! What a joy! What a Savior He is!*

A cornerstone in a building,
That will unite two walls of stone,
Is a starting place to build it,
Put in place as foundation stone

It's also representative
Of something indispensable,
A necessity we must have,
To help our life be viable.

Therefore we look to LORD Jesus,
In our temple the Cornerstone;
For He's the rock of our salvation,
Uniting us to Him alone.

To our life He's indispensable,
As we look to Him on the throne.
We have this solid foundation,
For Jesus is our Cornerstone.

LM

PRAYER AND PRAISE: *LORD Jesus, our precious King, all glory belongs to You! Help me be a living stone in Your spiritual house as a part of Your Holy Priesthood. I offer my sacrifice of praise to You!*

Week 45 ❖ Day 6   Theme: Jesus   Nov 9

KNOCKING ON YOUR HEART

HIS WORD: "Here I am! I stand at the door and knock.
If anyone hears my voice and opens the door,
I will come in and eat with him, and he with me."
Revelation 3:20

MY CHALLENGE: What a beautiful invitation Jesus gives me in His words above!
My challenge is to a) answer the knock, b) hear His voice,
c) open the door of my heart and d) allow Him to come in!

To My Loving Friend

As I am knocking on your heart,
Please open up today.
My voice is gently speaking, now
Invite me in to stay.

As you have opened your heart's door,
Receive Me to abide.
We'll walk together, you and I,
For you're My loving bride!

Since you have opened your heart's door,
I am living within.
I'll eat with you and you with Me.
Forever we are kin.

Please make your cares and wants be known.
I'll guide you to the end.
I want the very best for you.
I'm much more than a friend.

Now hear My Voice that calls your name.
It's gentle and with love.
I do not speak a worldly way,
But call you from above.

Thank you, child, that you hear My call,
Have opened your heart's door.
You've made My Heart leap high with joy,
For you, I've so much more.

Your Loving Friend, Jesus

CM

PRAYER AND PRAISE: Lord, I hear You. I hear Your hand tapping on the door of my heart.
I answer it now with this request: Please come in and dwell forevermore.
Though I've answered it many times before, I confess I've found ways to shut You out!
But now I'm determined to do all possible to abide in Your Will!

Week 45 ❖ Day 7   Theme: Jesus   **Nov 10**

46

VICTORY

The greatest victory of all,

Is victory over sin;

Our Jesus paid the total price,

For new life to begin.

WALKING ALL ALONE

HIS WORD: "He holds victory in store for the upright,
he is a shield to those whose walk is blameless,
for he guards the course of the just
and protects the way of his faithful ones."
Proverbs 2:7-8

MY CHALLENGE: To stand on God's promises!
In those times of feeling all alone, I have a choice to make.
I can continue to feel sorry for myself
or I can stand on God's promises
and rise above my circumstances, and win the victory.

To My Understanding Lord:

Why is the lonely pain so great,
When walking all alone,
When wondering what shall happen next,
To which I might be prone?

What must I do to aid the cause,
To help my aching soul,
To walk again the most high road,
To once again be whole?

Then, at the darkest point of night,
A light comes shining through.
While basking in that wondrous Light,
I knew that it was You!

You are the answer to my pain.
You are life's gift to me.
I joy in Your Presence, Lord.
You are my victory.

Your Loving Child
CM

PRAYER AND PRAISE: In gaining the victory, my Lord, I pray for strength and wisdom to carry on in that which You have won for me.
Thanks be to You, my God, for You've given me victory!

Week 46 ❖ Day 1   Theme: Victory   Nov 11

DELAYED ANSWER

HIS WORD: "Then the high priest stood up before them and asked Jesus, 'Are you not going to answer? What is this testimony that these men are bringing against you?' But Jesus remained silent and gave no answer."
Mark 14:60-61a

MY CHALLENGE: *To remain content, patient and trusting when I do not have an answer from the LORD. I am to trust in Father God, as Jesus did, and not in my fellow man.*
Jesus knew His mission. He knew His destiny.
He wasted not His time on frivolous and erroneous questions.

When answer to our prayer's delayed,
And faith is growing dim.
It's time to look up to the LORD,
To only trust in Him.

We know not reasons for delay.
Our hearts are pleading long.
Will the answer ever arrive
And sing the victor's song?

We know not what His timing be.
Our faith must still be strong
Till that day the answer comes,
Regardless of how long.

We thank You, LORD, for giving us
Your patience to endure,
That in Your perfect timing, LORD,
Your answer is assured.

CM

PRAYER AND PRAISE: *LORD, I ask for discernment. I pray for contentment as I wait for answers from You. I know the answer will come, and whatever it is, it will be the best one for me. This is so, even if I cannot see it now. But You are LORD, and I place myself into Your loving and caring hands. Thank You, LORD!*

Week 46 ❖ Day 2   Theme: Victory   Nov 12

VICTORY OVER SATAN

HIS WORD: "The sting of death is sin, and the power of sin is the law.
But thanks be to God!
He gives us the victory through our LORD Jesus Christ."
1 Corinthians 15:56-57

MY CHALLENGE: *To step out in my walk of faith each day, knowing I have the victory, and not allowing Satan to bring anything against me. The Word says it, and I claim it. I have the victory through Christ!*

I come against the evil one,
For all he might destroy;
For he has tried to conquer me,
With lies he does employ.

But I can take the upper hand,
With power from Above,
To win the victory over him,
With words of God's true love.

So I come against you, Satan,
In all your work today.
Jesus is the Name above all.
To Him you must obey.

There is no other Name on earth,
For all the world to see,
And bring about God's will for all,
To win the victory.

CM

PRAYER AND PRAISE: *I confess, LORD, I have been defeated at times—those times when I let Satan have his way. But I thank You now, as I come to You and claim Your victory in my life. Satan shall no longer have reign. He is finished, for You wrought the victory for me on the cross.*
Praise be to Your Holy Name!

Week 46 ❖ Day 3   Theme: Victory   **Nov 13**

FROM DEFEAT TO VICTORY - Part 1

HIS WORD: "With God we will gain the victory,
and he will trample down our enemies."
Psalm 60:12

MY CHALLENGE: *To know He gives me the victory. It's to my advantage to cling to Him, follow Him and trust in Him—for He IS my Victory!*

Are you trying to figure out the future?
Attempting to control your destiny?
Are you spending a lot of time planning,
Rather than communicating with Me?

It is a waste of time and energy
To plot out the future you wish to hold,
A frightful loss of natural resources,
Seeking to gather much of the world's gold.

Your energy is being exhausted,
Weakened and weary by rushing each day.
Relax in the middle of exhaustion.
Look to Me, My child, for I AM the Way.

There is a simple answer to your life
Of going in circles until strength is gone:
"My Jesus, I give it all up to You!"
Are words of release that beckon Me come.

You have opened a door that lets Me through.
It allows Me to come into your heart
To give you everything you need in life,
To walk My path of peace, ne'er to depart.

10 10.10 10

PRAYER AND PRAISE: *Thank You, my God! Thank You that I'm able to live a life of victory! No matter what the world may say or do; and regardless what others may think or say, I live in victory!*

Week 46 ❖ Day 4   Theme: Victory   **Nov 14**

FROM DEFEAT TO VICTORY - Part 2

HIS WORD: "With God we will gain the victory,
and he will trample down our enemies."
Psalm 108:13

MY CHALLENGE: To <u>know</u> God has trampled down my enemies,
and to live my life accordingly.

Putting your future into My control
Gives you freedom and peace you never knew.
Now you are walking and leaning on Me,
We both can look forward to life anew.

I love you, child, more than you'll ever know.
All facets of life are concern for Me.
I desire, more than you can ever imagine,
To help you in your walk to victory.

For it's My Way which will win the battles
In this life, as you keep plodding along.
It's My Way you need to follow, My child,
For My Way leads to your victory song.

It's My freedom which will cause you to sing
A new song, giving you new melody.
Your life of walking together with Me
Is living life in precious harmony.

Take joy, My child, in all you have learned,
In walking the road forever to see,
Our steps together, in walking as one,
The future assured is one of victory.

10 10.10 10

PRAYER AND PRAISE: Praise Your Name forever, for assurance is knowing
I have the victory in Jesus! Help me, LORD, to live it out each day,
as You have promised.

COMMUNE FOR VICTORY

HIS WORD: "When he was at the table with them, he took bread, gave thanks, broke it and began to give it to them. Then their eyes were opened and they recognized him, and he disappeared from their sight."
Luke 24:30-31

MY CHALLENGE: May my eyes also be opened each time I commune with Him, break bread and we fellowship with one another. Then I, too, can proclaim, "I saw Jesus!"

The most powerful weapon of all
Is communing with the LORD,
To talk with Him about everything,
Be, with Him, in sweet accord.

Don't wait till things have quieted down
And your spinning world has slowed.
Don't wait until that time to begin.
Make it constant episode.

This is a battle we are fighting
With the devil, you have heard.
We fight the enemy on his own turf,
By bombing Him with God's Word.

Talk with the LORD about anything,
Whatever is on your mind.
Be with Him in constant dialogue,
And this is what you will find.

That you are on the victorious side.
The enemy is below.
The LORD has trampled him underfoot,
Has given him final blow.

Know this victory He wrought for us
And all the weapons in play,
By communing with Him all the time.
Make it habit every day.

97.97

PRAYER AND PRAISE: Yes LORD, open my eyes that I may see Your Glory and your Majesty, as I commune with You on a daily, even hourly, basis. Thank You, my LORD!

Week 46 ❖ Day 6   Theme: Victory   **Nov 16**

VICTORY

HIS WORD: "For everyone born of God overcomes the world.
This is the victory that has overcome the world, even our faith.
Who is it that overcomes the world?
Only he who believes that Jesus is the Son of God."
1 John 5:4-5

MY CHALLENGE: *To live out the victorious life He has wrought for me
and to continually give Him praise for it.
Yes, thanks be to God for the victory through our Lord Jesus Christ.
And what a victory it is! Nothing can compare!*

To My Victorious Child:

Victory is a celebration
Of life I give to thee,
To bring My Love and saving Grace,
To set completely free.

It hurts My heart to see the strife
That's caused by evil men.
I did not create them this way.
To Me they all offend.

The enemy has had his day,
Striving to bring you down,
Causing you to see evil ways,
Of seeking earthly crowns.

I have a way open to you,
To bring you victory,
If you will but open your heart,
My victory to receive.

I offer it to all who come.
Accept My Gracious Gift.
It is for all eternity.
Your life I will uplift.

Lift up your voice and shout it out
For all the world to see:
I have delivered you, My child.
Celebrate victory!

Your Winning Lord

CM

PRAYER AND PRAISE: *Lord, I celebrate the victory! I celebrate Your life in me.
I celebrate Your victory over evil. I pray to remain faithful and, thus,
to remain in celebration of eternal life. I give praise to You and give
You my devotion. I thank You for Your bountiful supply.
Thank You, JESUS!*

47

TRUST

"Trust in God; trust also in Me"

Are words that Jesus spoke.

It's up to us to obey His Word

And take to us His yoke.

HIS PATH OF TRUST

HIS WORD: "Trust in the LORD with all your heart and
lean not on your own understanding.
In all your ways acknowledge him,
and he will make your paths straight."
Proverbs 3:5-6

MY CHALLENGE: To trust in Him and Him alone. I <u>know</u> I should trust in Him.
I know I shouldn't trust in my own understanding. Yet I do.
I know that I should acknowledge Him in all my ways.
Yet, do I? That's also my challenge!

To My Helping LORD:

I trust You, Jesus.
Forgive me for my slack.
I love You, Jesus.
Help me to keep on track.

I walk Your straight path
With simple acts of faith.
It's a narrow path,
To walk a slower pace.

I render to You
My whole life and my heart.
My trust is in You.
I know we'll never part.

I know it is true
To trust You is a must.
I keep You in view,
To walk Your Path of Trust!

Your Trusting Child
56.56

PRAYER AND PRAISE: It is my prayer, LORD, to trust in You for all things at all times, so that I am completely at peace. This is the path You ask us to take. This is the path I desire to walk. Thank You for Your help.

Week 47 ❖ Day 1   Theme: Trust   Nov 18

THAT'S WHAT IT'S ALL ABOUT

HIS WORD: "Put your trust in the light while you have it, so that you may become sons of light."
John 12:36a

MY CHALLENGE: To put my <u>complete</u> trust in Him.
Jesus is the Light of the World, and
I am to trust Him for <u>everything!</u>
The question is: Can I? Will I?

My future is hid from my view.
I cannot see down the road.
It leaves me having to trust in Him,
To carry all of my load.

I try to shine a light of sorts,
To see what is coming next;
But it leaves me with bloodshot eyes,
A strain that is too complex.

I must simplify my living
And trust in His loving care,
Not to worry about tomorrow,
Nor fretting that will ensnare.

I give my life and all to Him,
Which will free me from all doubt;
Loving and trusting in Jesus,
For that's what it's all about.

87.87

PRAYER AND PRAISE: My prayer my, LORD, is to learn to trust You for everything. I confess that in my humanness I tend to want to trust in my thinking. But when I do, I make many mistakes. I need You, LORD. I need You to help me trust in You for all things, all the time. Thank You, LORD, for Your guidance.

Week 47 ❖ Day 2   Theme: Trust   Nov 19

IN HIM PUT YOUR TRUST

HIS WORD: "Do not let your hearts be troubled.
Trust in God, trust also in me."
John 14:1

MY CHALLENGE: *To give up all my troubles to Him
and put my life completely in His hands.*

Has doubt and fear had control of your life?
Anxiety got you down?
Does your heart beat hard and your breath come short,
Your mind on a merry-go-round?

The eternal life God designed for you
is peace and tranquility,
Of trusting in Him for all things you need,
Living free of agony.

It all boils down to one thing in your life,
One thing that will set you free:
Release all your troubles, giving all to Him,
Determined freedom to see.

It is surrender of your will to Him.
Give up your focus on self.
Take all the cares and worries you have
And put them all on the shelf.

It is easier said than to do at times,
But doing it is a must.
Make up your mind, no matter what may come,
In Him you will put your trust.

10 7.10 7

PRAYER AND PRAISE: *Okay, Lord, I give up. I've gone my own way far too long.
From here on out, I put my complete trust in You.
Hear my prayer, Lord, and help me keep on track. Your track.
Thank You, Lord. Amen!*

Week 47 ❖ Day 3   Theme: Trust   Nov 20

I HOLD YOUR HAND

HIS WORD: "Trust in the LORD and do good;
dwell in the land and enjoy safe pasture.
Delight yourself in the LORD and
he will give you the desires of your heart."
Psalm 37:3-4

MY CHALLENGE: *To discover and experience the joy of the LORD,
while trusting completely in Him.
When I do that, I have the promise He will give me the desires of my heart.
The first step is to trust in Him. That's my challenge.*

I hold Your hand and trust in You.
Your Presence I enjoy.
My earthly fears have passed away,
As Your Word I employ.

I know that as I trust in You,
For all things great and small,
I go on to maturity,
In answer to Your call.

It's then I see the greater view,
A picture that's Divine.
As I gaze upon Your Presence,
I'm Yours, and You are mine.

My heart sails beyond description,
To trust and take my stand.
I delight myself in You, O LORD,
Holding firmly to Your hand.

CM

PRAYER AND PRAISE: *I confess, my LORD, I must learn to delight myself in You
to a greater degree. I think too much about only delighting myself.
I promise You, LORD, that I will do my best to do this, and I thank You
for Your promise to grant me the desires of my heart.
Amen!*

Week 47 ❖ Day 4   Theme: Trust   Nov 21

WALK HIS WAY

HIS WORD: "When I am afraid, I will trust in you.
In God, whose word I praise,
in God I trust; I will not be afraid.
What can mortal man do to me?"
Psalm 56:3-4

MY CHALLENGE: *To trust in mortal man less and in God more.
In fact, when I trust in God, I <u>must</u> not be afraid,
only trust and obey, as I walk His way.*

Do we seek a fame and fortune,
To walk a lofty height?
Do we dream of gold and riches,
A life of ease delight?

It is great to have no worry,
No need to feel some guilt,
To relax and take life easy,
To rest on what we've built.

To walk the path He's given us,
A humble walk indeed.
Will we trod the road of service,
To fill a mighty need?

For His way is but to train us,
Bring honor and proclaim.
We're to trust in Him at all times,
Regardless of our fame.

Step aside from chasing rainbows,
To follow after Him.
We'll let His road lead us onward,
Until the final hymn.

CM

PRAYER AND PRAISE: L*ORD, my request is for the power of Your Holy
Spirit in my life, to walk Your path, trusting totally in You, and not fearing man.
I thank You for filling me, guiding me and teaching me, as I walk Your path.*

Week 47 ❖ Day 5   Theme: Trust   Nov 22

KEEP ME FOCUSED

HIS WORD: "May the God of hope fill you with all joy and peace as you trust in him, so that you may overflow with hope by the power of the Holy Spirit."
Romans 15:13

MY CHALLENGE: *To overflow with hope by the power of the Holy Spirit. What a thought! That I may <u>overflow</u> with <u>hope</u>! And that is by the power of the Holy Spirit. Not only that: I am <u>filled</u> with all <u>joy</u> and <u>peace</u> as I trust in Him. That is what I am challenged to receive.*

LORD, I pray to keep me focused,
To worship You alone,
That I fulfill my destiny,
To see Your golden throne.

I trust to keep my eyes on You,
In present time alone,
To watch Your Way and Will with Me,
For You're my Cornerstone.

I will focus on Your Presence
And not on things amassed.
I'll not worry about tomorrow,
Nor fret things of the past.

You are the basis for my faith,
To carry on each day,
And fill the time with trust in You,
To follow in Your Way.

CM

PRAYER AND PRAISE: *Okay, LORD, I want all You have for me—a filling of joy and peace and overflowing with hope. I like that. I receive that now. Thank You, LORD, for Your leading, as I follow in Your way, keeping my eyes on You.*

Week 47 ❖ Day 6   Theme: Trust   Nov 23

I AM ALL YOURS TODAY

HIS WORD: "But I will leave within you the meek and humble; who trust in the name of the LORD."
Zephaniah 3:12

MY CHALLENGE: To let go and let God. Since I know He is the great I AM, the Creator of all, I <u>know</u> I can trust in Him in every aspect of my life.

To My Trusting Child:

Forgive him, though he hurt you so.
Let Me the battle fight.
You are My child; I love you so.
Recall I AM the Light!

I have laid out the path for you.
Just walk My Holy line,
And you will see, at final end,
The victory is Mine!

I've given you My Holy Word,
To bless your soul, dear one,
That you would get to know Me well,
As you and I are one.

I AM the Great and Mighty One,
The Creator of all,
And yet I come to live within
Your heart, though be it small.

This may be hard to comprehend,
Difficult to fathom,
Yet it's true; I designed it so,
That you would overcome.

So trust Me, my child, at all times.
Trust Me in every way.
For you, I've won the victory.
I AM all yours today.

Your Concerned Dad.

CM

PRAYER AND PRAISE: My heavenly "Dad," I make a promise to You. Day by day, I will learn to walk closer to You, trusting in Your care, knowing Your love, and giving up self, to be filled with You to a greater degree. Thank You, my LORD!

Week 47 ❖ Day 7   Theme: Trust   Nov 24

48

THANKS

Give thanks to God for everything,

No matter what it takes.

Our destiny is in His hands.

Give thanks for our own sake.

I THANK YOU, LORD

HIS WORD: "Rejoice in the Lord always. I will say it again: Rejoice!
Let your gentleness be evident to all. The Lord is near.
Do not be anxious about anything, but in everything,
by prayer and petition, with thanksgiving,
present your requests to God."
Philippians 4:4-6

MY CHALLENGE: *To rejoice and give thanks to God for everything!
It takes determination, it takes practice, and it takes
spiritual maturity to give thanks to God—always, for everything.
When I learn to give thanks and rejoice in Him for <u>everything</u>,
I find He grants me great inner peace and joy.*

To My Lord:

I thank You, Lord, for everything,
With heart and mind and soul.
I thank You for the words You give,
To keep me in control.

I thank You, Lord, for giving me,
Life on earth to enjoy.
I thank You for the strength You give,
To maintain my employ.

Thank You, Lord, for forgiving me
My sins and everything.
I thank You, Lord, for Your great love.
Your praise I'll always sing.

I thank You, Lord, for Your great gifts
And all You've given me.
It matters not the world around.
My thanks is all to Thee.

Your Loving Child
CM

PRAYER AND PRAISE: *My prayer? At this time, Lord, it's simply to take the time to thank You and praise You for all I have received in the past, for all I have now, and for all I'll ever be given. You are the Lord of lords, and I am so grateful to know You and to be assured of my future in the eternal home You have prepared for me and all those who believe.*

Week 48 ❖ Day 1   Theme: Thanks   **Nov 25**

THANK HIM

HIS WORD: "Give thanks in all circumstances,
for this is God's will for you in Christ Jesus."
1 Thessalonians 5:18

MY CHALLENGE: *To give thanks in <u>all</u> circumstances.
It is a most difficult thing at first, until I come to understand that God is in every aspect of my life. As I can accept and believe that, I can give Him thanks for ALL things, because I know that He will bring about the best for me, although the current situation may not be to my liking.
Giving thanks for all things and trusting Him for all things go hand in hand.*

Thank Him in all circumstances,
Be they bad or be they good.
We rejoice in His Providence,
Living in His brotherhood.

In giving thanks for everything
Can be oh so difficult.
When things are bad and hurting so,
Know He'll bring the best result.

We give Him our thanks continually,
Whatever the case may be.
Thanking Him for even the worst
Brings home the victory.

He deals with us so patiently,
Grabbing victory from defeat.
If we will but give all to Him,
We will rest in Him complete.

87.87

PRAYER AND PRAISE: *L<small>ORD</small>, I confess I often find it difficult to give You thanks in the middle of my trials for whatever may be happening. Help me, I ask, to practice giving You thanks for everything all the time. In Jesus Name!
Amen!*

Week 48 ❖ Day 2   Theme: Thanks   Nov 26

THANKS FOR LIBERTY

HIS WORD: "Thanks be to God for His indescribable gift!"
2 Corinthians 9:15

MY CHALLENGE: To give my God thanks for His indescribable gift of grace! Too often I ignore giving thanks to God. Everything I receive from Him is a gift. Don't I always make certain to give thanks to the one who has given me a gift? My challenge is to see that God receives my thanks EVERY day.

I don't know why	Therefore I look
I even try	To Him Who took
To do things my own way;	My sins and set me free;
For when I do,	For then I give
Before I'm through,	My thanks, to live
Something has gone astray.	With Him forever be.
And then I see	I praise You, LORD,
It must be me,	That You have poured
In going all alone.	Your love and grace on me.
It's time I must	Now here I stand,
Put all my trust	As You have planned,
In Him Who's on the throne.	In thanks for liberty.

446.446

PRAYER AND PRAISE: LORD, I dare to ask You to do whatever is necessary with me, to help me remember to give You thanks for all things at all times, regardless of the situation or how hopeless it may seem. I give You thanks for giving me liberty from sin. I know, LORD, that all I have is from You. Thank You!

Week 48 ❖ Day 3   Theme: Thanks   Nov 27

GIVE HIM THANKS

HIS WORD: "And whatever you do, whether in word or deed,
do it all in the name of the Lord Jesus,
giving thanks to God the Father through him."
Colossians 3:17

MY CHALLENGE: *To give Him thanks in <u>whatever</u> I do, in word and deed,
as I <u>do it all</u> in the name of the Lord Jesus.
That's it!*

Let not problems you face control your life,
For they will diminish your trust.
Give thanks to Him in all circumstances.
Faith in Him an absolute must.

When your life seems to be going all wrong,
Circumstances out of control,
Just give Him thanks for all of your trials;
For in living that is your role.

We may not understand the reason for all,
But it's enough for us to know
That we can put our whole life in His hands,
As all earthly things we let go.

As we let go and look to His giving,
To provide everything we need,
We rejoice for His care in every day.
We give Him Thanks for all indeed.

10 8.10 8

PRAYER AND PRAISE: *Lord, I confess I have not given You thanks for
everything I have done in word and deed. It has not all been done in Your name,
nor glory given to You.
But I am determined to be in line with Your Word and do as
Your scripture commands. I ask You now to help me in giving me
the power, knowledge and wisdom to give You thanks in all I do,
as I follow Your Word. Thank You, Lord!*

Week 48 ❖ Day 4   Theme: Thanks   Nov 28

GRATITUDE AND THANKS

HIS WORD: "Let the peace of Christ rule in your hearts, since as members of one body you were called to peace. And be thankful. Let the word of Christ dwell in you richly as you teach and admonish one another with all wisdom, and as you sing psalms, hymns and spiritual songs with gratitude in your hearts to God."
Colossians 3:15-16

MY CHALLENGE: *To consistently live my life in such a way that it allows Christ to rule in my heart.*
Am I allowing His word to dwell in me richly?
Am I worshiping Him with singing and with gratitude in my heart?

I give to You my gratitude
And overwhelming thanks
For all You have provided me,
In overcoming angst.

I know that fear is not from You;
It's from the enemy,
To help destroy my faith in You
And bring disharmony.

I rise up with Your Sword in hand.
Your Word I do apply.
The enemy is scattered thus.
Your Word He must comply.

I thank You for the victory.
In praise I give my due,
To give You gratitude and thanks,
All gained in service to You.

CM

PRAYER AND PRAISE: *I can't thank You enough, LORD!*
As I continue to serve You with my whole mind, will and strength,
I will give You thanks and praise.
That is my prayer.

I EXALT YOU

HIS WORD: "O Lord, You are my God;
I will exalt you and praise your name,
for in perfect faithfulness you have done marvelous things,
things planned long ago."
Isaiah 25:1

MY CHALLENGE: *To exalt His Name continually.
To thank Him in all circumstances for all things
and to remain faithful in giving Him the glory forevermore.*

I exalt You, my Lord Jesus.
I lift Your Name on high.
There is no other name on earth
In which to glorify.

How can I give you greater praise,
To show my gratitude,
And describe my joy in Your Love,
To sing it, as I should?

I know that it sets me apart,
Sometimes to feel alone;
But that's the price I need to pay,
To be one of Your own.

I care not what the world may think;
It matters not it's way.
I only care to praise Your Name,
Exalt Your life each day.

CM

PRAYER AND PRAISE: *I ask You, Lord, to fill me so full of Your Holy Spirit
and so fill my heart with love that I'll soar on high, praising You,
giving You all the glory.
My thanks, my gratitude and my praise is Yours, my Lord!*

Week 48 ❖ Day 6   Theme: Thanks   Nov 30

THANK YOU, MY CHILD

HIS WORD: "'At that time I will deal with all who oppressed you;
I will rescue the lame and gather those who have been scattered.
I will give them praise and honor in every land where they were put to shame.
At that time I will gather you; at that time I will bring you home.
I will give you honor and praise among all the peoples of the earth
when I restore your fortunes before your very eyes,' says the LORD."
Zephaniah 3:19-20

MY CHALLENGE: *To remain faithful in my praise and thanksgiving,
until the very end, when Jesus comes in all His glory.*

To My Thankful Child:

I thank you for your praise to Me.
You have right attitude.
And with the praise you've lifted up,
You've shown your gratitude.

My Day is coming soon enough.
There's plenty we must do,
To save the lost and bring them in,
So they will know Me too.

The time to gather is in view,
To burn the weeds in fire,
Then bring the wheat into My barn,
Fulfilling My desire.

So, as you keep your eyes on Me
And wait for My return,
Keep on with sowing and reaping.
It is for you I yearn.

Again, I praise My faithful child.
My thanks for all your works,
Until that Day you will receive
All your heavenly perks.

Until the time I call you home,
I praise My faithful one,
To keep on serving Me, your God,
Until the victory's won.

Your Appreciative Father
CM

PRAYER AND PRAISE: *My glorious heavenly Father, what a wonderful delight
to thank You for all things and praise You for Who You are!
Amen!*

Week 48 ❖ Day 7   Theme: Thanks   Dec 1

49

HIS LIGHT

Jesus is the Light of the World.

We're to reflect His light,

To share it with others around us,

To make their lives aright.

HIS GUIDING LIGHT

HIS WORD: "Your word is a lamp to my feet and a light for my path."
Psalm 119:105

MY CHALLENGE: *To follow that guiding light—the light of His Word.*
When I truly follow it, I cannot stumble or fall,
for His light brightens my way, as I follow each day.

To My Guiding Light:
You meet us at our point of need,
And lift above the fray.
You guide us with Your gentle touch,
To follow in Your Way.

It is Your guiding Light we see,
The path marked out for us,
To walk Your Way and live Your life,
A living stimulus.

Your Word is a lamp to our feet
And a light for our way.
As we follow Your path for us,
You bless us every day.

We thank You, LORD, for leading us,
On pathway that is right;
For it is reassuring,
To follow Your guiding light.

Your Loving Child
CM

PRAYER AND PRAISE: *I pray to keep my eyes open, as I walk on Your lighted path for my life, that I would not waiver to the left or to the right, but keep on in Your perfect will for me. Thank You, LORD, for Your light!*

Week 49 ❖ Day 1 Theme: His Light **Dec 2**

LIGHT PIERCES DARKNESS

HIS WORD: "Therefore judge nothing before the appointed time; wait till the Lord comes. He will bring to light what is hidden in darkness and will expose the motives of men's hearts. At that time each will receive his praise from God."
1 Corinthians 4:5

"But you, brothers, are not in darkness so that this day should surprise you like a thief. You are all sons of the light and sons of the day. We do not belong to the night or to the darkness."
1 Thessalonians 5:4-5

MY CHALLENGE: *To allow His light to shine within me, exposing that which needs to be removed, replacing it with new life.*

When life is like a forest dense,
Naught but undergrowth and trees,
So thick that sunlight cannot reach,
And devoid of any breeze.

The darkness has prevailed below,
Kept the light from coming in.
Then there are times a tree may fall,
To expose all things within.

And that is how it is with us,
With our darkness black as coal.
There always is that spark of hope,
That His Light will pierce our soul.

When a tree of sin falls today,
Then Jesus' Light enters in,
Penetrates to the greatest depths.
New life He creates within.

87.87

PRAYER AND PRAISE: *As I come to You now, my Lord Jesus, I confess my sins to You. I repent of them, and I thank You for giving me new life within. I praise You for Your forgiveness and for Your Light that dispels all darkness. All glory to You, my Lord!*

Week 49 ❖ Day 2   Theme: His Light   **Dec 3**

HIS FREEDOM LIGHT

HIS WORD: "It is for freedom that Christ has set us free. Stand firm, then, and do not let yourselves be burdened again by a yoke of slavery."
Galatians 5:1

"In him and through faith in him we may approach God with freedom and confidence."
Ephesians 3:12

MY CHALLENGE: *To know without a doubt He has set me free, as His Light dispels the darkness of my world.*

Has fear and worry come your way?
And, filling up your life,
Is it wrapping you up in knots
And causing you much strife?

Do you feel your heart beating hard
And tightening of your chest?
The whole world coming against you,
With no time now to rest?

There is good news to give to you:
It need not be that way.
Jesus wants to deliver you,
To live free in Him today.

You think it's easier said than done.
What is it you will choose?
So cast yourself upon the LORD.
What have you got to lose?

Jesus is our Bondage Breaker.
He makes our burden light.
If we but cast it all on Him,
He'll set our life aright.

He brings to us the victory
And frees us from our fright,
As we give up our trials to Him,
To receive His freedom light.

CM

PRAYER AND PRAISE: *My Jesus, I come to You on bended knee, asking for Your strength in my body, Your power in my spirit and Your illumination in my mind, that I may live victoriously, as You have promised in Your Word.*

Week 49 ❖ Day 3 Theme: His Light **Dec 4**

HIS GOLDEN LIGHT

HIS WORD: "Then Jesus told them,
'You are going to have the light just a little while longer.
Walk while you have the light, before darkness overtakes you.
The man who walks in the dark does not know where he is going.
Put your trust in the light while you have it,
so that you may become sons of the light.'"
John 12:35-36a

MY CHALLENGE: *To do just as scripture says: To walk in the Light while I have it, by putting my trust in the light—that is, Jesus!*

Bask in the golden Light of God,
To feel His Presence nigh.
We bring to Him our praises sing,
To lift His Name on high.

It is with joy and peace o'er all
We come to Him today,
To lay our burdens at His feet
And look to Him, we pray.

There is no other way on earth
To give our all to God,
Submit our lives to His great cause
And cast out all facade.

We thank You, LORD, for Who You are
And for Your glorious might.
Your precious Presence gives us joy,
To bask in golden Light.

CM

PRAYER AND PRAISE: *Thank You, LORD, as this is a reminder to praise You more in my prayer time, expressing my joy for Jesus and my pleasure in Your Presence. What a beautiful vision it is to see ourselves basking in Your golden Light, as we bow in prayer and praise to You. May my praise today lift Jesus higher!*

Week 49 ❖ Day 4   Theme: His Light   **Dec 5**

IN THE LIGHT OF HIS PRESENCE

HIS WORD: "When Jesus spoke again to the people, he said, 'I am the light of the world. Whoever follows me will never walk in darkness, but will have the light of life.'"
John 8:12

"While I am in the world, I am the light of the world."
John 9:5

MY CHALLENGE: *To walk in His Light: that is, to follow Him every step of the way in this path of life, for He is my Light of Life.*

I walk in the Light of His Presence.
He guides the way for my sake.
His Light illuminates my pathway
And shows me the steps to take.

For it's only by His guidance
I can be assured of this:
With His Holy Light to lead me,
I'll be in heavenly bliss.

I know not what's ahead of me,
Nor troubles that may ensue.
I only know to follow Him
And to keep His Light in view.

He's the only Light of this world.
No other will take His place.
I look to that beautiful Day
When I see Him face to face.

87.87

PRAYER AND PRAISE: *My Lord, what more is there to ask for than to walk in the Light of Your Presence? To walk continually in Your Light means that I'll always know the way to go. I'll never need to worry because I know that You will take care of me and all my needs.*
Come to think of it, Lord, that's exactly what You want me to do, isn't it? And so my promise to You is to do the best I can to be there!
Amen!

Week 49 ❖ Day 5 Theme: His Light **Dec 6**

FOCUS ON HIS PRESENCE

HIS WORD: "Blessed are those who have learned to acclaim you,
who walk in the light of your presence, O LORD."
Psalm 89:15

MY CHALLENGE: *To be blessed by walking in His Presence.
No, more than that—to walk in the light of His Presence!*

Focus on His Presence in you,
His light filling your soul.
Let your spirit soar unto Him,
To let Him have control.

Now you can take the negatives,
Worries that consume your life.
Then sit quietly in His Presence,
Removing all cares and strife.

Not only is He the Light of Life,
The Savior of your soul.
He is also the Light in you,
For He has made you whole.

That Light of His Presence in you,
May it so shine in you,
That others may see and come to Him.
They, too, His life pursue.

CM

PRAYER AND PRAISE: *My prayer is to spend more time focusing on You
and less time on my own pursuits of so called "lights." I praise You now for shining
Your light in me, s That I may see more clearly Your way for me.
Thank You, LORD!*

Week 49 ❖ Day 6   Theme: His Light   **Dec 7**

IN YOUR QUEST

HIS WORD: "Then Jesus cried out, 'When a man believes in me, he does not believe in me only, but in the one who sent me. When he looks at me, he sees the one who sent me. I have come into the world as a light, so that no one who believes in me should stay in darkness.'"
John 12:44-46

"But you are a chosen people, a royal priesthood, a holy nation, a people belonging to God, that you may declare the praises of him who called you out of darkness into his wonderful light."
1 Peter 2:9

MY CHALLENGE: To walk a closer walk with Him in His Light.

To My Questing Child:

In your quest for a closer walk,
A life of perfection,
Do not worry, dear child of Mine.
I am your Holy Bastion.

So worry not the perfect life,
For you're my pure delight.
I have covered you with My blood.
You're perfect in My sight.

The trials on earth may be difficult,
Gives chance for you to learn.
To trust in Me for everything
Is not something you can earn.

In your quest for a perfect life
And closer walk with Me,
Let's walk the path of earth as one,
To live in harmony.

The time will come for you someday.
A date I have for you,
That you will live in My embrace
And find this all is true.

For then your quest will be fulfilled,
The day you take to flight,
To the place I've prepared for you,
Forever in My Light.

Your Light-Giving LORD

CM

PRAYER AND PRAISE: Thank You, my LORD, for Your great light, in fulfilling my quest to You. You have given all I need to see a new breakthrough. Thank You, Jesus, my LORD!

Week 49 ❖ Day 7   Theme: His Light   Dec 8

50

JOY

He is the joy of the whole earth,

This Jesus, Friend of mine.

I praise Him for His joy in me,

For He's my Lord Divine.

I LOVE YOU, LORD JESUS

HIS WORD: "As the Father has loved me, so have I loved you. Now remain in my love. If you obey my commands, you will remain in my love, just as I have obeyed my Father's commands and remain in his love. I have told you this so that my joy may be in you and that your joy may be complete. My command is this: Love each other as I have loved you. Greater love has no one than this, that he lay down his life for his friends."
John 15:9-13

MY CHALLENGE: *To have my joy overflowing, by loving others, as Jesus has loved me, and so to remain in His love.*

To My Loving LORD:

I love You. I love You. I love You, LORD.
I Love You with all my heart.
I love You, LORD Jesus, with all my soul,
Till the day that I depart.

It matters not the many problems here,
If I follow Your commands.
I lean on You, with blessed assurance.
You have the whole world in Your hands.

So, why do I worry about things in my life,
When I know You're in control?
I look to You and all Your promises,
That Your Word I will extol.

As I live out my life, full of Your joy,
I have to express anew:
I love You. I love You. I love You, LORD.
I joy in my life with You.

Your Loving Child
10 7.10 7

PRAYER AND PRAISE: *I have nothing but praise for You, my LORD. My life, for me, You have restored. I find, when I praise You right from the start, my joy swells up within my heart. Praise to You for Your joy!*

Week 50 ❖ Day 1   Theme: Joy   Dec 9

GOD'S PURE JOY

HIS WORD: "Shout for joy to the Lord, all the earth.
Worship the Lord with gladness; come before him with joyful songs.
Know that the Lord is God.
It is he who made us, and we are his;
we are his people, the sheep of his pasture.
Enter his gates with thanksgiving and his courts with praise;
give thanks to him and praise his name.
For the Lord is good and his love endures forever;
his faithfulness continues through all generations."
Psalm 100

MY CHALLENGE: *To shout for joy to the Lord and come before Him with joyful songs!*

Inject a dose of Your pure joy
Into my life today.
Then cause it flow throughout my veins,
On to my heart to stay.

Infuse Your joy and make it mine,
A Holy act of Love,
To give me joy unspeakable,
A gift from You above.

There is no greater joy than this,
To live a life fulfilled,
Completing all You have for me,
In that which You have willed.

Therefore I give my life to You,
To work as Your envoy,
As I live out Your will for me,
A life of Your pure joy.

CM

PRAYER AND PRAISE: My praise to You for the joy I have in my heart. That joy is far above all happiness and comes from You, not from some earthly stimulation. Thank You, my Lord, for filling me with Your joy and love.
Amen!

Week 50 ❖ Day 2   Theme: Joy   **Dec 10**

MY SOUL AWAKE TO JOY

HIS WORD: "Though you have not seen him, you love him; and even though you do not see him now, you believe in him and are filled with an inexpressible and glorious joy. For you are receiving the goal of your faith, the salvation of your souls."
1 Peter 1:8-9

MY CHALLENGE: To believe in Him with an inexpressible and glorious joy!

Awaken your soul to His joy,
That joy He has for you.
As you open your heart to Him,
Give Him your love that's due.

Thrill to the joy of His Presence.
Sense His love in your heart.
He loves you with intensity.
You know He'll ne'er depart.

Stay ever so close to the LORD,
By spending time alone,
Just soaking in His Presence there,
While all your cares have flown.

There's nothing in this world of ours
Will truly satisfy,
To give us peace and comfort too,
Our wants to gratify.

Yield to the LORD your hearts with joy.
Your life is filled with Him.
Shout to the LORD your heartfelt love,
And sing a glorious hymn.

Let's sense His closeness to us now,
With words of love employ.
Then we can speak that lovely phrase:
"My soul, awake to joy!"

CM

PRAYER AND PRAISE: What a wonderful thing—to give You thanksgiving and praise for the joy You give! My life is so rich with You and empty without You. Therefore I am pleased, as my soul awakens to Your life in me each day. Amen!

Week 50 ❖ Day 3 Theme: Joy **Dec 11**

SEEKING SUCCESS

HIS WORD: "The joy of the Lord is your strength."
Nehemiah 8:10c

"Yet I will rejoice in the Lord, I will be joyful in God my Savior."
Habakkuk 3:18

"Be joyful always."
1 Thessalonians 5:16

MY CHALLENGE: *To be joyful in all I do, at all times, for everything.*

If success is what you're seeking,
You're chasing it non-stop,
And looking down upon others,
That you can be on top.

There is a problem straight ahead.
You may not be aware.
A crash is coming to your life,
To alter your affairs.

However, it need not happen.
There's one thing you can do,
To help save yourself and loved ones
And to yourself be true.

There is a secret some have learned
In life as their format:
No matter what stage of your life,
"Be happy where you're at!"

Take joy in all your possessions,
Be that little as it may.
It matters not what others think.
They'll think it anyway.

Be joyful always for all things.
All times freely confess:
It's only Jesus Who matters.
Then you will have success.

CM

PRAYER AND PRAISE: *Lord, I confess that I do have problems, and I know that there are more down the road. But I take You at Your Word and am determined to be joyful in all I do, at all times, for everything, no matter the circumstance. Thank You for being with me all the way. Amen!*

Week 50 ❖ Day 4   Theme: Joy   **Dec 12**

LET US JOY!

HIS WORD: (Jesus speaking to His Father) "I am coming to you now, but I say these things while I am still in the world, so that they may have the full measure of my joy within them. I have given them your word and the world has hated them, for they are not of the world any more than I am of the world."
John 17:13-14

MY CHALLENGE: To accept this full measure of joy that Jesus has promised us.

Let us joy in the assurance,
His perfect love for us,
That we'll always be confident.
In Him we'll fully trust.

Let us joy in Him evermore,
Till we take our last breath.
The law of His Spirit of life
Frees us from sin and death.

Let us joy in the confidence
We always have in Him,
To follow His leading upward,
Singing His Royal Hymn.

Let us joy in His victory,
Our Holy Viceroy.
We will always be His subjects.
Forever let us joy!

CM

PRAYER AND PRAISE: My LORD Jesus, as I come to You, I must admit that so many times I do not feel joy. In fact, I feel quite the opposite. I get burdened down with the concerns of this life, and I struggle to find any joy whatsoever. However, I know Your Word is true, and it is for me today. Therefore I accept the full measure of joy You have promised. As I open up to Your filling, I empty myself of all struggle and strife. I am Yours to do with as You know best. I look to You, filled with Your joy and thanksgiving, for You have answered my prayers again. Thank You, my precious LORD!

Week 50 ✦ Day 5   Theme: Joy   **Dec 13**

JESUS AND HUMOR

HIS WORD: "I tell you the truth, you will weep and mourn while the world rejoices. You will grieve, but your grief will turn to joy. A woman giving birth to a child has pain because her time has come; but when her baby is born she forgets the anguish because of her joy that a child is born into the world. So with you: Now is your time of grief, but I will see you again and you will rejoice, and no one will take away your joy."
John 16:20-22

MY CHALLENGE: *To look forward to that time when life will be all joy with Him for eternity. What a true joy that will be!*

I think of Jesus and His twelve
And their close comradeship.
How they must have had times of joy,
With constant fellowship!

Sometimes Jesus showed His humor.
The disciples did the same,
Threw back their heads and laughed awhile,
While they enjoyed the game.

It balanced out their troubled lives,
In all their Kingdom work,
To bring lost souls to saving grace,
And heal those sick and hurt.

So Jesus oft took them apart,
That they would get their rest,
To relax from all their worldly cares,
To do the very best.

In times like this in privacy
And strength need be restored,
Jesus helped them recuperate,
With humor as His sword.

And so it is with us, My friend.
Don't ever let it fail,
To bring some humor into life
And let your joy prevail.

CM

PRAYER AND PRAISE: *My LORD, I do notice that those who are filled with Your joy also have a wonderful holy humor that makes them a delight to be with. I pray that Your joy within me will create such a thing. Thank You, LORD!*

THERE IS JOY

HIS WORD: "For the kingdom of God is not a matter of eating and drinking, but of righteousness, peace and joy in the Holy Spirit, because anyone who serves Christ in this way is pleasing to God and approved by men."
Romans 14:17-18

MY CHALLENGE: *To serve Christ in the joy of the Holy Spirit, as this is pleasing to God.*

To My Joyful Child:

There is joy in the world today,
If you will comprehend.
The world knows not the joy I have,
To those I call My friend.

You are a friend of Mine, dear child.
You're in My family.
You prayed to Me; I entered in
For all eternity.

This joy of mine I give to you,
Sustains you through your life,
Gives inner strength to carry you,
Regardless of your strife.

My joy came to the world one day,
A Babe in Bethlehem,
But grew to prove He was My Son.
To death He was condemned.

My joy would not allow defeat.
I rose Him from the dead,
Then brought new meaning to My Grace,
To prove we are God-Head.

Our Holy Spirit works within,
Our strength to you deploy,
That you may share with us always,
Our great eternal joy.

Your Joy-Giving Father
CM

PRAYER AND PRAISE: *My praise to You, my Lord and God, for Your great eternal joy. Thank You for helping me to see how important it is to me to have Your joy permeating my life. It's essential for me, and it's a good witness to others. Praise Your Holy Name!*

51

HIS FINAL RETURN

He will return in His perfect time,

To bring about His peace;

He'll give the wicked their fair due,

And give His own release.

HIS FINAL RETURN

HIS WORD: "At that time the sign of the Son of Man will appear in the sky, and all the nations of the earth will mourn. They will see the Son of Man coming on the clouds of the sky, with power and great glory.
And he will send his angels with a loud trumpet call, and they will gather his elect from the four winds, from one end of the heavens to the other."
Matthew 24:30-31

MY CHALLENGE: *To be ready for His final return.*
With eyes fixed on His glory and ears listening for the trumpet call,
I'm to keep on serving Him until it's over and done.

To My Coming King:

Oh, glory, glory, glory, Lord,
We're ready to comply.
As You return to gather us,
We raise Your name on high.

For You have made us ready, Lord,
Receiving You as King.
Fulfill our joy with You, our Lord.
A new world You will bring.

We wait for the descending scene.
Last trumpet has been blown,
As You appear for all to see
And now Your name be known!

We hear Your voice that You have come.
We see Your glorious light.
Now judge the people on the earth.
Divide them left and right.

You take Your throne right here on earth
To rule a thousand years.
What joy is ours to see this sight
And know that we are Yours!

So as we live our life on earth,
And from Your Word we learn,
We, who believe, proclaim Your Name,
Awaiting Your return.

Your Waiting Child
CM

PRAYER AND PRAISE: *Yes, my Lord, I wait in great expectation for Your appearance. In the meantime, I pray to be ready. I pray for my loved ones. I pray for our leaders. I pray for the lost. I pray for the sick. There's so much more to do before Your return.*

Week 51 ❖ Day 1   Theme: His Final Return   Dec 16

FOR ALL THOSE WHO BELIEVE

HIS WORD: "Surely he took up our infirmities and carried our sorrows, yet we considered him stricken by God, smitten by him, and afflicted. But he was pierced for our transgressions, he was crushed for our iniquities; the punishment that brought us peace was upon him, and by his wounds we are healed."
Isaiah 53:4-5

"For the Lamb at the center of the throne will be their shepherd; he will lead them to springs of living water. And God will wipe away every tear from their eyes."
Revelation 7:17

MY CHALLENGE: *To hold on in the present, with my vision for the future. This I can do because Christ has my future in His hands.*

Christ defeated death and disease.
He took them to the grave,
Forever disposing of them.
To us, new life He gave.

Wounded for all our transgressions,
Crushed for iniquities,
He bore the cross that brought us peace.
With His stripes we are healed.

He'll wipe every tear from our eyes,
And death will be no more.
No more pain and suffering decay
On His heavenly shore.

Our life without death and disease
Will soon be ours to live,
When He returns in His glory,
For all those who believe.

CM

PRAYER AND PRAISE: My LORD, even though I know the time will come when there will be no pain and sorrow, the fact remains that I have it right now, and it's very real.
My LORD, I believe, therefore I thank You for touching me now, to bring health, healing and deliverance. I thank You, as I look forward to Your Day of return.
Amen!

Week 51 ❖ Day 2   Theme: His Final Return   Dec 17

OUR LIVING KING

HIS WORD: "The seventh angel sounded his trumpet, and there were loud voices in heaven, which said: 'The kingdom of the world has become the kingdom of our Lord and of his Christ, and he will reign for ever and ever.'"
Revelation 11:15

MY CHALLENGE: *To keep my eye on the coming living King, in great anticipation of His glorious arrival.*

Some people may be millionaires,
With worldly goods galore.
We believe we are billionaires—
All that and so much more.

It matters not our gathering up
Of earth's temporal fare.
The Lord has prepared, for His own,
Riches beyond compare.

On streets of gold and air so pure
And a house of our own,
Built by The Master Carpenter,
To be for us alone.

That beauty we can not describe,
While living here below.
We simply look forward by faith,
To our heavenly chateau.

Be swayed not by earth's enticements.
Keep your eye on the goal.
He has given us His promise
To satisfy our soul.

So now we give our all to Him.
His glories we will sing,
His power within to carry on,
For He's our Living King!

CM

PRAYER AND PRAISE: As I come to You, my Lord, I must admit that I'm not always living my life as though You were coming soon. I confess this, and I repent of it. Thank You for forgiving me—that I can be set free to experience the anticipation of You returning to earth in all Your Glory!
Amen!

Week 51 ❖ Day 3 Theme: His Final Return **Dec 18**

A GLORIOUS LIFE BEGUN

HIS WORD: "And the twenty-four elders, who were seated on their thrones before God, fell on their faces and worshiped God, saying: 'We give thanks to you, Lord God Almighty, the One who is and who was, because you have taken your great power and have begun to reign.'"
Revelation 11:16-17

MY CHALLENGE: *To be ready in this life to live the glorious life to come. Jesus helps me prepare for that time. Therefore I look to Him.*

The time is coming soon enough,
His glory to be known,
As all the world beholds it. Then
He comes to gather own.

He'll make the shout with clarion call.
The trumpet sounds it's blast.
The world looks up to see Him come,
Eternal King at last.

There never was a sight like this
Since all the world began,
The promise that He would return,
Fulfilled by God's own hand.

He'll judge the world and all within
There on the Judgment Seat.
The sheep and goats will stand apart,
As all bow at His feet.

He'll rule the world a thousand years,
As peace He brings to bear.
He rules supreme, as life goes on,
To finish out the years.

Then, as this time comes to the end,
With final battle won,
He brings to us New Heav'n and Earth,
A glorious life begun.

CM

PRAYER AND PRAISE: *I humble myself under Your mighty hand, as I contemplate Your glorious coming. It's beyond anything I can imagine at this time and more glorious than I can picture. So, I pray, my Lord, to be ready for whatever may come my way, that I may be a good and faithful servant of Yours, prepared for Your glorious return.*
Amen!

OUR GLORY STROLL

HIS WORD: "Then I saw a new heaven and a new earth, for the first heaven and the first earth had passed away, and there was no longer any sea.
He will wipe every tear from their eyes. There will be no more death or mourning or crying or pain, for the old order of things has passed away.
He who overcomes will inherit all this,
and I will be his God and he will be my son.
The twelve gates were twelve pearls, each gate made of a single pearl.
The great street of the city was of pure gold, like transparent glass.
The city does not need the sun or the moon to shine on it, for the glory of God gives it light, and the Lamb is its lamp."
Revelation 21:1,4,7,21,23

MY CHALLENGE: *To catch a glimpse of this glory, and then to pass it on to others, in the hope they will also see it.*

On streets of gold, with His great Light,
A glory stroll we'll take.
We'll meet old friends and family.
Eternal friends we'll make.

No aches, no pains, no worry at all,
No earthly cares to fight,
We'll bask in the Light of His Love,
In pure holy delight.

We don't look back, but forward gaze
At Christ's eternal throne,
Praising Him for His Majesty,
His Holy Name intoned.

We know it's the land of Glory.
Our names are on the scroll.
We walk the path of earth, awaiting
To take our Glory stroll.

CM

PRAYER AND PRAISE: *My LORD, it is my prayer many people would catch a glimpse of this glory to come. I pray to be Your helping hand, so that others can see it and be prepared. Thank You, LORD!*

Week 51 ❖ Day 5   Theme: His Final Return   Dec 20

STAND FIRM, KEEP WATCH, BE READY

HIS WORD: "But he who stands firm to the end will be saved. Therefore keep watch, because you do not know on what day your LORD will come. So you also must be ready, because the Son of Man will come at an hour when you do not expect him."
Matthew 24:13,42,44

CHALLENGE: *To do as the Word says: stand firm, keep watch and be ready.*

An admonition is given us.
There's much for us to learn.
Stand firm, keep watch and be ready,
In waiting His return.

He who stands firm unto the end
Will be saved, He has said.
He'll keep us through the great distress,
Not fear what is ahead.

Keep watch because you do not know
What day Your LORD will come.
No one knows the day nor the hour,
Not angels nor the Son.

So you must also be ready,
Faithful and wise servant;
For He shall come in all His Glory,
To bring the Final Judgement.

Believers need not fear at all,
For Christ will cover them.
He'll gather all of them to Him,
As chicks with mother hen.

Now, as we look for Him to come,
We're sure to all agree:
We're to follow His words for us:
Stand firm, keep watch, be ready.

CM

PRAYER AND PRAISE: *As I come to You, I know I need You, because this is so necessary to do. That is—to stand firm, keep watch and be ready. Help me, LORD, to stand firm in my faith, as I walk Your path. Help me keep watch of these times and to be ready for whatever may come to be. Thank You, my LORD!*

Week 51 ❖ Day 6 Theme: His Final Return **Dec 21**

I'M COMING SOON, I'M COMING SOON

HIS WORD: "'Behold, I am coming soon! My reward is with me, and I will give to everyone according to what he has done. I am the Alpha and the Omega, the First and the Last, the Beginning and the End.'
The Spirit and the bride say, 'Come!'
And let him who hears say, 'Come!' Whoever is thirsty, let him come; and whoever wishes, let him take the free gift of the water of life."
Revelation 22:12-13,17

MY CHALLENGE: *To be thirsty, waiting and ready for His soon coming!*

To My Waiting Child:

I'm coming soon. I'm coming soon,
For all the world to see.
It wonders Me. It wonders Me
They listen not to Me.

Listen, my child. Listen, my child.
Listen to what I say.
Hear Me, my child. Hear Me, my child.
Soon coming is the Day.

Stand firm your faith. Stand firm your faith,
For time is running out.
Get ready now. Get ready now.
Get ready for My shout!

I will be heard. I will be heard.
The earth will come to end.
Keep watch for Me. Keep watch for Me.
My glory will descend.

Thank you, my child. Thank you, my child,
For spreading forth the news,
That I AM LORD, that I AM LORD.
There is no time to lose.

I'm waiting for that perfect hour,
When time is opportune.
I'm looking for the world to change,
As I AM coming soon.

Your Soon-Coming LORD

CM

PRAYER AND PRAISE: *To see Your glory tomorrow is beyond description today. But I have the blessed assurance of tomorrow, so I thank You, LORD, this day. I am ready to see Your glory. I am ready to be used of You. Even so, come, LORD Jesus!*

Theme: His Final Return

52

HIS PRESENCE AND PEACE

When we have His Presence in our lives,

His inner Peace will reign;

For you can't separate the two,

When you live in His domain.

HIS PRESENCE AND PEACE

HIS WORD: "The LORD replied,
'My Presence will go with you, and I will give you rest.'"
Exodus 33:14

"Surely you have granted him eternal blessings and made him glad
with the joy of your presence."
Psalm 21:6

MY CHALLENGE: To live in His Presence, with His peace of heart.

To My LORD:

There is peace within my heart
That only You can give;
For You have birthed Your love in me.
Eternal life I live.

One day, so many years ago,
God came to live on earth.
Mary and Joseph, chosen ones,
Jesus came in human birth.

You came into a hostile world.
'Twas full of muck and mire.
God had a plan, a way to cleanse.
You sent the Spirit's fire!

You came to live that You would die
And pay the ransom price,
To shed Your blood as perfect lamb,
Your own life sacrificed.

You have a way of forgiveness,
At times we go astray.
Oh, Jesus, and Your love for us —
You've made for us the way.

Now we wait Your coming again,
When joys shall never cease.
Forever more we'll sing Your praise,
Your Presence and Your peace.

Your Appreciative Child

CM

PRAYER AND PRAISE: Only by Your grace I come into Your Presence.
I praise You for the peace of heart You grant to me. To show my gratitude,
may I fulfill the mission You've called me to. Thank You, Jesus!

Week 52 ❖ Day 1   Theme: His Presence and Peace   Dec 23

REARVIEW MIRROR

HIS WORD: "And there were shepherds living out in the fields nearby, keeping watch over their flocks at night. An angel of the LORD appeared to them, and the glory of the LORD shone around them, and they were terrified. But the angel said to them, 'Do not be afraid. I bring you good news of great joy that will be for all the people.'"
Luke 2:8-10

MY CHALLENGE: To know the LORD speaks peace to my heart. Because He resides in me and comforts me, I need not be terrified. I can simply enjoy His Presence within.

As we look in our rearview mirror,
While living straight ahead,
We see, taking place in ages past,
LORD working in our stead.

He came into this cruel world,
In lowly birth indeed.
The shepherds knew their Savior came.
His star had given lead.

The wisemen came at later time,
Some precious gifts they brought,
Thereby supplying all their needs,
As Egypt's land they sought.

They did return and raised their Son,
Was human and Divine,
Who gave His life and gave it all.
It was by God's design.

So as you learn from past events
And build your faith on them,
You keep your eyes ahead, until
Your Savior comes again.

That day will come just like a thief,
But believers not surprised;
For they have known His coming soon,
Have waited for the prize!

We take our eyes off rearview mirror
And look on down the road.
We see Him coming once again.
All praise to Him explode!

CM

PRAYER AND PRAISE: *I confess that I need to keep my eyes on You, in order to have Your peace in my heart. LORD, melt and mold my heart while I wait in Your Presence. All praise to You!*

Week 52 ❖ Day 2   Theme: His Presence and Peace   Dec 24

IT'S ALL ABOUT JESUS

HIS WORD: "Today in the town of David a Savior has been born to you; he is Christ the Lord. This will be a sign to you: You will find a baby wrapped in cloths lying in a manger. Suddenly a great company of the heavenly host appeared with the angel, praising God and saying, 'Glory to God in the highest, and on earth peace to men on whom his favor rests.'"
Luke 2:11-14

MY CHALLENGE: *To acknowledge the Peace of all peaces, that is, the King of all kings, and celebrate His coming to earth for my sake, and for the sake of all mankind.*

It's all about Jesus, our Savior and King,
From beginning of time to the end,
Left the throneroom of heaven to come to earth.
Began as a Babe in Bethlehem.

Born of virgin Mary, with Joseph by her side.
Shepherds heard angels sing their refrain.
Born in the most humble circumstance of all,
Yet as King of all kings o'er all He'd reign.

Though many years have gone by since He was here,
There's salvation to all who believe.
It's all about Jesus, our Savior and King.
Will you reach out to Him and receive?

They named that baby Jesus, as they were told,
And raised Him for the Lord God above.
They reared Him to manhood as God's only Son,
Gave Him as a sacrifice of love

11 9.11 9

PRAYER AND PRAISE: *I joy in You, my Jesus, for Your Presence on earth changed the course of history as Savior to mankind. I am eternally grateful. I look forward to that time when Your Presence on earth again will again change the course of history and time. Praise Your Holy Name!*

Week 52 ❖ Day 3   Theme: His Presence and Peace   **Dec 25**

JESUS, SAVIOR OF MANKIND

HIS WORD: "They said to the woman, 'We no longer believe just because of what you said; now we have heard for ourselves, and we know that this man really is the Savior of the world.'"
John 4:42

MY CHALLENGE: To know, beyond a shadow of a doubt, that this man Jesus is really the Savior of the world. I know that I know because of the Holy Spirit being a witness to me. Therefore I will stand firm in my faith and commitment to Him.

There are those who would gladly kill
The Christian and the Jew,
To take this world for other gods
That are not real or true.

Their basis is the evil one.
Does nothing but distort.
He lies and kills and robs God's sheep.
His time is running short.

He'll not give up his evil deeds
Until the very last hour.
He leads the blind as captured men,
In looking to devour.

There is no other such as Jesus,
Our Savior, LORD and Guide,
Who wins the victory over all,
When comes the final tide.

We do not fear opposing ones,
Who threaten us with strife;
For He has won it all for us,
With His eternal life.

Their minds cannot conceive the fact
That He's the Mastermind;
For Jesus is our One True God,
The Savior of mankind.

CM

PRAYER AND PRAISE: *Jesus, the honor of serving You is out of this world! There are those who would silence Your believers today, just as in ages past. Therefore I ask for Your protection for all believers, even knowing that You have chosen some to be martyrs. Thank You, LORD!*

Week 52 ❖ Day 4   Theme: His Presence and Peace   **Dec 26**

HE'S BEEN THERE ALL THE TIME

HIS WORD: "To him who is able to keep you from falling and to present you before his glorious presence without fault and with great joy—to the only God our Savior be glory, majesty, power and authority, through Jesus Christ our Lord."
Jude 1:24-25

MY CHALLENGE: To bask in His glorious Presence, knowing that He is always with me and in me and will always be there for me.

You love the Lord with all your heart;
You've told Him o'er and o'er.
You've reached out in that mighty Name,
As many times before.

You've shared His Word with many folk
And spent much time in prayer.
You've praised His Name in word and song,
Received His mighty care.

Sometimes there's a quietness
In your relationship.
You haven't conversed as one on one,
In your close fellowship.

You know that God is still above,
His Presence everywhere.
He hasn't moved from where He's been.
He's waiting for you there.

You make your turn and rush to Him,
Forsaking all alarms.
You feel the warmth of His embrace,
Inside His waiting arms.

You've learned your lesson once again,
As oft in your lifetime.
Received His blessed assurance:
He's been there all the time.

CM

PRAYER AND PRAISE: I thank You, Lord, for the assurance that You are always present and waiting to hear from me. Therefore, I come to You, confessing to You again my shortcomings and broken promises. Thank You for forgiving me and giving me another chance. You certainly are the God of second chances! Thank You, Lord!

Week 52 ❖ Day 5   Theme: His Presence and Peace   Dec 27

LET MY SPIRIT SOAR

HIS WORD: "For God did not give us a spirit of timidity, but a spirit of power, of love and of self-discipline."
2 Timothy 1:7

MY CHALLENGE: To accept the truth of this scripture, that when God gave me the gift of His Holy Spirit, it was a spiritual gift of power, love and self-discipline. AND He gave it to me to use, not to hide.

Rest my body and still my mind.
Then let my spirit soar,
As I spend time alone with Him
And praise Him o'er and o'er.

It matters not what others think.
Give my all to Him alone.
Then let His Spirit take control,
To make His love be known.

Then, as my spirit soars to Him,
He makes it crystal clear
That He alone has captured me,
To feel His Presence near.

There is no other here on earth,
Nor in heaven above
Who will redeem the time we've lost,
Because of His great love.

That's why we must give praise to Him
And make our voice be heard,
That Jesus Christ is LORD o'er all.
He is God's Holy Word!

Oh, how I give my thanks to Him,
And will forevermore.
Until I see Him face to face,
I'll let my spirit soar.

CM

PRAYER AND PRAISE: My God, I confess, that I couldn't do any kind of ministry in Your Name without Your power. It is so essential. Therefore I give You thanks and honor for it now. I continue to pray that You would continue to keep me full of Your power and love and, yes, even self-discipline. Amen!

Week 52 ❖ Day 6   Theme: His Presence and Peace   **Dec 28**

MY INFUSING PEACE

HIS WORD: "You will keep in perfect peace him whose mind is steadfast, because he trusts in you."
Isaiah 26:3

MY CHALLENGE: *To keep my mind focused on Him, knowing that by my doing so, He will grant me perfect peace.*

To My Beloved Child:

Let the peace of My Presence infuse you now.
My peace to you I love to impart.
That peace of Mine beyond your understanding
Is always ready to calm your heart.

Open up your heart and receive My blessings.
I pour them out for you to receive.
My blessings to you of My Presence and Peace,
Oh, My child, if you'll only believe.

The world cannot fathom My wonderful peace,
That's ready and waiting for My own.
As you receive and are completely fulfilled,
May you share My Word and make Me known.

Rest quietly in the peace of My Presence.
Thereby all problems to Me release.
There is nothing greater I can do for you.
To You, My child, I infuse My Peace!

Your Loving Dad
11 9.11 9

PRAYER AND PRAISE: Yes, my LORD, that's what I pray for—to rest quietly in the peace of Your Presence, by releasing all my problems to You. Thank You for taking my burdens and setting me free.

Week 52 ❖ Day 7 Theme: His Presence and Peace   **Dec 29**

IN RHYTHM WITH ETERNITY

HIS WORD: "The Lord reigns, he is robed in majesty;
the Lord is robed in majesty and is armed with strength.
The world is firmly established; it cannot be moved.
Your throne was established long ago;
you are from all eternity."
Psalm 93:1-2

"He has made everything beautiful in its time.
He has also set eternity in the hearts of men;
yet they cannot fathom what God has done from beginning to end."
Ecclesiastes 3:11

MY CHALLENGE: *To be in rhythm with my heavenly, eternal Father,
for He has given me life—for eternity!
I accept it by faith, for it is beyond my comprehension.*

In rhythm with eternity,
My Savior walks along with me,
Holding my hand.
I understand
His way is best for destiny.

My Father in glory above,
Through Your eyes of passionate love,
You guide my way
Above the fray,
Giving me Your heavenly Dove.

As I worship Your Reverence,
I receive Your Holy Presence,
Working in me,
Growing to be,
A sample of Your excellence.

Although I cannot comprehend
Fully Your way, calling me friend,
I hear Your voice,
I've made the choice,
In rhythm with eternity.

88.448

PRAYER AND PRAISE: *Although I can't fully comprehend the concept of eternity, I receive Your eternal life by faith. I thank You, Lord, for this greatest of gifts.*

A NEW YEAR LOOMS AHEAD

HIS WORD: "You were taught, with regard to your former way of life, to put off your old self, which is being corrupted by its deceitful desires; to be made new in the attitude of your minds; and to put on the new self, created to be like God in true righteousness and holiness."
Ephesians 4:22-24

MY CHALLENGE: To prepare myself in body, mind and spirit, for the new year to come.

As the old year comes to an end,
The new one looms ahead.
Is our future holding some hope?
Or is it one we dread?

Have we some plans to carry out,
Some goals that can be met?
Or are we simply walking blind,
With no direction set?

God has called us to follow Him.
Let's learn of all His ways.
We're His child and called to serve Him
And give Him all the praise.

For Jesus has a plan for us,
But we must seek it out.
Therefore we must spend time in prayer.
That's what it's all about.

As we enter the coming new year,
Let's cast our cares aside.
Lean on Him, for He cares for us.
Let's follow at His side.

If things are to change in our lives,
There's one thing we must do.
That first thing is to change ourselves.
Let Christ make all things new.

That means to cast the dross aside.
Let Him create anew.
For He'll show us the steps to take
And what we are to do.

Then, as we follow after Him,
And with His Word we're fed,
We need not fear what is facing us,
As new year looms ahead.

CM

PRAYER AND PRAISE: And now, my LORD, let my one new year's resolution be to become more like You in this coming year. I am determined. By Your help, I will.
Amen! Amen! And Amen!

TIME ALONE
Postlude

To My Beloved Child:

    And now, My child, as you walk on
    Each day to honor Me,
    Spend time alone with Me each day,
    Your first priority.

    Look not at the hands of the clock,
    To limit us in our time;
    But look to Me, your One True God.
    Let's keep an open line.

    This book will not say good-bye,
    As we may part our ways;
    For it is the goal of these words,
    To daily give Me praise.

    I thank you now for times of worth,
    And for our comradeship.
    As we alone together spent
    Our time in fellowship.

    With this book, a "so-long" for now,
    But trust you will return.
    Now keep on talking with Me, child.
    You are of My concern.

    As you have made your way each day
    Through messages compiled,
    It's purpose is for you to know
    You're My beloved child!

                      Your Loving Heavenly Dad

THEMES, ALPHABETICAL INDEX

THEME	WK	DATE
Be Still/Quietness	3	Jan 15-Jan 21
Beginning a New Journey	1	Jan 1-Jan 7
Call, His	32	Aug 5-Aug 11
Comfort	36	Sep 2-Sep 8
Contentment	43	Oct 21-Oct 27
Eternity	52+	Dec 30-Dec 31
Faith	5	Jan 29-Feb 4
Fear Not	20	May 13-May 19
Follow Him	9	Feb 26-Mar 3
Forgive/Pardon	26	Jun 24-Jun 30
Friend	37	Sep 9-Sep 15
Gathering	34	Aug 19-Aug 25
Giving	24	Jun 10-Jun 16
Grace	8	Feb 19-Feb 25
Healing/Miracles	23	Jun 3-Jun 9
Heaven Bound	19	May 6-May 12
Heaven Ahead	40	Sep 30-Oct 6
Help from the LORD	22	May 27-Jun 2
Hope	6	Feb 5-Feb 11
Jesus	45	Nov 4-Nov 10
Jesus, Our	28	Jul 8-Jul 16
Journey	1	Jan 1-Jan 7
Joy	50	Dec 9-Dec 14
Light, His	49	Dec 2-Dec 8
Love	7	Feb 12-Feb 18
Love, In His	38	Sep 16-Sep 22
Need	12	Mar-18 Mar 24
Plan, His	11	Mar 11-Mar 17
Peace, His	10	Mar 4-Mar 10
Praise	44	Oct 28-Nov 3
Prayer	15	Apr 7-Apr 14
Presence and Peace, His	52	Dec 23-Dec 29
Presence, His	16	Apr 14-Apr 21
Release	30	Jul 22-Jul 28
Renewal	41	Oct 7-Oct 13
Rest, His	35	Aug 26-Sept 1
Resurrection, Gratitude for	14	Apr 1-Apr 7
Return, His Final	51	Dec 15-Dec 22
Righteousness	18	Apr 28-May 5
Salvation	39	Sep 23-Sep 29
Serve	13	Mar 25-Mar 31
Submission	17	Apr 22-Apr 28
Thanks	48	Nov 25-Dec 1
Thanksgiving	33	Aug 12-Aug 18
Trust	47	Nov 18-Nov 24
Victory, He Is My	25	Jun 17-Jun 23
Victory	46	Nov 11-Nov 17
Voice, His	4	Jan 22-Jan 28
Voice, His Clear	27	Jul 1-Jul 7
Voice, Listen to His	21	May 20-May 26
Walk with Him	2	Jan 8-Jan 14
Will, His	29	Jul 15-Jul 21
Witness	31	Jul 29-Aug 4
Word, His	42	Oct 14-Oct 20

TITLE INDEX

TITLE	DATE
A Communication of Comfort	Sep 3
A Daily Journey with Jesus	Jan 1
A Dance of Victory	Oct 5
A Good Helpmate	Mar 29
A Field of Love	Sep 17
A Glorious Life Begun	Dec 19
A Home Prepared	May 12
A Jesus Impression	Jul 12
A Life of Righteousness	May 5
A Life of Victory	Jun 18
A Living Sacrifice	Jun 10
A Message for the World	Aug 3
A New Beginning	Jan 2
A New Year Looms Ahead	Dec 31
A Peace of Praise	Nov 3
A Time of Praise	Nov 1
A Touch of Healing	Jun 6
A Training Ground	Jan 4
An Inner Peace	Mar 7
Answer My Call	Aug 11
Answered Prayer	Apr 13
Are You Ready	Aug 24
As Ambassadors	Jul 31
As Your Extended Hands	Jul 29
Attitude of Prayer	Apr 9
Awaiting that Day	Jan 3
Bask in My Beauty	Jul 21
Be a Witness	Jul 30
Be Content in Life	Oct 27
Be Content with What You Have	Oct 26
Be Open to God	Jul 19
Be Still	Jan 15
Be What God Called You to Be	Jan 31
Beautiful Day of Thanks	Aug 12
Believers Delight	May 7
By Faith in His Name	Jun 7
By My Grace	Feb 25
Check in Your Spirit	Jul 6
Closet of Prayer	Apr 8
Come, Follow Me	Mar 3
Commanded to Love	Feb 14
Commune for Victory	Nov 16
Completeness in His Rest	Aug 30
Constant Companion	Jan 14

TITLE	DATE
Dare to Be	Mar 27
Delayed Answer	Nov 12
Delight Ourselves in Him	Sep 14
Desire to Rest in Him	Aug 27
Dialogue with Him	Jul 20
Do Not Fear	May 14
Don't Believe the Devil	Oct 16
Draw Near to Me	Aug 18
Empowered by Him	Jun 3
Enjoy the Victory	Jun 23
Enter His Rest	Aug 29
Exalt My Word	Apr 14
Exalted Prayer	Apr 12
Face to Face	May 8
Faucet of Thanksgiving	Aug 15
Fear Not	May 13
Fear of the LORD	May 17
Fill Us as We Go	Mar 26
Focus on His Presence	Dec 7
Focusing on the Future	Aug 23
Follow after Him	Feb 29
Follow His Lead	Feb 27
Follow You Implicitly	Feb 26
For All Those Who Believe	Dec 17
Forgive	Jun 30
Forgiven Eternally	Jun 25
Forgiveness to Perfection	Jun 29
Founding Fathers, USA	Jul 4
Four "C"'s to Christ	Sep 28
Fourth Watch of the Night	May 22
From Defeat to Victory, Part 1	Nov 14
From Defeat to Victory, Part 2	Nov 15
Fulfill Your Plan	Mar 11
Garden of My Heart	Jul 3
Gather His Elect	Aug 20
Gather the Wheat	Aug 22
Gift of Contentment	Oct 25
Gift of Perfect Peace	Mar 10
Give All You Can	Jun 13
Give Him Thanks	Nov 28
Give Him Thanks for All	Aug 17
Give Thanks for Everything	Aug 14
Give Thanks, The Way to Go	Aug 13

TITLE	DATE	TITLE	DATE
Give You Honor Due	Jan 18	His Plan, Part #2	Mar 13
Giving Him Praises Today	Jun 15	His Plan, Part #3	Mar 14
Giving in His Will	Jun 14	His Presence and His Peace	Dec 23
Giving Is a Way of Life	Jun 11	His Quiet Rest	Aug 28
God's Love	Feb 18	His Sovereignty	Jul 18
God's Pure Joy	Dec 10	His Unfailing Love	Sep 25
Graduation into Glory	Oct 4	His Unmerited Grace	Feb 21
Gratitude and Thanks	Nov 29	His Voice Comes	
Gratitude for Resurrection	Apr 5	Breaking Through	Jan 25
		His Will for You	Jul 17
Hail, Your Majesty	Oct 18	Holding His Hand	Feb 4
Hallelujah, I'm Alive	Oct 2	Hope in His Unfailing Love	Feb 7
Having All that You Need	Oct 24	Hope that is Overflowing	Feb 6
He Calls on Us	Aug 7	Hope Is an Anchor	Feb 9
He Gives His Peace	Mar 9	Hope of Heaven	Oct 1
He Has Set Me Free	Jun 28		
He Is Risen	Apr 6	I Abide in Your Peace	Mar 4
Hear His Call	May 23	I Am All Yours Today	Nov 24
Hear His Loving Voice	Jan 26	I Am Ready	Feb 28
Help Me, My LORD, Part #1	May 28	I Am Your God	Apr 28
Help Me, My LORD, Part #2	May 29	I Am Your Hope	May 19
Help Me, Holy Spirit	May 27	I Bask in Your Presence	Apr 15
Help Me to Listen	May 20	I Exalt You	Nov 30
Helping Hands	Jun 12	I Follow Only You	Sep 23
Hear His Gentle Voice	Jan 23	I Have Longed to Gather	Aug 25
Hear His Voice	Jan 22	I Hold Your Hand	Nov 21
Hear My Voice	Jan 28	I Humble Myself	Oct 7
Hear the Voice of God	Jul 5	I Love You, LORD Jesus	Dec 9
He's Been there All the Time	Dec 27	I Make Your Life Anew	Jun 9
His Awesome Grace	Feb 23	I Offer My Devotion	Jan 16
His Awesome Presence	Apr 19	I Owe My Life to You	Sep 18
His Call	Aug 8	I Seek Your Voice	Jul 1
His Clarion Call	Aug 6	I Sing Your Song	Feb 15
His Final Return	Dec 16	I Surrender My All	Apr 23
His Forgiveness Forever	Jun 27	I Thank You, LORD	Nov 25
His Freedom Light	Dec 4	I Want to Live	Sep 13
His Gentle Voice	Jul 2	I Will Gather You	Aug 19
His Glorious Grace	Feb 24	I Will Supply Need	Mar 24
His Guiding Light	Dec 2	I Would Follow	Mar 2
His Golden Light	Dec 5	I'll Call You Home	Oct 6
His Mighty Mercy	Jan 19	I'm Coming Soon, I'm Coming	Dec 22
His Name Is Jesus	Jul 13	In Footsteps of His Grace	Feb 20
His Native Tongue Is Love	Feb 16	In Him We Live and Move	May 18
His Open Door	Jul 16	In Him Put Your Trust	Nov 20
His Path of Trust	Nov 18	In Humble Service	Jan 17
His Peace Is Contentment	Oct 23	In Light of Your Love	Sep 20
His Peaceful Presence	Sep 6	In My Closet of Prayer	Oct 10
His Perfect Love	Feb 13	In My Prayer Time, O LORD	Apr 27
His Perfect Way	Jan 20	In Rhythm with Eternity	Dec 30
His Plan, Part #1	Mar 12	In the Light of His Presence	Dec 6

TITLE	DATE	TITLE	DATE
In Your Quest	Dec 8	My Hope Is in You	Feb 5
Inhabits Our Praise	Oct 31	My Infusing Peace	Dec 29
It's All about Jesus	Dec 25	My Lord	Mar 25
		My Neediness	Mar 18
Jesus	Nov 4	My Presence	Apr 21
Jesus and Humor	Dec 14	My Precious Jesus	Apr 26
Jesus Fills Our Need	Mar 22	My Secret Solitude	Apr 11
Jesus, Help Me	Jun 1	My Soul, Awake to Joy	Dec 11
Jesus Is His Name	Nov 8	My Weakness, I Rejoice	Jan 5
Jesus Is My Friend	Sep 12	My Word for You	Oct 20
Jesus, Jesus, Jesus	Aug 26		
Jesus, My Friend, I Confess	Sep 10	Need	Mar 20
Jesus, Our Victory	Jun 20	Need a Miracle	Jun 5
Jesus, Savior of Mankind	Dec 26	No Greater Love	Sep 21
Jesus, the Great "I AM"	Jun 4	No One Can Take His Place	July 9
Jesus, the Word of God	Oct 19		
		On Stepping Stones of Faith	Feb 3
Keep Jesus on Your Throne	Oct 11	On the Road to Damascus	Jul 7
Keep Me Focused	Nov 23	Our Beautiful Robe	Apr 30
Knocking on Your Heart	Nov 10	Our Blessed Cornerstone	Sep 30
		Our Blessed Hope	Jul 11
Lay It All at His Feet	Apr 25	Our Circle of Life	Aug 2
Learning to Release	Jul 26	Our Driving Force	Oct 9
Let His Peace Rule	Mar 6	Our First Resort	Jan 9
Let My Love Take Hold	Sep 22	Our Glory Stroll	Dec 20
Let My Spirit Soar	Dec 28	Our Holy Anthem	Jul 10
Let Not Your Heart Be Troubled	Mar 1	Our Living King	Dec 18
Let Us Joy	Dec 13	Our Praise to You Alone	Oct 29
Life, a Love Song	Sep 16	Our Precious Cornerstone	Nov 9
Light Pierces Darkness	Dec 3	Our Shepherd-King	Jul 8
Listen	May 25	Overflowing Love	Sep 19
Listen for Discernment	Jan 21		
Listen for the Prompting	May 21	Patiently We Wait	May 11
Listen to His Voice	May 24	Peace and Contentment	Mar 5
Live Free in Him	Jun 26	Peace in His Light	Mar 8
Live in Simplicity	Jan 7	Peace in His Presence	Apr 17
Love Our Mates	Aug 9	Please Your Heart	Apr 4
		Praise of Psalm 150	Oct 28
Made Perfect Forever	May 3	Praise, Pathway to Peace	Oct 30
Marching to His Call	Aug 5	Praise You, Praise You	Nov 2
More Than Enough	Apr 3	Private Devotional Time	Oct 12
My Banner Unfurled	Aug 4	Psalm 119:33-40	Oct 15
My Best Friend	Sep 15	Purifying Hope	Feb 10
My Best Plans	Mar 16	Put Your Hope in Me	Feb 11
My Blessed Rest	Sep 1	Rear View Mirror	Dec 24
My Comfort in Perfect Time	Sep 8	Refill Your Tank	Oct 13
My Comforting Words	Sep 4	Release from Fear	Jul 27
My Great Plan	Mar 17	Release It All Today	Jul 22
My Help Comes from the Lord	May 30	Release Your Past	Jul 28

TITLE	DATE	TITLE	DATE
Releasing Anxiety	Jul 23	The Only Way Is You	May 31
Rest Content	Oct 22	The Open Door	Jul 16
Resurrection Power	Apr 7	The Road of His Love	Feb 17
Righteousness	May 4	The Sacrifice of Gratitude	Apr 2
Robe of Righteousness	Apr 29	The Time to Reconnect	Oct 8
Rhythm of Life	Oct 21	The Two-Sided Coin	Jul 24
		There Is Joy	Dec 15
Salvation	Feb 2	Tough Faith	Jan 29
Salvation to My Child	Sep 29	To Him All Things Release	Jul 25
Saved by Grace	Sep 26	To My LORD	Jun 24
Seeds from Solomon	Jan 6	To Walk In Victory	Jun 17
Seeking Success	Dec 12	True Grace of God	Feb 19
Serve Me	Mar 31	Turn Problems into Peace	Jun 2
Sojourners in the Faith	Sep 27		
Serving as a Friend	Sep 11	Until Our Sabbath-Rest	Aug 31
Serving Him	Mar 30		
Shield of Faith	Feb 1	Victory	Nov 17
Shouting Victory	May 6	Victory Over All	Jun 22
Someone Wonderful	Nov 6	Victory Over Satan	Nov 13
Some Things	Jan 30		
Song of Life	Nov 7	Waiting for His Nod	May 10
Stand Firm, Keep Watch,	Dec 21	Walk His Way	Nov 22
Steadfast in Our Faith	Mar 28	Walk in His Light	Jan 10
Stormin' Heaven	May 26	Walk in Your Love	Feb 12
Streets of Purest Gold	May 9	Walk in Victory	Jun 19
Supplies My Every Need	Mar 19	Walk with Him	Jan 8
Surrender	Apr 24	Walk Your Way	Jan 11
Surrender to Serve	Jul 15	Walking All Alone	Nov 11
		Walking the Road of Life	Jan 13
Take It to Jesus	Mar 23	We Bow to You	Apr 22
Tell the Whole World	Aug 1	We Wait in Hope	Feb 8
Thank Him	Nov 26	Wear His Righteous Robe	May 2
Thank You, My Child	Dec 1	We're Royal Family	May 1
Thanks for Liberty	Nov 27	When God Is Silent	Oct 17
Thanks for My Salvation	Sep 24	With Him as One	Jan 12
Thanksgiving, Language of Love	Aug 16	Words of Comfort and Hope	Sep 5
Thanksgiving Praise	Aug 18		
That Loving, Gentle Voice	Jan 27	You Alone	Nov 5
That's What It's All About	Nov 19	You Are Unique	Jan 24
The Art of Giving	Jun 16	Your Comfort in Service	Sep 7
The Final Call	Aug 10	Your Extended Hand	Sep 9
The Gathering Day Warning	Aug 21	Your Holy Presence	Apr 16
The Gift of Life	Feb 22	Your Place of Prayer	Apr 10
The Greater the Victory	Jun 21	Your Presence	Apr 20
The Greatest Miracles	Jun 8	Your Resurrection Power	Apr 1
The Ladder of the LORD	Oct 3	Your Walk Alone, #1	May 15
The LORD Is in this Place	Jul 14	Your Walk Alone, #2	May 16
The Marvelous Plan of God	Mar 15	Your Word to Me	Oct 14
The Mystery of God	Apr 18	You're My Comfort	Sep 2
The Need of a Savior	Mar 21		

SCRIPTURE INDEX
Old Testament

Reference	Date	Reference	Date	Reference	Date
Gen 4:7	Oct 11	Psalm 60:12	Nov 14	Prov 21:31	Jun 21
Gen 28:16-17	Jul 14	Psalm 77:14	Jun 5	Prov 22:11	Sep 12
Gen 41:37-40	Mar 15	Psalm 86:15-17	Sep 7	Eccl 2:26, 3:11	Jan 6
Exo 33:14	Dec 23	Psalm 89:15	Jan 8	Eccl 3:11	Dec 30
Deut 30:19b-20a	Jan 22	Psalm 89:15	Apr 18	Song of Songs 6:8-9	Jan 24
1 Sam 29:12-14a	Apr 27	Psalm 89:15	Jun 23	Isaiah 2:5	Jan 10
1 Kings 19:12-13	May 25	Psalm 89:15	Dec 7	Isaiah 6:8	Mar 11
1 Chron 28:9	Jan 16	Psalm 93:1-2	Dec 30	Isaiah 9:6	Nov 6
Ezra 3:11	Nov 2	Psalm 95:1-2	Nov 1	Isaiah 12:2	Nov 7
Ezra 3:11	Aug 15	Psalm 95:1-3	Aug 12	Isaiah 12:2-3	Sep 29
Nehemiah 8:10c	Dec 12	Psalm 95:1-3	Sep 24	Isaiah 24:14-16	Apr 12
Job 22:21	Apr 22	Psalm 95:6-8	Jan 26	Isaiah 25:1	Nov 30
Job 42:1-2	Mar 16	Psalm 99:5,9	Apr 14	Isaiah 26:3	Dec 29
Psalm 16:11	Apr 21	Psalm 95:6-7	Oct 21	Isaiah 40:1	Sep 5
Psalm 18:6	May 31	Psalm 100	Oct 31	Isaiah 40:31	Feb 11
Psalm 18:30-32	Jan 20	Psalm 100	Dec 10	Isaiah 40:31	Apr 27
Psalm 18:35	Jun 22	Psalm 103:2-4	Jun 24	Isaiah 40:31	May 15
Psalm 21:6	Dec 23	Psalm 107:43	Feb 16	Isaiah 41:10	Jul 27
Psalm 21:6-7	Apr 19	Psalm 108:13	Nov 15	Isaiah 41:10,13	May 14
Psalm 22:3	Oct 31	Psalm 111:10	Feb 29	Isaiah 41:13-14	Jun 2
Psalm 23	Sep 6	Psalm 118:6	May 28	Isaiah 42:8-12	Oct 29
Psalm 25:3-5, 21	Feb 5	Psalm 118:7	May 29	Isaiah 43:2-3a	May 16
Psalm 25:15	Jul 28	Psalm 118:14	Nov 7	Isaiah 43:1	May 13
Psalm 27:1	Jul 18	Psalm 118:14-15	Jun 20	Isaiah 43:4-7	Aug 19
Psalm 29:11	Mar 9	Psalm 118:28-29	Aug 16	Isaiah 53:4-5	Dec 17
Psalm 31:14-16,21	Sep 25	Psalm 119:33-36	Feb 27	Isaiah 61:1-2	Jul 25
Psalm 33:1-3	Feb 15	Psalm 119:33-40	Oct 15	Isaiah 61:10	Apr 29
Psalm 33:12a	Jul 4	Psalm 119:105	Dec 2	Jer 6:16	Aug 27
Psalm 33:18-22	Feb 7	Psalm 121:1,2	May 30	Jer 29:11a	Mar 12
Psalm 34:1-2	Nov 3	Psalm 139:8-10	Feb 4	Jer 29:11b	Mar 13
Psalm 34:14	Mar 5	Psalm 150	Oct 28	Jer 29:11c	Mar 14
Psalm 37:3-4	Nov 21	Prov 2:7-8	Jun 23	Jer 29:12-14a	Apr 27
Psalm 37:3-6	Sep 14	Prov 2:7-8	Nov 11	Jer 30:8-9	Jul 24
Psalm 40:1-4a	Oct 17	Prov 3:5-6	Nov 18	Jer 31:11-13	Sep 8
Psalm 41:12	Apr 16	Prov 16:9	Mar 17	Habakkuk 3:18	Dec 12
Psalm 44:6-8	Jun 18	Prov 18:24	Jul 9	Zeph 3:12	Nov 24
Psalm 46:10	Jan 15	Prov 18:24	Sep 12	Zeph 3:17	Jul 10
Psalm 56:3-4	Nov 22	Prov 19:23	Oct 22	Zeph 3:19-20	Dec 1

SCRIPTURE in Biblical Order
New Testament

Reference	Date	Reference	Date	Reference	Date
Mat 1:21	Nov 4	Luke 8:38-39	Jul 12	John 20:13-16	Jul 3
Mat 3:17	Sep 21	Luke 9:23	Jan 1	John 20:31	Nov 4
Mat 5:9	May 4	Luke 9:57	Jan 13	John 21:5-6	Sep 13
Mat 5:48	Jun 29	Luke 11:4ab	Jun 26	Acts 1:4-5,8	Jun 3
Mat 6:6	Apr 8	Luke 12:29-31	Mar 24	Acts 1:8	Jul 30
Mat 6:5-6	Oct 10	Luke 12:35-36	Mar 31	Acts 2:1-4	Oct 9
Mat 6:7-8	Mar 23	Luke 12:35-38	Feb 28	Acts 3:16	Jun 7
Mat 6:31-32	Mar 20	Luke 13:34-35	Aug 25	Acts 4:8-10	Oct 20
Mat. 6:31-34	Jul 17	Luke 16:13	Mar 27	Acts 4:12	Sep 29
Mat. 7:13-14	Jan 11	Luke 17:15-16	Apr 25	Acts 5:41-42	Aug 4
Mat 10:26-27	Aug 1	Luke 24:6-8	Apr 6	Acts 7:30-32	Jul 5
Mat 11:28-29	Aug 26	Luke 24:30-31	Nov 16	Acts 16:13	Apr 10
Mat 11:29	Jan 27	John 1:1-5	Oct 18	Acts 17:27-28	May 18
Mat 13:30	Aug 22	John 1:51	Oct 3	Acts 20:34-35	Jun 16
Mat 13:40-43	Aug 22	John 3:16-17	Feb 18	Acts 22:9,14	Jul 7
Mat 14:25-27	May 22	John 4:42	Dec 26	Acts 22:14-16	Jul 29
Mat 15:25-28	Jun 1	John 6:38-39	Jul 15	Acts 26:22-23	Jan 9
Mat 17:5	Jul 1	John 8:12	Dec 6	Acts 27:23-24	Mar 28
Mat 20:25-28	Mar 25	John 8:36	Jun 28	Rom 1:17	Jan 29
Mat 22:37-39	Feb 12	John 9:5	Dec 6	Rom 6:22	Jun 28
Mat 23:12	Oct 7	John 10:2-3	Jan 23	Rom 7:4-6	Mar 26
Mat 24:13,42,44	Dec 21	John 10:3-4	May 21	Rom 8:6	Mar 4
Mat 24:30-31	Aug 20	John 10:3-4	Jul 2	Rom 8:23-25	Feb 8
Mat 24:30-31	Dec 16	John 10:4	Jan 27	Rom 10:9-10	Feb 2
Mat 24:42-44	Aug 24	John 10:14-16	Jan 25	Rom 12:1-2	Jun 10
Mat 28:5-7	Apr 7	John 10:27-30	May 24	Rom 14:17-18	Dec 15
Mat 28:18-19	Aug 2	John 10:37-38	Jun 8	Rom 15:5-6	Mar 2
Mat 28:19-20	Aug 3	John 11:24-26	Jun 4	Rom 15:13	Feb 6
Mark 1:16-18	Mar 3	John 11:25-26	Apr 5	Rom 15:13	Mar 5
Mark 1:16-18	Aug 8	John 12:25-26	Sep 23	Rom 15:13	May 19
Mark 1:35	Oct 8	John 12:35-36a	Dec 5	Rom 15:13	Nov 23
Mark 5:27-29	Jun 6	John 12:36a	Nov 19	Rom 15:17	Mar 30
Mark 8:34-35	Mar 31	John 12:44-46	Dec 8	1 Cor 4:5	Dec 3
Mark 13:26-27	Aug 23	John 14:1	Mar 1	1 Cor 9:24-25	Jan 4
Mark 14:60-61a	Nov 12	John 14:2-3	May 12	1 Cor 13:12	May 8
Mark 16:15-16	Aug 5	John 14:1	Nov 20	1 Cor 15:56-57	Nov 13
Mark 16:15-16	Sep 27	John 14:11	Jun 5	1 Cor 15:57	Jun 19
Luke 1:78-79	Mar 8	John 14:27	Mar 9	1 Cor 15:58	Jun 14
Luke 2:8-10	Dec 24	John 15:9-13	Dec 9	2 Cor 1:3-4	Sep 2
Luke 2:11-14	Dec 25	John 15:10-12	Feb 14	2 Cor 1:5-6	Sep 3
Luke 2:14	Mar 8	John 15:12-13	Sep 9	2 Cor 1:7	Sep 4
Luke 4:18-19	Jul 26	John 15:13-14	Sep 21	2 Cor 5:9	Apr 4
Luke 4:42	Apr 11	John 15:14	Sep 10	2 Cor 5:20a	Jul 31
Luke 5:20	Jul 9	John 15:15	Sep 11	2 Cor 4:13-14	Apr 20
Luke 6:37	Jun 26	John 15:15	Sep 22	2 Cor 5:1-5	Oct 6
Luke 6:37	Jul 22	John 15:16	Aug 11	2 Cor 6:1-2	Sep 28
Luke 6:38	Jun 13	John 16:20-22	Dec 14	2 Cor 6:16	Jan 14
Luke 6:45	Sep 19	John 17:13-14	Dec 13	2 Cor 9:8	Oct 24
Luke 6:47-48	Nov 8	John 17:20-23	Jan 12	2 Cor 9:6-7	Jun 11

Reference	Date	Reference	Date	Reference	Date
2 Cor 9:10-11	Mar 19	1 Thes. 5:4-5	Dec 3	1 Peter 5:6-7	Oct 7
2 Cor 9:13-15	Feb 22	1 Thes. 5:14-15	Jun 12	1 Peter 5:10	Mar 28
2 Cor 9:15	Nov 27	1 Thes. 5:16	Dec 12	1 Peter 5:10-11	Aug 10
2 Cor. 12:9	Apr 23	1 Thes. 5:16-18	Jun 9	1 Peter 5:10-12	Feb 19
2 Cor. 12:9-10	Jan 5	1 Thes. 5:18	Aug 17	2 Peter 1:10-11	Aug 7
2 Cor. 13:11bc	Mar 4	1 Thes. 5:18	Nov 26	2 Peter 1:3-4	Mar 18
Gal. 3:26-27	Apr 30	2 Thes. 1:11-12	May 23	1 John 1:7	Jan 10
Gal. 5:1	Dec 4	2 Thes. 2:1-2	Aug 21	1 John 2:1-2	Oct 11
Gal. 5:25	Jul 6	1 Tim. 4:4-5	Aug 18	1 John 2:5-6	Feb 17
Eph. 1:2, 13-14	Feb 24	1 Tim. 6:6-10	Oct 25	1 John 2:12	Jun 25
Eph. 1:7-8	Jun 27	1 Tim. 6:13-16	Jan 18	1 John 3:2-3	Feb 10
Eph. 2:8-9	Feb 25	2 Tim. 1:7	Dec 28	1 John 3:19-20	Apr 15
Eph. 2:8-10	Sep 26	2 Tim. 1:14	May 27	1 John 4:7-11	Sep 18
Eph. 2:14-18	Mar 7	Titus 2:11-13	Feb 21	1 John 4:12-16	Sep 20
Eph. 2:19-22	Sep 30	Titus 2:11-14	Jul 11	1 John 4:16b-18a	Feb 13
Eph. 3:12	Dec 4	Titus 2:12-14	May 11	1 John 5:3-5	Jun 17
Eph. 3:16-19	Sep 17	Titus 3:4-5	Jan 19	1 John 5:4-5	Nov 17
Eph. 3:20-21	Apr 3	Heb. 4:1-3	Aug 28	2 John 1:6	Sep 15
Eph. 4:2-4	Jan 31	Heb. 4:4-6	Aug 29	2 John 1:12-14	Jan 2
Eph. 4:11-13	Mar 29	Heb. 4:7-8	Aug 30	Jude 1:20-21	Feb 3
Eph. 4:22-24	Dec 31	Heb. 4:9-11	Aug 31	Jude 1:24-25	Dec 27
Eph. 5:1-2	Sep 16	Heb. 4:16	Feb 23	Rev. 3:4-5	Jul 21
Eph. 5:17-18	Oct 13	Heb. 4:16	Mar 21	Rev. 3:8	Jul 16
Eph. 5:19-20	Aug 14	Heb. 6:18-20a	Feb 9	Rev. 3:20	May 20
Eph. 5:25-26,33	Aug 9	Heb. 10:5-7	Jul 19	Rev. 3:20	Nov 10
Eph. 6:7	Mar 27	Heb. 10:13-14	May 3	Rev. 5:12-13	Oct 30
Eph. 6:16	Jan 29	Heb. 11:13-16	Oct 4	Rev. 7:13-14	May 2
Eph. 6:16	Feb 1	Heb. 12:1-3	Jan 30	Rev. 7:17	Dec 17
Eph. 6:16	Jun 22	Heb. 12:1-3	Oct 27	Rev. 11:15	May 7
Eph. 6:19-20a	Jul 31	Heb. 12:9-11	Apr 28	Rev. 11:15	Dec 18
Phil. 1:9-11	Jan 21	Heb. 13:5	Oct 26	Rev. 11:16-17	Dec 19
Phil. 2:3-5 (-8)	Jan 17	Heb. 13:15-16	Apr 2	Rev. 12:10-11	May 6
Phil. 2:9-11	Apr 26	Heb. 13:15	Jun 15	Rev. 14:7	May 17
Phil. 2:10-11	Jul 13	Heb. 13:20-21	Jul 8	Rev. 14:13	Sep 1
Phil. 3:10-11	Apr 1	James 1:22-25	May 26	Rev. 15:4	Nov 5
Phil. 3:20-21	Jan 3	James 2:23	Sep 15	Rev. 19:1	Oct 2
Phil. 4:4-6	Nov 25	James 3:18	May 4	Rev. 19:6	Oct 2
Phil. 4:6-7	Feb 21	James 4:5-6	Feb 20	Rev. 19:11-13	Oct 1
Phil. 4:6-7	Mar 10	James 4:7	Oct 16	Rev. 19:13-16	Oct 19
Phil. 4:11-12	Oct 23	James 4:7-8	Apr 24	Rev. 20:1-3	Oct 16
Phil. 4:19	Mar 22	James 4:7-8a,10	Apr 27	Rev. 21:1-4	Oct 5
Col. 1:9-12	Jul 20	James 5:17-18	Apr 13	Rev. 21:3-4	Jan 28
Col. 1:28	Jun 29	1 Peter 2:4-6	Nov 9	Rev. 21:1,4,7,21,23	Dec 20
Col. 3:13	Jun 30	1 Peter 1:8-9	Dec 11	Rev. 21:18,21	May 9
Col. 3:15	Mar 6	1 Peter 2:9	Dec 8	Rev. 22:3-4	May 8
Col. 3:15	Apr 17	1 Peter 2:9	May 1	Rev. 22:7,14	May 10
Col. 3:15-16	Nov 29	1 Peter 2:13-14	Jul 4	Rev. 22:12-13,17	Dec 22
Col. 3:15-17	Oct 14	1 Peter 2:19-21	Aug 6		
Col. 3:17	Aug 13	1 Peter 2:24	May 5		
Col. 3:17	Nov 28	1 Peter 2:18-21	Feb 26		
Col. 4:2	Apr 9	1 Peter 3:14-16	May 19		
1 Thes. 3:12-13	Sep 19	1 Peter 5:6	Oct 12		
1 Thes 4:11-12	Jan 7	1 Peter 5:7	Jul 23		

METRICAL INDEX

METER	DATE
SM (66.86)	Feb 25, Apr 19, May 20, May 27, Jun 19, Aug 26, Oct 26
CM (86.86)	
JAN:	1,2,4,7,8,10,11,12,13,14,15,16, 17,18,21,22,23,25,28,29,30,
FEB:	1,2,3,4,5,6,7,8,9,10,11,13,14, 16,18,20,23,28,29,
MAR:	2,3,4,6,7,8,9,10,11,12, 13,14,15,16,17,18,19,20,21,22, 24,25,26,28,29,31,
APR:	1,2,4,5,6,7,9,10,12,14,18, 20, 21,22,23,25,28,29
MAY:	1,2,4,5,6,7,9,10,11,12,13,14, 18,19,21,22,24,25,28,29,30,31
JUN:	1,2,3,4,5,7,8,9,11,12,13,14, 16,17,18,20,21,22,23,24,25,30
JUL:	1,2,5,6,7,8,9,11,12,14,15,18,22, 24,25,26,27,28,30,31
AUG:	2,3,4,5,7,9,10,11,12,13,14,15, 16,18,19,20,22,23,24,25, 28,30,31
SEP:	6,7,9,11,12,13,14,15,16,17,18, 19,21,22,23,24,25,26,27,29,30
OCT:	1,2,4,5,6,8,9,11,13,14,16,18, 20,22,23,27,28,29,30,31
NOV:	1,3,6,10,11,12,13,17,21,22,23, 24,25,29,30
DEC:	1,2,4,5,7,8,10,11,12,13,14,15, 16,17,18,19,20,21,22,23,24, 26,27,28,31
LM (88.88)	Jan 5, Jan 19, Feb 5, Apr 30, Jun 15, Jun 26, Jun 28, Jul 4, Jul 17, Aug 27, Sep 28, Nov 5, Nov 9,
Irr. (Irregular)	Apr 26, Apr 27, Jul 13, Sep 10, Oct 19, Nov 4

METER	DATE
4 4.6.4 4 6	Nov 27,
5 5 8.5 5 8	Oct 10
5 6.5 6	Nov 18
6 6 8.6 6 8	Jan 31, Apr 13,
7 5.7 5	Aug 17, Nov 2, Nov 8,
7 6.7 6	Jan 3, Jan 27, Jul 3, Nov 7,
7 7.7 7	Feb 12, Feb 15,
7 7.4 4 7	Aug 8
8 7.8 7	Jan 24, Jan 26, Feb 26, Apr 3, Apr 8, Apr 15, Jun 6, Jun 29, Jul 10, July 29, Sep 1, Sep 20, Oct 21, Oct 24, Nov 19, Nov 26, Dec 3, Dec 6,
8 8	May 8,
8 8.4 4 8	Dec 30
9 7.9 7	Feb 19, Feb 21, Feb 22, Mar 23, Mar 27, Apr 11, Jul 16 Jul 20, Sep 3, Sep 5, Sep 8, Oct 3, Oct 15, Oct 17, Oct 25, Nov 16,
9 8.9 8	Jul 19,
9 9.5 5 9	Aug 1,
10 6.10 6	Mar 30, May 23,
10 7.10 7	Jan 6, Feb 24, Mar 1, Apr 17, May 26, Jun 27, Jul 23, Nov 20, Dec 9,
10 8.10 8	Feb 27, Mar 5, Apr 16, May 3, Jun 10, Jul 21, Aug 21, Sep 2, Nov 28,
10 10 7 7 10	Jan 9,
10 10.10 10	Nov 14, Nov 15
11 7.11 7	Jan 20, Apr 24,
11 8.11 8	Feb 17, May 15, May 16, Aug 29, Oct 12,
11 9.11 9	May 17, Sep 4, Oct 7, Dec 25, Dec 29
12 8.12 8	Aug 6

May God Himself,
the God of peace,
sanctify you through and through.
May your whole spirit,
soul and body
be kept blameless
at the coming of our
Lord Jesus Christ.
The one who calls you
is faithful
and he will do it.

1 Thess 5:23-24

Amen!